THE JUDICIAL COMMITTEE AND THE
BRITISH NORTH AMERICA ACT

THE
JUDICIAL COMMITTEE
AND THE
BRITISH NORTH AMERICA
ACT

An Analysis of the
Interpretative Scheme for the
Distribution of Legislative Powers

G. P. BROWNE

UNIVERSITY OF TORONTO PRESS

© University of Toronto Press 1967
Printed in Canada

PREFACE

Between 1867 and 1949, the final court of appeal for Canadian constitutional cases was the Judicial Committee of the Privy Council. This study is an attempt to analyse the resulting interpretative scheme for the distribution of legislative powers. While the emphasis is on the 173 major judgments listed in the Analytical Table, all the judgments delivered by the Board—from *The Queen* v. *Coote*, 1873, to *Ponoka— Calmar Oils* v. *Earl F. Wakefield Co.*, 1960—have been taken into account.

My reason for producing yet another analysis is that the currently orthodox interpretation seems at least debatable in three respects: on the jurisprudential level, the "constituent statute" argument has been advocated to the point of obscuring other, and particularly precedent, considerations; on the textual level, W. F. O'Connor's "two-compartment" proposals have been accepted without due attention to the Judicial Committee's "three-compartment" view, or even to the *O'Connor Report* itself; but most serious of all, there has been virtually no attempt to relate the two levels, and so to reveal how the first affected, and was affected by, the second. This analysis is primarily designed to examine those fundamental, but undebated, problems.

Although the resulting conclusions could be used to bolster various political and social opinions, my object is simply to determine the most plausible legal hypotheses. These hypotheses consequently should not be presumed to stem from any particular viewpoint—other than a feeling, perhaps, that the law should not be bent in the interests of either policy or history, and can be interpreted in the light of neither.

The work is a revised version of my D.Phil. thesis, which was accepted in 1963. Above all, I am indebted to my supervisors, Dr. A. F. Madden, Reader in Commonwealth Government at Oxford, and Professor Bryan Keith-Lucas, formerly Senior Lecturer in Local Government at Oxford, and now Professor of Government at the University of Kent. I was encouraged by Professor Margaret Ormsby and the late

Professor Gilbert Tucker, both of the University of British Columbia; by Dean David Farr, of Carleton University; and by my examiners, Professor F. H. Lawson, the former Professor of Comparative Law at Oxford, and Dr. K. C. Wheare, the Rector of Exeter. I was assisted by the staffs of the Bodleian Library, the Carleton University Library, the Privy Council Office, the Public Archives of Canada, the Library of the Supreme Court of Canada, and the Library of the Parliament of Canada. I benefited, in many ways, from association with the University of British Columbia, Merton College, Nuffield College, Carleton University and the University of Wisconsin. I was subsidized by the Imperial Oil Company, the Canada Council, and the Administrators of the Beit Fund. And I am obliged to the Queen's Printer, Ottawa, for permission to reproduce Mr. E. A. Driedger's *Consolidation of the British North America Acts, 1867–1952*. I was helped through the final stages by Miss Prudence Tracy, of the University of Toronto Press, and Mrs. James Steele, who read and edited the proofs. To all these persons and institutions I am more grateful than I can say.

This volume has been published with the help of grants from the Publications Fund of the University of Toronto Press and the Social Science Research Council, using funds provided by the Canada Council.

G. P. B.

CONTENTS

TABLE OF CASES

xvi

LIST OF ABBREVIATIONS

CBR   *Canadian Bar Review*

CHR   *Canadian Historical Review*

CJEPS   *Canadian Journal of Economics and Political Science*

CLT   *Canadian Law Times*

LQR   *Law Quarterly Review*

PPCPSA   *Papers and Proceedings of the Canadian Political Science Association*

QQ   *Queen's Quarterly*

UTLJ   *University of Toronto Law Journal*

THE JUDICIAL COMMITTEE AND THE
BRITISH NORTH AMERICA ACT

Chapter One

JURISPRUDENTIAL ASSUMPTIONS: I

1. The English Rule of Precedent

Although many of the following assumptions must be well known, most of them have been disregarded in accounts of the Judicial Committee's interpretative scheme. But it should not be forgotten that if all legal systems require a balancing of stability and equity, the English system places a premium on the former object. In English law, precedents are not merely persuasive, but binding.[1]

This emphasis does not mean that the system is rigid; for the distinguishing process gives the courts some discretionary power,[2] and under certain conditions, overrulings are possible.[3] Nevertheless, it is still useful to describe *stare decisis* as "the 'sacred principle' of English law"[4]; for the relative emphasis implicit in this description is significant. In by far the majority of cases, the Rule of Precedent exerts almost absolute authority, while in the few, though sometimes critical exceptions, it represents the norm from which deviations are made.[5] In fact, English judges are so inhibited that the one "court" which is not theoretically bound by precedent—the Judicial Committee of the Privy Council—has behaved, in practice, as if it were.[6]

The influence of *stare decisis* is noticeable even in the interpretation of statutes. By focusing attention on the act itself, the "Rules of Statutory

[1]See Cross, *Precedent*, Intro. and chap. 1.
[2]See Joanes, *CBR*, XXXVI (1958), 197.
[3]For recent discussion of these conditions, with particular reference to Canada, see Cross, *Precedent*, chap. IV; Friedmann, *Legal Theory*, 321–26, and *CBR*, XXXI (1953), 731–35; Laird, *CBR*, XII (1935), 3–8; Schmitthoff, *CBR*, XXX (1952), 58–60. See also *Nordenfelt* v. *Maxim Nordenfelt Guns and Ammunition Co.*, [1894] A.C. 535, *Young* v. *Bristol Aeroplane Co.*, [1944] K.B. 718, and Mr. Cross' comment on these two judgments, at 126–46.
[4]P. G. Osborne, *A Concise Law Dictionary* (London, 1954), 317.
[5]Until as late as 1966, the final court of appeal in England, the House of Lords, was actually bound by its own previous decisions: see *London Street Tramways Co.* v. *London County Council*, [1898] A.C. 375, at 380.
[6]See below, chap. 2, sec. 1.

Interpretation" might be expected to modify that doctrine. Since the words of an act are usually construed according to precedent,[7] however, *stare decisis* still applies. Moreover, an English court will always "be slow to override a previous decision on the interpretation of a statute when it has long been acted on, and it will be more than usually slow to do so when Parliament has, since the decision, re-enacted the statute in the same terms":[8]

It seems to follow that, subject to the existence of some additional reasons for treating a case as authority for no more than that which it decides, in the sense of Lord Halsbury's speech in *Quinn* v. *Leathem*, there is no reason for regarding the present operation of the English doctrine of precedent as any different in relation to statutory interpretation from its operation in other cases.[9]

The most acceptable justification for the Rule of Precedent today is that it makes for certainty in the law.[10] During *London Street Tramways* v. *London County Council*,[11] 1898, for instance, Lord Halsbury approved the strict application of *stare decisis* on these grounds:

Of course I do not deny that cases of individual hardship may arise, and there may be a current of opinion in the profession that such and such a judgment was erroneous; but what is that occasional interference with what is perhaps abstract justice, as compared with the inconvenience—the disastrous inconvenience—of having each question subject to being reargued and the dealings of mankind rendered doubtful by reason of different decisions, so that in truth and in fact there would be no real final Court of Appeal. My Lords, "interest rei publicae" that there should be "finis litium" at some time, and there could be no "finis litium" if it were possible to suggest in each case that it might be reargued, because it is "not an ordinary case," whatever that may mean.

In contrast, during *Beamish* v. *Beamish*,[12] 1861, Lord Campbell argued that unless the House of Lords was bound by its previous decisions, it could be charged with not merely interpreting, but making the law:

If it were competent to me, I would now ask your Lordships to reconsider the doctrine laid down in *The Queen* v. *Millis*. . . .
But it is my duty to say that your Lordships are bound by this decision as much as if it had been pronounced *nemine dissentiente*, and that the rule of law which your Lordships lay down as the ground of your judgment, sitting

---

[7]See *Stephenson* v. *Higginson* (1852), 3 H.L.C. 638, at 686; also Cross, *Precedent*, 170 and 188–97.

[8]Denning L.J. (as he then was), in *Royal Crown Derby Porcelain Co.* v. *Raymond Russell*, [1949] 2 K.B. 417, at 429.

[9]Cross, *Precedent*, 194.   [10]See *ibid.*, 106–7 and chap. VIII.

[11][1898] A.C. 375, at 380.   [12]9 H.L.C. 274, at 338.

judicially, as the last and supreme Court of Appeal for this Empire, must be taken for law till altered by an act of Parliament, agreed to by the Commons and the Crown, as well as by your Lordships. The law laid down as your *ratio decidendi*, being clearly binding on all inferior tribunals, and on all the rest of the Queen's subjects, if it were not considered as equally binding upon your Lordships, this House would be arrogating to itself the right of altering the law, and legislating by its own separate authority.

This difference of justification is largely a reflection of historical development. Throughout the eighteenth and early nineteenth centuries, English courts were less confined by the Rule of Precedent than they came to be later on;[13] for so long as the "Declaratory Theory of Precedent" was accepted, precedents that conflicted with "general rules and principles" were not considered binding.[14] Accordingly, since the House of Lords was not bound by its previous decisions until the *Beamish* judgment,[15] Lord St. Leonards could make this statement as late as 1852: "you are not bound by any rule of law which you may lay down, if upon a subsequent occasion you should find reason to differ from that rule; that is, that this House, like every Court of Justice possesses an inherent power to correct an error into which it may have fallen."[16]

From about the middle of the nineteenth century onwards,[17] however, the principle of *stare decisis* gradually acquired the status demonstrated by *Beamish* v. *Beamish*. In this case, a decision[18] that had been reached in a hurry, for doubtful historical reasons, without much previous authority, and on an even division, was followed solely because of precedent. Lord Campbell was sufficiently upset to make the following protest:

> If it were competent to me, I would now ask your Lordships to reconsider the doctrine laid down in *The Queen* v. *Millis*, particularly as the judges who were then consulted, complained of being hurried into giving an opinion without due time for deliberation, and the Members of this House who heard the argument, and voted on the question, "That the judgment appealed against be reversed," were equally divided; so that the judgment which decided the marriage by a Presbyterian clergyman of a man and woman, who both belonged to his religious persuasion, who both believed that they

---

[13]See Cross, *Precedent*, 17–18; also Holdsworth, *LQR*, L (1934), 180.
[14]See Cross, *Precedent*, 21–30 and 119–21.
[15]9 H.L.C. 274, at 338. Though this question was now "virtually settled," it was not "finally established" until *London Street Tramways Co.* v. *London County Council*, [1898] 375, at 380: see Cross, *Precedent*, 7–8 and 106–8.
[16]*Bright* v. *Hutton* (1852), 3 H.L.C. 341, at 388.
[17]See Cross, *Precedent*, 18; also Goodhart, *LQR*, L (1934), 42 and 198.
[18]Viz., *R.* v. *Millis* (1844), 10 Cl. and F. 534.

were contracting lawful matrimony, who had lived together as husband and wife, and who had procreated children while so living together as husband and wife, to be a nullity, was only pronounced on the technical rule of your Lordships' House, that where, upon a division, the numbers are equal, *semper praesumitur pro negante.*

It might be added that the courts are now retreating to a less restrictive position:[19] the notion of "implied overruling" has been recognized in several decisions;[20] judges seem more willing to acknowledge the fact of mutually conflicting decisions;[21] greater stress is placed on the exceptions to *stare decisis,*[22] and while the House of Lords continues to treat its previous decisions as "normally" binding, it has finally abolished the rule that it is absolutely bound by its former judgments on points of law.[23]

These developments in the English Rule of Precedent should also be related to the altered status of the Theory of the Separation of Powers. Even if that theory is no longer acceptable in its original form, it is still influential in the more limited sense of the Theory of Judicial Restraint. For when the following of precedent leads to individually unfair or socially undesirable effects, it can still be argued that the basic remedy lies with the legislature, rather than the judiciary. This argument— developed by Austin,[24] Salmond,[25] and Gray,[26] and accepted by Halsbury,[27] Atkin,[28] Macmillan,[29] Asquith,[30] and Jowitt[31]—was summed up by Parke B., in *Egerton* v. *Brownlow,*[32] 1853, as follows:

It is the province of the statesman, and not the lawyer, to discuss, and of the legislature to determine, what is best for the public good, and to provide

[19]See Friedmann, *Legal Theory,* 329–32, and Schmitthoff, *CBR,* XXX (1952), 52–53.
[20]See Cross, *Precedent,* 121–23.
[21]See *ibid.,* 128–30.
[22]Especially since *Young* v. *Bristol Aeroplane Co.,* [1944] K.B. 718: cf. Schmitthoff, *CBR,* XXX (1952), 52, and Paton and Sawyer, *LQR,* LXVIII (1947), 480–81.
[23]This step was taken at the quasi-judicial sitting of 26 July, 1966. For examples of the argument against the old practice, see Lord Reid, in *Nash* v. *Tamplin and Sons Brewery Brighton,* [1952] A.C. 231, at 250; Lord Denning, *From Precedent to Precedent;* Cross, *Precedent,* 30–32 and 253–58; Gardiner and Jones, *Law Reform Now,* 16.
[24]Austin, *Jurisprudence,* 184–91 and 372–75.
[25]Williams, ed., *Salmond,* 139–41.
[26]Gray, *Nature of the Law,* 139–44.
[27]See *Janson* v. *Dreifontein Consolidated Mines,* [1902] A.C. 484, at 495–96.
[28]See *Fender* v. *St. John-Mildmay,* [1938] A.C. 1, at 10–12.
[29]See *Read* v. *J. Lyons and Co.,* [1947] A.C. 156, at 175.
[30]See *Candler* v. *Crane, Christmas and Co.,* [1951] 2 K.B. 164, at 195.
[31]See his comments on Justice W. K. Fullagar's paper, "Liability for Representations at Common Law," *Australian Law Journal,* XXV (1951), 296.
[32]4 H.L.C. 1, at 123.

for it by proper enactments. It is the province of the judge to expound the law only; the written from the statutes: the unwritten or common law from the decisions of our predecessors and of our existing courts, from textwriters of acknowledged authority, and upon the principles to be clearly deduced from them by sound reason and just inference; not to speculate upon what is best, in his opinion, for the advantage of the community.

While the debate over this argument is irrelevant for present purposes,[33] one criticism might be examined. This criticism amounts to a denial, not of the desirability of the restraining position, but of its possibility.[34] Because the process of interpreting a law must affect the nature of that law, the question is not whether a judge ought to "legislate," but whether he can avoid doing so. After all, even Austin recognized that "there can be no law without a legislative act";[35] and Salmond agreed: "where judges establish a new principle by means of judicial decision, they may be said to exercise legislative, and not merely judicial power."[36]

The argument that judges are not concerned with ideology is consequently held to represent an ideological point of view itself, an acceptance of what might be termed "legal positivism."[37] And the followers of Austin, Salmond, and Gray are said to be as much legal "philosophers" as their critics. At the same time, by being less self-aware than the "liberals," these legal positivists are actually more liable to the influence of "extraneous" factors: as Mr. Friedmann points out, "their self-delusion makes it psychologically easier for them to mould the law in accordance with their beliefs and prejudices without feeling the weight of responsibility that burdens lawyers with greater consciousness of the issues at stake."[38]

But this criticism surely misses the point. It is not a question of whether judicial legislation can be avoided, but of the extent to which it should be restrained; and the liberals themselves admit that some restraint is possible. As a matter of fact, they not only assume that by recognizing the inevitability of judicial legislation a judge can control it, but also debate the degree to which he should consider public opinion in

[33]The standard accounts might be supplemented with these: Friedmann, *CBR*, XXXI (1953), 723–51; Joanes, *CBR*, XXXVI (1958), 198; Lloyd, *LQR*, LXIV (1948), 472, 475–77, 482–84; McWhinney, *Australian Journal of Comparative Legislation*, II (1953), 37; Schmitthoff, *CBR*, XXV (1952), 51.
[34]See Friedmann, *Legal Theory*, chap. XXIII, and *Law and Social Change*, chap. VI.
[35]Quoted in Williams, ed., *Salmond*, 139.
[36]*Ibid.*
[37]Friedmann, *Legal Theory*, 292.
[38]*Ibid.*; see also *Law and Social Change*, chap. VI.

his law-making. With the introduction of such considerations, however, the debate returns to the stage it had reached when the "possibility criticism" was raised.

2. The Rules of Statutory Interpretation

The difference between applying a common law precedent and interpreting a statute might be summed up like this: in the former case, the court compares the facts before it with the facts that lay behind the precedent; in the latter, it compares the facts before it with the abstract rules laid down by the statute. In the interpretation of statutes, therefore, the problem of judicial restraint becomes especially pressing: since the court is now confronted with the express intentions of the framers, the danger is not that the judiciary and the legislature might overlap, but that they might conflict.

The "Rules of Statutory Interpretation" are supposed to prevent such conflicts.[39] The cardinal rule is that statutes "should be construed according to the intent of the Parliament which passed them."[40] However, since it must disregard both the presumed objectives of the framers and the possible effect of its decision, the court must gather that intent from the "literal words."[41] Mr. Cross makes a pertinent comment on this "Literal Rule":

It is easy to make fun of the rule, but it has great merits up to a point. It is productive of certainty in the sense that it renders the decision of a court easier to predict than would be the case if the judges assumed that they have a roving commission to carry out the object of legislation, irrespective of the words used. The literal rule presupposes that it is possible to draw a sharp line between interpreting a statute and carrying out its object. The rule also supposes that all or most words and phrases have a meaning apart from the object with which they are used. Neither proposition is fully justified, but the literal rule is, none the less, something which should not be departed from lightly.[42]

This does not mean that a statute must always be given its "ordinary and grammatical" construction. On the contrary, if certain words appear

[39]The following account is based on "Craies' rules" (as found in Odgers, ed., *Craies*); see also Cross, *Precedent*, 179–81.

[40]Tindal C.J., in *Sussex Peerage* Case (1844), 11 Cl. and F. 85, at 143.

[41]More precisely, from the "ordinary and legal meaning" (preference being given to the latter, if the meanings are at variance): see Cross, *Precedent*, 179–81.

[42]Cross, *Precedent*, 179.

obscure, ambiguous, or "manifestly absurd," the court must reconcile them with the "general sense" of the act.[43] Thus in *Grey* v. *Pearson*,[44] 1857, Lord Wensleydale formulated the "Golden Rule" like this: "in construing wills, and indeed statutes, and all written instruments, the grammatical and ordinary sense of the words is to be adhered to, unless that would lead to some absurdity, or some repugnancy or inconsistency in the rest of the instrument, in which case the grammatical and ordinary sense of the words may be modified, so as to avoid that absurdity and inconsistency, but no farther." Mr. Cross supplies another explanation:

> Two qualifications on the application of the golden rule must be mentioned. In the first place, the question whether the result of a literal adherence to the words of a statute is absurd must be determined in the light of the circumstances existing when the statute was passed. The second qualification is that, according to a large body of opinion, the rule can only be applied when the meaning of the statutory words is ambiguous, i.e. it is not a gloss on the literal rule as the formulation above suggests, but a precept for solving an ambiguity when *ex hypothesi* the literal rule cannot be applied.[45]

The "Mischief Rule" provides a third directive for interpreting statutes. This rule presumes, not that a literal reading would lead to absurdity, but that the effects of such a reading would be contrary to the purpose of the impugned legislation.[46] The solution for this difficulty (first indicated in *Heydon's* Case,[47] 1584) was summed up by Lord Selborne, in *Caledonian Railway* v. *North British Railway*,[48] 1881: "The more literal construction of a statute ought not to prevail, if . . . it is opposed to the intentions of the Legislature, as apparent by the statute; and if the words are sufficiently flexible to admit of some other construction by which that intention will be better effectuated." Mr. Cross explains when the Mischief Rule comes into force: "there is authority for the view that it, too, like the golden rule as understood by Lord Esher, is not a gloss on the literal rule, but a rule which should only be applied in cases of ambiguity, i.e. when the literal rule is, *ex hypothesi*, inapplicable."[49]

Despite these basic directives, however, the Rules of Statutory Interpretation not only permit, but require a "resort to extrinsic aids." If by "attempting to give a meaning to every word, we should have to make

[43] See Odgers, ed., *Craies*, 82–83.
[44] 6 H.L.C. 61, at 106.
[45] Cross, *Precedent*, 182.
[46] See *ibid.*, 182–86.
[47] 3 Co. Rep. 7a. See Cross, *Precedent*, 183, and Odgers, ed., *Craies*, 91–92.
[48] 6 A.C. 114, at 122. See Odgers, ed., *Craies*, 80.
[49] Cross, *Precedent*, 183; see also 185–86.

the Act of Parliament insensible,"[50] the court may reject words outright, as surplusage. It should also maintain the principle *ex visceribus actus* (literally, "within the four corners of the Act," or, "in view of the context of the passage").[51] And it should generally abide by such presumptions as the *ejusdam generis* rule, the maxim *expressio unius est exclusio alterius*, and the proposition that, whenever possible, statutes must be construed in accordance with the common law.[52]

On the other hand, a court should be sceptical of any reference to the "history" of acts, even as a guide to the "intent of the Parliament which passed them."[53] In *South Eastern Railway* v. *Railway Commissioners*,[54] 1880, Lush J. decided that "we must look, not at one phrase or one section only, but at the whole of the Act, and must read it by the light which the state of the law at that time . . . throws upon it." In *Gorham* v. *Bishop of Exeter*,[55] 1850, Alderson B. went further— to assert that "we do not construe Acts of Parliament by reference to history." And although Craies notes that "in several cases public history as distinguished from the history of the law has been admitted in aid,"[56] at least one prohibition is definite: "It is not permissible, however, in discussing the meaning of an obscure enactment, to refer to 'the parliamentary history' of a statute, in the sense of the debates which took place in Parliament when the statute was under consideration."[57]

The use of contemporary, as opposed to current meaning is more controversial. According to Craies, words should be read in the light of their meaning at the date of the passing of the Act.[58] During *Clyde Navigation* v. *Laird*,[59] 1883, however, Lord Watson declared that "*contemporanea expositio* ought rarely, if ever, to be applied to modern Acts." It has also been argued that the "contemporary meaning" rule should be qualified in the case of constituent statutes.[60] And there is no

[50]Odgers, ed., *Craies*, 100. Craies is paraphrasing Coleridge J., in *R.* v. *Inhabitants of East Ardsley* (1850), 14 Q.B. 793, at 801.
[51]See Odgers, ed., *Craies*, 93.
[52]See Cross, *Precedent*, 186–87.
[53]See Odgers, ed., *Craies*, 120.
[54]5 Q.B.D. 217, at 240.
[55]5 Ex. 630, at 667.
[56]Odgers, ed., *Craies*, 120; cf. Farwell L.J., in *R.* v. *West Riding of Yorkshire County Council*, [1906] 2 K.B. 676, at 716–17.
[57]Odgers, ed., *Craies*, 121.
[58]See *ibid.*, 78; cf. Cross, *Precedent*, 175–76.
[59]8 A.C. 658, at 673.
[60]See *A.-G. Ont.* v. *A.-G. Can.*, [1947] A.C. 127, at 154. Mr. Cross confuses this case with *A.-G. Ont.* v. *Canada Temperance Federation*, [1946] A.C. 193: see *Precedent*, 176, n. 3. For further discussion of this argument, see below, 12–13 and chap. 2, sec. 2.

denying that the application of the Mischief Rule, especially, has often led to uncontemplated interpretations.[61]

Another rule states that a new construction should not be given to an ambiguous passage if the change would materially affect transactions based on an earlier current of interpretation.[62] In theory, this rule applies only when the previous judgments have been uniform; otherwise, the court decides which current of interpretation ought to prevail, and construes the statute accordingly. In practice, however, the court usually takes account of the date, duration, number, and prestige of previous judgments; the nature and effect of the transactions based on them; the degree of conviction as to the error involved, or inconvenience entailed; and the prevailing attitude towards the Rule of Precedent. Thus in *Bourne v. Keane*, [63] 1919, Lord Buckmaster made the following summary:

> Firstly, the construction of a statute of doubtful meaning, once laid down and accepted for a long period of time, ought not to be altered unless your Lordships could say positively that it was wrong and productive of inconvenience;
> Secondly, that the decisions upon which title to property depends, or which by establishing principles of construction or otherwise form the basis of contracts, ought to receive the same protection;
> Thirdly, decisions that affect the general conduct of affairs, so that their alteration would mean that taxes had been unlawfully imposed, or exemption unlawfully obtained, payments needlessly made, or the position of the public materially affected, ought in the same way to continue.

There are also certain minor rules. In *Stephenson v. Taylor*,[64] 1861, Cockburn C. J. declared that "on the Parliament Roll there is no punctuation, and we therefore are not bound by that in the printed copies." Craies adds, somewhat confusingly, that "this statement seems to be also applicable to the vellum prints"; that punctuation in the latter might be regarded "to some extent at least, as *contemporanea expositio*"; and that in the official copies of modern statutes, "punctuation forms no part of the Act."[65] As for "general words," while these may not be limited in meaning except in so far as such limitation is required by the subject, context, or other parts of the statute,[66] they must be limited if they occur along with particular words that would be overruled by

---

[61]Thus the Telegraph Act of 1869 was applied to telephones, despite the fact that the latter were invented after that date: see *A.-G. v. Edison Telephone Co.* (1881), 6 Q.B.D. 244, at 254. This example is suggested in Cross, *Precedent*, 176.

[62]See Odgers, ed., *Craies*, 146.

[63][1919] A.C. 815, at 874.

[64] 1 B. and S. 101, at 106.

[65]Odgers, ed., *Craies*, 185.

[66]See *ibid.*, 171–72.

allowing the general words their most comprehensive sense.[67] Likewise, since an "excepting" proviso serves to exclude from the preceding portion of an act something which, but for that proviso, would be within it, "such a proviso cannot be construed as enlarging the scope of an enactment when it can be fairly and properly construed without attributing to it that effect."[68] And quasi-technical terms may be interpreted by reference to contemporary literary definitions.[69]

Last of all, with regard to the application of these Rules of Statutory Interpretation, some authorities would confine them to "ordinary," as distinct from "constituent" statutes. This approach has been justified on the ground that a "constituent" statute creates not merely a law, but a state. Such a statute must therefore be given an "organic" construction, so that the distribution of legislative powers is continuously related to times and circumstances: for "constitutions are not intended to be construed *in vacuo* but as living instruments of government."[70]

While this "constituent statute argument" has become increasingly influential in the United States,[71] English courts have been generally unresponsive. They are tending to apply the Rule of Precedent a little less rigorously than formerly; they seem to make more frequent allowances for the special nature of the legislation in question; and they usually construe penal statutes in favour of the subject.[72] Yet neither the extent nor the significance of such developments should be exaggerated. As Mr. Cross points out, it is questionable whether the latter argument "is anything more than a presumption of doubtful strength"; allowances are made because "to some extent, the object of a statute plays an integral part in its construction"; and in any event, "this is a far cry from having different rules of interpretation for different statutes."[73]

Admittedly, the Judicial Committee allowed that "to such an organic statute [as the B.N.A. Act] the flexible interpretation must be given

[67]i.e., "general language yields to particular expression": see *ibid.*, 205–6.
[68]See *ibid.*, 201–2.
[69]See *ibid.*, 151–52.
[70]MacDonald, *CBR*, XXIX (1951), 1030.
[71]Especially through the efforts of Brandeis and Cardozo JJ.: see Brandeis J., dissenting, in *Burnet* v. *Coronado Oil and Gas Co.* (1932), 285 U.S. 393, at 405 ff.; Cardozo, *Judicial Process, passim*; and Stone and Cardozo JJ., in *St. Joseph Stockyard Co.* v. *United States* (1936), 298 U.S. 38, at 94. On the other hand, the doctrine of *stare decisis* has also played a part in American constitutional interpretation, and protests have been made against facile departures from it: see *Mahnich* v. *Southern S. S. Co.* (1944), 321 U.S. 96, at 112, and *United States* v. *Rabinowitz* (1950), 339 U.S. 56, at 86.
[72]See Friedmann, *Legal Theory*, 311, and Cross, *Precedent*, 177–78.
[73]Cross, *Precedent*, 177–78.

that changing circumstances require."[74] Nevertheless, it is questionable whether the Board really accepted the argument of "another special rule of flexible interpretation in the case of constitutional statutes."[75] For if Lord Jowitt's "organic" recommendations—in the *Privy Council Appeals* judgment of 1947—are by no means unique,[76] the degree to which this sentiment has influenced actual decisions is another matter.[77]

Of course the constituent statute argument could be ostensibly rejected, but actually adopted. Suppose, for example, that the enforcement of the Rules of Statutory Interpretation served to safeguard the autonomy of one of the various legislative authorities in a federal constitution. Suppose, too, that a court accepted the "co-ordinate and independent"[78] view of federal government, and also felt that the original intention, or politic outcome, was for a particular constitution to be "federal" in this "autonomous" sense. Such a "philosophy" might lead it to apply the Rules of Statutory Interpretation—though for very different, if not contradictory, reasons to those from which these rules are theoretically derived. On the other hand, since the connection could be coincidental, the mere fact that a court applied the rules would not prove that it had such motives—even though it might have accepted such a philosophy.

[74]*A.-G. Ont.* v. *A.-G. Can.*, [1947] A.C. 127, at 154.
[75]Cross, *Precedent*, 177.
[76]For other examples of this "liberal" approach, see below, chap. 2, sec. 2.
[77]As will become evident when the solutions for each of the major problems are analysed. Meanwhile, a good example of this gap between theory and practice can be seen in the contrast between some of Lord Wright's opinions and certain of his judgments: cf. *Cambridge Law Journal*, VIII (1944), 135, and *Co-operative Committee on Japanese Canadians* v. *A.-G. Can.*, [1947] A.C. 87 (which reaffirmed the Emergency Doctrine, and so upheld the three-compartment view: see below, 54, 155–56).
[78]See Wheare, *Federal Government*, chap. 1.

Chapter Two

JURISPRUDENTIAL ASSUMPTIONS: II

1. *Stare Decisis* and the Judicial Committee's Interpretative Scheme

If the Judicial Committee were bound by its previous decisions, the framework of its interpretative scheme was probably constructed in its earliest judgments. If an "alternative" scheme were developed later on, however, extraneous considerations could have appeared at that point. Finally, if the Supreme Court of Canada were not bound by the decisions of the Judicial Committee, a contrast between the two sets of judgments might serve to evaluate the common complaint that Canada was saddled with an "alien," as well as an unpractical, constitution.

In *Ridesdale* v. *Clifton*,[1] 1877, Lord Cairns decided that the Judicial Committee is not bound by its previous decisions. As Anglin J. pointed out in *Stuart* v. *Bank of Montreal*,[2] 1909, one reason for this rule is that those decisions take the form of advice tendered to the sovereign. Another is that the Board must frequently decide constitutional questions, which require at least some consideration of state needs.[3] Accordingly, in the *Canada Temperance Act* judgment[4] of 1946, Lord Simon affirmed Lord Cairns' theoretical rule: "Their Lordships do not doubt that in tendering humble advice to His Majesty they are not absolutely bound by previous decisions of the Board, as is the House of Lords by its own judgments. In ecclesiastical appeals, for instance, on more than one occasion, the Board has tendered advice contrary to that given in a previous case, which further historical research has shown to have been wrong."

[1] 2 P.D. 276, at 307. See also Lord Watson, in *Tooth* v. *Power*, [1891] A.C. 284, at 292, and Lord Halsbury, in *Read* v. *Bishop of Lincoln*, [1892] A.C. 644, at 654. For more recent examples of departures from previous decisions (which were not concerned with either ecclesiastical or constitutional appeals), see *Mercantile Bank of India* v. *Central Bank of India*, [1938] A.C. 287, and *Gideon Nkambule* v. *The King*, [1950] A.C. 379.

[2] 41 S.C.R. 516, at 545.

[3] See Cross, *Precedent*, 16.

[4] *A.-G. Ont.* v. *Canada Temperance Federation*, [1946] A.C. 193, at 206.

In practice, however, the Judicial Committee has not only tended to follow precedent, but has done so even in the case of constitutional appeals.[5] This tendency was naturally most pronounced during the late nineteenth and early twentieth centuries, when the Rule of Precedent and the Theory of Judicial Restraint were at the height of their influence. During the unreported *McCarthy Act Reference*[6] of 1885, for instance, the following exchange took place:

Sir Barnes Peacock: "Do I understand you correctly to admit that *Russell* v. *The Queen* is not overruled by *Hodge* v. *The Queen?*"
Mr. Davey: "Certainly. I do not know that your Lordships can overrule a previous decision of your Lordships. The House of Lords cannot!"
Sir Barnes Peacock: "Some of the decisions have been varied by subsequent decisions in the Privy Council."
Mr. Davey: "Your Lordships cannot overrule; you can explain."
Sir Barnes Peacock: "*Russell* v. *The Queen* is still in force."
Mr. Davey: "Undoubtedly."
Sir Montague Smith: "Both decisions, of course are in force, and they may well stand together. The question is whether this one comes nearer to one or the other."

Yet even when it was perfectly understood that the Judicial Committee could depart from previous decisions, qualifications were expressed. In the *Aeronautics* judgment[7] of 1932, Lord Sankey gave this warning:

While the decisions which the Board has pronounced in the many constitutional cases which have come under their consideration from the Dominion must each be regarded in the light of the facts involved in it, their Lordships recognize that there has grown up around the British North America Act a body of precedents of high authority and value as guides to its interpretation and application. The useful and essential task of taking stock of this body of authority and reviewing it in relation to the original text has been undertaken by this Board from time to time and notably, for example, in *Attorney-General for Ontario* v. *Attorney-General for Canada;*[8] *Attorney-General for Canada* v. *Attorney-General of Ontario;*[9] *City of Montreal* v. *Montreal Street Ry.;*[10] and in the same year *Attorney-General for Ontario* v. *Attorney-General for Canada.*[11]

In the *Canada Temperance Act* judgment[12] of 1946, Lord Simon actually concluded on a different note from that suggested above:

But on constitutional questions it must be seldom indeed that the Board

---

[5] Thus most reversals were made in ecclesiastical appeals.
[6] Canada, Dominion Liquor License Acts, 1883–4, *Report of Proceedings*, 118. For further information concerning this source, see below, 66, n. 32.
[7] *In re the Regulation and Control of Aeronautics in Canada*, [1932] A.C. 54, at 71.
[8] [1896] A.C. 348. [9] [1898] A.C. 247.
[10] [1912] A.C. 333. [11] [1912] A.C. 571.
[12] *A.-G. Ont.* v. *Canada Temperance Federation*, [1946] A.C. 193, at 206.

would depart from a previous decision which it may be assumed will have been acted on both by governments and subjects. In the present case the decision now sought to be overruled [viz., *Russell* v. *The Queen*[13]] has stood for over sixty years; the Act has been put into operation for varying periods in many places in the Dominion; under its provisions businesses must have been closed, fines and imprisonments for breaches of the Act have been imposed and suffered. Time and again the occasion has arisen when the Board could have overruled the decision had they thought it wrong. Accordingly, in the opinion of their Lordships, the decision must be regarded as firmly embedded in the constitutional law of Canada, and it is impossible now to depart from it.

And in the *Margarine* judgment[14] of 1951, Lord Morton of Henryton rejected an argument based on section 95 because "the authorities show that this contention is unsound."

This reluctance to upset a current of interpretation does not mean that the Judicial Committee never departed from precedent. But it does suggest why those departures were made so reluctantly, or with such a concern for stability, that they were seldom made outright. As a matter of fact, the Board never overruled a previous decision in a Canadian constitutional case.[15] Instead, it resorted to the methods normally employed by an English court when an awkward precedent is evaded: judgments were "distinguished," accepted only in part, or simply ignored altogether. Instances of distinguishing are sufficiently common to be left for later discussion, but the other two methods might be illustrated here.

In *British Coal Corporation* v. *The King*,[16] 1935, Lord Sankey held that because "the Statute [of Westminster] has removed the two difficulties which were decisive in *Nadan's* case," this precedent no longer applied. What Lord Sankey omitted to note, however, was that *Nadan* v. *The King*[17] raised three difficulties, and that the third had not been removed. For while it met the objections that the parliament of Canada may not legislate with extra-territorial effect, and that section 1025 of the Canadian Criminal Code was void under the Colonial Laws Validity

[13](1882), 7 A.C. 829.
[14]*Canadian Federation of Agriculture* v. *A.-G. Que.*, [1951] A.C. 179, at 198.
[15]Though it did "disassociate" itself from earlier views: see Lord Atkin, in *Proprietary Articles Trade Association* v. *A.-G. Can.*, [1931] A.C. 310, at 326 (re the construction placed on s. 91(2) by Lord Haldane, during *In re the Board of Commerce Act, 1919, and the Combines and Fair Prices Act, 1919*, [1922] 1 A.C. 191); also Lord Simon, in *A.-G. Ont.* v. *Canada Temperance Federation*, [1946] A.C. 193, at 204–6 (re Lord Haldane's interpretation of *Russell* v. *The Queen* (1882), 7 A.C. 829, in *Toronto Electric Commissioners* v. *Snider*, [1925] A.C. 396).
[16][1935] A.C. 500, at 516.
[17][1926] A.C. 482.

Act of 1865, the Statute of Westminster did not affect the argument that "if the prerogative is to be excluded, this must be accomplished by an Imperial statute."[18] Admittedly, Lord Sankey might have been denying that this third difficulty was a *ratio* of the *Nadan* judgment;[19] but it seems more probable that in the *British Coal Corporation* judgment of 1935, the Judicial Committee accepted a precedent only in part.[20]

Meanwhile, in the *Great West Saddlery* judgment[21] of 1921, the *Board of Commerce* judgment[22] of 1922, and the *Snider* judgment[23] of 1925, the Committee had practically eliminated the power of the federal parliament to regulate trade and commerce in the provinces. For Lord Haldane had reasoned that section 91(2) could not be held to "override" section 92(13) unless it were invoked in aid of one of the other heads of section 91. In contrast, during the *Dominion Trade and Industry Act* judgment[24] of 1937, Lord Atkin decided that section 91(2) enabled the federal parliament to create and to regulate a uniform law of trademarks, which are a form of property. Consequently, in *Re Alberta Legislation*,[25] 1938, Duff J. reopened the whole question of head 2 of section 91—and so, in effect, ignored a precedent:

. . . in a judgment delivered in *Re the Natural Products Marketing Act* we unanimously expressed the opinion, and our judgment proceeded in part, at least, upon the hypothesis, that we were bound by this pronouncement in the judgment in *Snider's* case and by similar pronouncements in the *Board of Commerce* case, as expressing the *ratio decidendi* of those decisions. It is clear now, however, from the reasons for the judgment in *Attorney-General for Ontario* v. *Attorney-General for Canada* that the Regulation of Trade and Commerce must be treated as having full independent status as one of the enumerated heads of section 91.

But the most convincing demonstration of the influence of *stare decisis* was given in the case of the Compartment Problem. In so far as it determines the limits within which the other problems must be solved, this is the fundamental problem in the interpretation of the British North America Act.[26] And here, despite current orthodoxy, the Judicial

[18]*Ibid.*, at 493.
[19]See Cross, *Precedent*, 49 and 86–89.
[20]See Varcoe, *Legislative Power*, 191, and Kennedy, in Oyler, *et. al.*, *CBR*, XIII (1935), 622–24.
[21]*Great West Saddlery Co.* v. *The King*, [1921] 2 A.C. 91, at 118–19.
[22]*In re the Board of Commerce Act, 1919, and the Combines and Fair Prices Act, 1919*, [1922] 1 A.C. 191, at 198.
[23]*Toronto Electric Commissioners* v. *Snider*, [1925] A.C. 396, at 409–10. For further discussion of the relation between these three judgments and s. 91(2), see below, chap. 7, sec. 2.
[24]*A.-G. Ont.* v. *A.-G. Can.*, [1937] A.C. 405.
[25][1938] S.C.R. 100, at 121.
[26]As will be shown below, in chaps. 3 and 4.

Committee substantially accepted one solution. Moreover, even on the orthodox assumption that the Compartment Problem evoked two contradictory solutions, it would still be remarkable that there were only two, and that those two occurred sequentially. In fact, by suggesting that the introduction of extraneous considerations provoked a revolutionary change in the Board's interpretative scheme, and that this change was then perpetuated through an unwillingness to disturb the current of authority, today's critics give a special emphasis to the influence of the Rule of Precedent.

As for the Supreme Court of Canada, in *Kelley* v. *Canadian Northern Railway*,[27] 1950, Smith J. referred to the "hitherto binding nature" of the Judicial Committee's decisions. In the *Farm Products Marketing Act* judgment[28] of 1957, Rand J. argued that the right to depart from precedent must have passed from the Judicial Committee to its successor. And the proposal to append an "instruction amendment" to the Act abolishing appeals—and so to preserve the Judicial Committee's interpretative scheme by specifically instructing the Supreme Court to supply the Rule of Precedent—was rejected.[29]

It might be doubted whether these "authorities" outweigh the succession of cases in which the Supreme Court affirmed its adherence to the principle of *stare decisis*.[30] It is also questionable whether this court may decline to follow the judgments of the Judicial Committee, as distinct from its own judgments. But at least before the abolition of appeals, in 1949, the Supreme Court of Canada was bound by both those sets of judgments—if not by the decisions of the House of Lords as well. Thus in *Robins* v. *National Trust Company*,[31] 1927, Lord Dunedin made the following statement:

... where an appellate Court in a colony which is regulated by English law differs from an appellate Court in England it is not right to assume that the Colonial Court is wrong. It is otherwise if the authority in England is that

[27][1950] 2 D.L.R. 760, at 770.

[28]*Reference re Farm Products Marketing Act, R.S.O. 1950, c. 131, as Amended,* [1957] S.C.R. 198, at 212. See also Rinfret C.J.C., dissenting, in *R.* v. *Storgoff,* [1945] S.C.R. 526, and Laskin, *Constitutional Law,* 189–92.

[29]Ostensibly on the ground that the Judicial Committee had not been bound by precedent: see Canada, Parliament, House of Commons, *Debates,* 1949 (2nd sess.), I, 18; Canada, Parliament, Senate, *Debates,* 1949 (2nd sess.), 132–33; *Winnipeg Free Press,* Oct. 5, 1949; Varcoe, *Legislative Power,* 187.

[30]See *Stuart* v. *Bank of Montreal* (1909), 41 S.C.R. 516; *Daoust, Lalonde and Co.* v. *Ferland,* [1932] S.C.R. 343; *A.-G. Can.* v. *Western Higbie,* [1945] S.C.R. 385; *Robert* v. *Marquis and Lussier,* [1958] S.C.R. 20. By emphasizing the *Farm Products Marketing Act* judgment at the expense of judgments like these, Mr. Cross gives a misleading impression: see *Precedent,* 17.

[31][1927] A.C. 515, at 519.

of the House of Lords. That is the supreme tribunal to settle English law, and that being settled, the Colonial Court which is bound by English law is bound to follow it. Equally, of course, the point of difference may be settled so far as the Colonial Court is concerned by a judgment of this Board.

This statement should be amplified. Despite Lord Dunedin's opening remarks, the judgments of the English Court of Appeal were normally treated as if binding on Canadian courts; indeed, they were sometimes followed in preference to the judgments of the Judicial Committee itself.[32] Likewise, a judgment of the House of Lords has been held to take precedence over one of the Board's decisions.[33] There was also some debate as to the binding effect of all the Judicial Committee's judgments (that is, those covering every part of the British Empire and Commonwealth, as opposed to those covering Canada alone). And the reason why Canadian courts were bound by judgments of the House of Lords, as well as the Court of Appeal, is that in 1867 it was still possible to assume an all-embracing body of "English Law."[35]

In general, though, it can be said that between 1867 and 1949, the Supreme Court of Canada was bound by the decisions of the Judicial Committee on the British North America Act. It therefore follows that the judgments delivered by the Supreme Court between those dates cannot be used either to weaken the "authority" of the Judicial Committee's interpretative scheme, or to show that this scheme was an alien

[32]This suggestion was in accord with *Negro* v. *Pietro's Bread Co.*, [1933] 1 D.L.R. 490, at 494–96—which was in turn preceded by an Australian case, *Trimble* v. *Hill* (1879), 5 A.C. 342, at 344. Canadian cases reflecting the same notion include *Lobb* v. *Rockwood Rural Credits Society* (1926), 35 M.R. 499, at 503–4; *McMillan* v. *Wallace*, [1929] 3 D.L.R. 367, at 369; *Re Cox*, [1950] 2 D.L.R. 449, at 468. Cf. the rejection of this notion in *Pacific Lumber Co.* v. *Imperial Timber Co.* (1916), 31 D.L.R. 748, at 749; *Radowitch* v. *Parsons* (1914), 19 D.L.R. 8, at 8–12; *Manitoba Bridge and Iron Works* v. *Minnedosa Power Co.*, [1917] 1 W.W.R. 731, at 738; *London* v. *Holeproof Hosiery Co.*, [1933] 3 D.L.R. 657, at 659; *Safeway Stores* v. *Harris*, [1948] 4 D.L.R. 187, at 202.

[33]Cf. *Will* v. *Bank of Montreal*, [1931] 3 D.L.R. 526, at 535–37, and *Jeremy and Jeremy* v. *Fontaine*, [1931] 4 D.L.R. 556, at 558.

[34]The "all parts" view was taken in *Negro* v. *Pietro's Bread Co.*, [1933] 1 D.L.R. 490, at 494–96, and in *Walsh* v. *Walsh*, [1948] 1 D.L.R. 630, at 647. Cf. the rejection of this view in *Lobb* v. *Rockwood Rural Credits Society* (1926), 35 M.R. 499, at 503.

[35]See *Trimble* v. *Hill* (1879), 5 A.C. 342, at 345. After the abolition of appeals in 1949, judgments delivered by the Judicial Committee were declared weightier than those of both the Court of Appeal and the House of Lords: see *Kelley* v. *C.N.R.*, [1950] 2 D.L.R. 760, at 770. It was also stated that the judgments of the latter courts, while of persuasive influence, did not have to be followed: see *Anderson* v. *Chasney*, [1949] 4 D.L.R. 71, at 91 and 95, and *Maltais* v. *C.P.R.*, [1950] 2 W.W.R. 145, at 160.

imposition. It is thus irrelevant, for present purposes, to observe that out of the 174[36] appeals analysed in this study, more than a quarter of those from the Supreme Court of Canada[37] (and more than a third of those from this court and the provincial supreme courts combined[38]) were reversed.

2. The Judicial Committee and the Constituent Statute Argument

Mr. V. C. MacDonald provides a good example of the "constituent statute argument":

> In matters pertaining to the distribution of legislative powers the Privy Council has adhered strictly to the two-fold view (a) that it must treat the B.N.A. Act "by the same methods of construction and exposition" as other statutes; and (b) that "if the text is explicit the text is conclusive . . . when the text is ambiguous . . . recourse must be had to the context and scheme of the Act". That is to say, the B.N.A. Act is a statute to be interpreted simply as such, and its intent and meaning are to be found from consideration of its own terms without extrinsic aid. Some instances there have been in the last twenty years of a recognition of the necessity of approaching the Act as a Constitution to which a more liberal construction should be given, and one allowing proper effect to extrinsic facts and developments. These new attitudes, however, appeared only in a few cases, which either involved no question of legislative power or involved matters outside sections 91 and 92, and thus had no considerable effect on the traditional attitude.[39]

The Judicial Committee adopted this literal approach in several judgments. In *Bank of Toronto* v. *Lambe*,[40] 1887, Lord Hobhouse declared that the courts must not only "treat the provisions of the Act in question by the same methods of construction and exposition which they apply to other statutes," but refuse to consider the possible abuse of power: "But whatever power falls within the legitimate meaning of classes 2 and 9, is, in their Lordships' judgment, what the Imperial Parliament intended to give; and to place a limit on it because the power may be used unwisely, as all powers may, would be an error, and would

[36]Since there was a joint appeal in *Winnipeg* v. *Barrett*, [1892] A.C. 445, there were 174 appeals involved in the 173 major judgments.
[37]Out of 89 appeals, 25 were reversed, 63 affirmed, 3 varied, and 1 not allowed. These figures do not add up correctly because some appeals were allowed in part, others dismissed in part, and others varied in part.
[38]Out of the 174 appeals, 63 were reversed, 110 affirmed, 7 varied, and 3 not allowed. The explanation for these figures is the same as for those in n. 37.
[39]MacDonald, *CBR*, XXIX (1951), 1028–29.
[40]12 A.C. 575, at 579 and 586.

lead to insuperable difficulties, in the construction of the Federation Act." In *Brophy* v. *Attorney-General of Manitoba*,[41] 1895, Lord Herschell developed a similar argument:

It was not doubted that the object of the 1st sub-section of sect. 22 [i.e. of the Manitoba Public Schools Act, 1890] was to afford protection to denominational schools, or that it was proper to have regard to the intent of the Legislature and the surrounding circumstances in interpreting the enactment. But the question which had to be determined was the true construction of the language used. The function of a tribunal is limited to construing the words employed; it is not justified in forcing into them a meaning which they cannot reasonably bear. Its duty is to interpret, not to enact. It is true that the construction put by this Board upon the 1st sub-section reduced within very narrow limits the protection afforded by that sub-section in respect of denominational schools. It may be that those who were acting on behalf of the Roman Catholic community in Manitoba, and those who either framed or assented to the wording of that enactment, were under the impression that its scope was wider, and that it afforded protection greater than their Lordships held to be the case. But such considerations cannot properly influence the judgment of those who have judicially to interpret a statute. The question is, not what may be supposed to have been intended, but what has been said. More complete effect might in some cases be given to the intentions of the Legislature, if violence were done to the language in which their legislation has taken shape; but such a course would on the whole be quite as likely to defeat as to further the object which was in view.

In the *Companies* judgment[42] of 1912, Lord Loreburn—remarking that "if the text is explicit the text is conclusive, alike in what it directs and what it forbids"—also accepted the "ordinary statute" contention:

A Court of law has nothing to do with a Canadian Act of Parliament, lawfully passed, except to give it effect according to its tenor. No one who has experience of judicial duties can doubt that, if an Act of this kind were abused, manifold evils might follow, including undeserved suspicion of the course of justice and much embarrassment and anxiety to the judges themselves. Such considerations are proper, no doubt, to be weighed by those who make and by those who administer the laws of Canada, nor is any Court of law entitled to suppose that they have not been or will not be duly so weighed. So far as it is a matter of wisdom or policy, it is for the determination of the Parliament. It is true that from time to time the Courts of this and of other countries, whether under the British flag or not, have to consider and set aside, as void, transactions upon the ground that they are against public policy. But no such doctrine can apply to an Act of Parliament. It is applicable only to the transactions of individuals. It cannot be too strongly put that with the wisdom or expediency or policy of an Act, lawfully passed, no Court has a word to say. All, therefore, that their Lordships can consider

---

41[1895] A.C. 202, at 215–16.
42*A.-G. Ont.* v. *A.-G. Can.*, [1912] A.C. 571, at 582–83.

21

in the argument under review is whether it takes them a step towards proving that this Act is outside the authority of the Canadian Parliament, which is purely a question of the constitutional law of Canada.

And in *Edwards* v. *Attorney-General for Canada*,[43] 1930, Lord Sankey agreed that "the question is, not what may be supposed to have been intended, but what has been said."

The most extreme examples of the Judicial Committee's literal approach, however, are probably the *Labour Conventions*[44] and *Natural Products Marketing Act*[45] judgments of 1937. In the former, Lord Atkin decided that the advance in Canada's imperial and international status (consequent on the Imperial Conference of 1926 and the Statute of Westminster, 1931) did not affect the distribution of legislative authority. For this reason, the new ability of the federal government to enter into treaties with foreign powers did not enable the federal parliament to pass legislation implementing those treaties:

While it is true, as was pointed out in the *Radio* case, that it was not contemplated in 1867 that the Dominion would possess treaty-making powers, it is impossible to strain the section so as to cover the uncontemplated event. . . .

It follows from what has been said that no further legislative competence is obtained by the Dominion from its accession to international status, and the consequent increase in the scope of its executive functions. It is true, as pointed out in the judgment of the Chief Justice, that as the executive is now clothed with the powers of making treaties so the Parliament of Canada, to which the executive is responsible, has imposed upon it responsibilities in connection with such treaties, for if it were to disapprove of them they would either not be made or the Ministers would meet their constitutional fate. But this is true of all executive functions in their relation to Parliament. There is no existing constitutional ground for stretching the competence of the Dominion Parliament so that it becomes enlarged to keep pace with enlarged functions of the Dominion executive. If the new functions affect the classes of subjects enumerated in s. 92 legislation to support the new functions is in the competence of the Provincial Legislatures only. If they do not, the competence of the Dominion Legislature is declared by s. 91 and existed ab origine. In other words, the Dominion cannot, merely by making promises to foreign countries, clothe itself with legislative authority inconsistent with the constitution which gave it birth.
. . . While the ship of state now sails on larger ventures and into foreign waters she still retains the water-tight compartments which are an essential part of her original structure.[46]

---

[43][1930] A.C. 124, at 137. Cf. the interpretation given this judgment below, 24–25.
[44]*A.-G. Can.* v. *A.-G. Ont.*, [1937] A.C. 326.
[45]*A.-G. B.C.* v. *A.-G. Can.*, [1937] A.C. 377.
[46][1937] A.C. 326, at 350, 352, 354.

Similarly, in the *Natural Products Marketing Act* judgment of 1937, Lord Atkin decided that no matter how desirable marketing control might be, the distribution of legislative authority must be maintained according to the literal terms of the British North America Act:

> The Board were given to understand that some of the Provinces attach much importance to the existence of marketing schemes such as might be set up under this legislation: and their attention was called to the existence of Provincial legislation setting up Provincial schemes for various Provincial products. It was said that as the Provinces and the Dominion between them possess a totality of complete legislative authority, it must be possible to combine Dominion and Provincial legislation so that each within its own sphere could in co-operation with the other achieve the complete power of regulation which is desired. Their Lordships appreciate the importance of the desired aim. Unless and until a change is made in the respective legislative functions of Dominion and Province it may well be that satisfactory results for both can only be obtained by co-operation. But the legislation will have to be carefully framed, and will not be achieved by either party leaving its own sphere and encroaching upon that of the other.[47]

On the other hand, the Judicial Committee occasionally expressed quite opposite sentiments; and in some judgments, these sentiments might have actually affected the decision. In *Attorney-General of Ontario* v. *Mercer*,[48] 1883, for example, Lord Selborne took into account the "consistent and probable," as well as the "proper," construction:

> Their Lordships, for the reasons above stated, assume the burden of proving that escheats, subsequent to the Union, are within the sources of revenue excepted and reserved to the provinces, to rest upon the provinces. But, if all ordinary territorial revenues arising within the provinces are so excepted and reserved, it is not à priori probable that this particular kind of casual territorial revenue (not being expressly provided for) would have been, unless by accident and oversight, transferred to the Dominion. The words of the statute must receive their proper construction, whatever that might be; but, if this is doubtful, the more consistent and probable construction ought, in their Lordships' opinion, to be preferred. And it is a circumstance not without weight in the same direction, that while "duties and revenues" only are appropriated to the Dominion, the public property itself, by which territorial revenues are produced (as distinct from the revenues arising from it), is found to be appropriated to the provinces.

In the *Brophy* judgment[49] of 1895, Lord Herschell qualified his approval of the literal approach with this admission: "Whilst, however, it is necessary to resist any temptation to deviate from sound rules of construction in the hope of more completely satisfying the intention of the

[47][1937] A.C. 377, at 389.
[48]8 A.C. 767, at 774–75.
[49]*Brophy* v. *A.-G. Man.*, [1895] A.C. 202, at 216.

23

Legislature, it is quite legitimate where more than one construction of a statute is possible, to select that one which will best carry out what appears from the general scope of the legislation and the surrounding circumstances to have been its intention." And in the *Companies* judgment[50] of 1912, Lord Loreburn—describing the British North America Act as an "organic instrument"—expanded his remark that "if the text is explicit the text is conclusive":

> When the text is ambiguous, as, for example, when the words establishing two mutually exclusive jurisdictions are wide enough to bring a particular power within either, recourse must be had to the context and scheme of the Act. Again, if the text says nothing expressly, then it is not to be presumed that the Constitution withholds the power altogether. On the contrary, it is to be taken for granted that the power is bestowed in some quarter unless it be extraneous to the statute itself (as, for example, a power to make laws for some part of His Majesty's dominions outside of Canada) or otherwise is clearly repugnant to its sense. For whatever belongs to self-government in Canada belongs either to the Dominion or to the provinces, within the limits of the British North America Act.

But it was not until Lord Sankey's judgment in *Edwards* v. *Attorney-General for Canada*,[51] 1930, that the "constituent statute argument" was explicitly approved, and possibly adopted:

> The British North America Act planted in Canada a living tree capable of growth and expansion within its natural limits. The object of the Act was to grant a Constitution to Canada. "Like all written constitutions it has been subject to development through usage and convention": Canadian Constitutional Studies, Sir Robert Borden (1922), p.55.
>
> Their Lordships do not conceive it to be the duty of this Board—it is certainly not their desire—to cut down the provisions of the Act by a narrow and technical construction, but rather to give it a large and liberal interpretation so that the Dominion to a great extent, but within certain fixed limits, may be mistress in her own house, as the Provinces to a great extent, but within certain fixed limits, are mistresses in theirs. "The Privy Council, indeed, has laid down that Courts of law must treat the provisions of the British North America Act by the same methods of construction and exposition which they apply to other statutes. But there are statutes and statutes; and the strict construction deemed proper in the case, for example, of a penal or taxing statute or one passed to regulate the affairs of an English parish, would be often subversive of Parliament's real intent if applied to an Act passed to ensure the peace, order and good government of a British Colony": see Clement's Canadian Constitution, 3rd ed., p.347.
>
> The learned author of that treatise quotes from the argument of Mr. Mowat and Mr. Edward Blake before the Privy Council in *St. Catherine's Milling and Lumber Co.* v. *The Queen*: "That Act should be on all occasions

---

[50]*A.-G. Ont.* v. *A.-G. Can.*, [1912] A.C. 571, at 583.
[51][1930] A.C. 124, at 136–37.

24

interpreted in a large, liberal and comprehensive spirit, considering the magnitude of the subjects with which it purports to deal in very few words." With that their Lordships agree. . . .

According to Sir Ivor Jennings, this decision "wiped out the rule that the Canadian Constitution is a statute, to be interpreted like other statutes."[52] But even if the *Labour Conventions* and *Natural Products Marketing Act* cases of 1937 did not prove otherwise, this estimate would still be extreme. For Lord Sankey qualified his description, "mistress within her own house," by inserting the phrase, "but within certain fixed limits." Furthermore, the purpose of the Mowat-Blake argument[53] was to support the contention that the "federal union" of Canada consisted of "several entities"; that the original object of this union was "to preserve the Provinces, not as fractions of a unit, but as units of a multiple"; and that the provinces must consequently "be on an equal footing." Above all, as Lord Sankey himself observed, the *Edwards* judgment of 1930 was not concerned with the distribution of legislative authority: "It must be remembered, too, that their Lordships are not here considering the question of the legislative competence either of the Dominion or its Provinces which arise under ss. 91 and 92 of the Act providing for the distribution of legislative powers and assigning to the Dominion and its Provinces their respective spheres of Government."[54]

The "constituent statute argument" was also approved in *British Coal Corporation* v. *The King*,[55] 1935, and *Attorney-General for Ontario* v. *Attorney-General for Canada*,[56] 1947. In the former case, Lord Sankey decided that section 91 of the British North America Act invested the federal parliament with authority to prohibit criminal appeals to the King in Council. Quoting from Lord Loreburn's *Companies* judgment[57] of 1912, as well as from his own argument in the *Edwards* case,[58] he added these comments:

What is the extent of the legislative competence in the relevant regard conferred on the Canadian Parliament, putting out of the question the limitations which are now removed, must be ascertained from the words of the constituent Act. In construing the words of that Act, it must be remembered what the nature and scope of the Act are. They are indicated in

---

[52]Jennings, *LQR*, LII (1936), 181.
[53]See *St. Catherine's Milling and Lumber Co.* v. *The Queen* (1889), 14 A.C. 46, at 50.
[54][1930] A.C. 124, at 137.
[55][1935] A.C. 500.
[56][1947] A.C. 127.
[57]*A.-G. Ont.* v. *A.-G. Can.*, [1912] A.C. 571.
[58]*Edwards* v. *A.-G. Can.*, [1930] A.C. 124.

the words used by Lord Loreburn L.C. in delivering the judgment of the Judicial Committee in *Attorney-General for Ontario* v. *Attorney-General for Canada*: "In 1867 the desire of Canada for a definite Constitution embracing the entire Dominion was embodied in the British North America Act. Now, there can be no doubt that under this organic instrument the powers distributed between the Dominion on the one hand and the provinces on the other hand cover the whole area of self-government within the whole area of Canada. It would be subversive of the entire scheme and policy of the Act to assume that any point of internal self-government was withheld from Canada.

. . . Indeed, in interpreting a constituent or organic statute such as the Act, that construction most beneficial to the widest possible amplitude of its powers must be adopted. This principle has been again clearly laid down by the Judicial Committee in *Edwards* v. *Attorney-General for Canada* [here the second paragraph quoted above from the *Edwards* judgment is repeated].[59]

While the *British Coal Corporation* judgment was not concerned with the distribution of legislative power either, it did provide a basis for the *Privy Council Appeals* decision of 1947. Lord Jowitt then held that the federal parliament had authority to abolish all appeals to the Privy Council, and so to give the Supreme Court of Canada "exclusive" and "ultimate" appellate jurisdiction. Repeating Lord Sankey's arguments as to the removal of previous "fetters" by the Statute of Westminster,[60] approving Lord Loreburn's "organic instrument" remarks in the *Companies* case[61] of 1912, and upholding the power of the federal parliament to abolish appeals by virtue of section 101,[62] he concluded with the following statements:

Giving full weight to the circumstances of the Union and to the determination shown by the provinces as late as the Imperial Conferences, which led to the Statute of Westminster, that their rights should be unimpaired, nevertheless, it appears to their Lordships that it is not consistent with the political conception which is embodied in the British Commonwealth of Nations that one member of that Commonwealth should be precluded from setting up, if it so desires, a Supreme Court of Appeal having a jurisdiction both ultimate and exclusive of any other member. The regulation of appeals is, to use the words of Lord Sankey in the *British Coal Corporation* case a "prime element in Canadian sovereignty," which would be impaired if at the will of its citizens recourse could be had to a tribunal, in the constitution of which it had no voice. It is, as their Lordships think, irrelevant that the question is one that might have seemed unreal at the date of the British North America Act. To such an organic statute the flexible interpretation must be given

---

[59][1935] A.C. 500, at 517 and 518.
[60][1947] A.C. 127, at 146–50.   [61]*Ibid.*, at 150.
[62]*Ibid.*, at 152–53. Section 101 was relied on notwithstanding ss. 92(13), 92(14), 92(16), and 129.

which changing circumstances require, and it would be alien to the spirit, with which the preamble to the Statute of Westminster is instinct, to concede anything less than the widest amplitude of power to the Dominion legislature under s. 101 of the Act.

. . . It is, in fact, a prime element in the self-government of the Dominion, that it should be able to secure through its own courts of justice that the law should be one and the same for all its citizens. This result is attainable only if s. 101 now authorizes the establishment of a court with final and exclusive appellate jurisdiction. The words used by Lord Macmillan in delivering the opinion of the Board in *Croft* v. *Dunphy*, on a question that arose in regard to one of the specific subjects enumerated in s. 91 are equally applicable in the consideration of s. 101; "their Lordships," he said, "see no reason to restrict the permitted scope of such legislation by any other consideration than is applicable to the legislation of a fully sovereign state."[63]

These statements illustrate another way in which the Judicial Committee revealed "liberal" sympathies. By tending to presume in favour of the validity of a statute (that is, by hesitating to declare legislation *ultra vires*), the Board effectively took into account the interpretation placed on disputed legislation by the enacting body. As early as *Valin* v. *Langlois*,[64] 1879, Lord Selborne observed that "it is not to be presumed that the Legislature of the dominion has exceeded its powers, unless upon grounds really of a serious character." And in *Hodge* v. *The Queen*,[65] 1883, Sir Barnes Peacock applied the same principle to provincial legislation:

It appears to their Lordships, however, that the objection thus raised by the appellants is founded on an entire misconception of the true character and position of the provincial legislatures. They are in no sense delegates of or acting under any mandate from the Imperial Parliament. When the British North America Act enacted that there should be a legislature for Ontario, and its legislative assembly should have exclusive authority to make laws for the Province and for provincial purposes in relation to the matters enumerated in sect. 92, it conferred powers not in any sense to be exercised by delegation from or as agents of the Imperial Parliament, but authority as plenary and as ample within the limits prescribed by sect. 92 as the Imperial Parliament in the plentitude of its power possessed and could bestow. Within these limits of subjects and area the local legislature is supreme, and has the same authority as the Imperial Parliament, or the Parliament of the Dominion, would have had under like circumstances to confide to a municipal institution or body of its own creation authority to make by-laws or resolutions as to subjects specified in the enactment, and with the object of carrying the enactment into operation and effect.

---

[63]*Ibid.*, at 153–54 and 154–55.

[64]5 A.C. 115, at 118.

[65]9 A.C. 117, at 132. This line of reasoning was also adopted, with reference to extra-territorial legislation by the federal parliament, in *A.-G. Can.* v. *Cain*, [1906] A.C. 542, at 546–47, and *Croft* v. *Dunphy*, [1933] A.C. 156, at 163.

As for federal legislation, in *Citizens Insurance Company* v. *Parsons*,[66] 1881, Sir Montague Smith developed this proposition: "The declarations of the dominion parliament are not, of course, conclusive upon the construction of the British North America Act; but when the proper construction of the language used in that Act to define the distribution of legislative powers is doubtful, the interpretation put upon it by the dominion parliament in its actual legislation may properly be considered." Similarly, in *Russell* v. *The Queen*,[67] 1882, Sir Montague emphasized the "declared object" of the federal parliament, "that there should be uniform legislation in all the provinces respecting the traffic in intoxicating liquors, with a view to promote temperance in the Dominion." Then, in the *Fort Frances* judgment[68] of 1923, Lord Haldane recommended not only that the need for emergency legislation should be gauged in the "interests of the Dominion generally," but that "as to these interests the Dominion Government, which in its Parliament represents the people as a whole, must be deemed to be left with considerable freedom to judge." And in *Abitibi Power and Paper Company* v. *Montreal Trust Company*,[69] 1943, Lord Atkin summed up this tendency to presume in favour of the validity of a statute, and so to consider the "constituent" character of the British North America Act:

It was pressed on their Lordships that the real substance of the legislation was an attempt to coerce the bondholders into accepting a plan of reconstruction, and that arrangements such as were contemplated by the report of the Royal Commission were within the exclusive field of dominion legislation. So they are, but this Board must have cogent grounds before it arising from the nature of the impugned legislation before it can impute to a provincial legislation some object other than what is to be seen on the face of the enactment itself. In the present case their Lordships see no reason to reject the statement of the Ontario legislature, contained in the preamble to the Act, that the power to stay the action is given so that an opportunity may be given to all the parties concerned to consider the plan submitted in the report of the Royal Commission.

Even so, the question is not whether the Judicial Committee was occasionally affected by the constituent statute argument, but whether it applied that argument in its "determinant" decisions. And this question is really undebatable. In by far the majority of cases it was the approach adopted in *Bank of Toronto* v. *Lambe*, rather than the one reflected in

[66]7 A.C. 96, at 115–16.

[67]7 A.C. 829, at 841.

[68]*Fort Frances Pulp and Power Co.* v. *Manitoba Free Press Co.*, [1923] A.C. 695, at 705.

[69][1943] A.C. 536, at 548. But note that the impugned legislation was a provincial, and not a federal, statute.

Edwards v. *Attorney-General for Canada*, that prevailed. It was also this literal approach that led to the resolution, if not the formulation, of the three major problems—Compartment, Ambit, and Consignment.[70] In short, the critics represented by Mr. V. C. MacDonald are basically correct: the Judicial Committee "has never seriously wavered from the principle that it was their function to interpret the 'intention of Parliament' as laid down in the Act and not to fit the Constitution to the changing conditions of social life."[71] Essentially, the Board rejected the "constituent statute argument."

3. The Judicial Committee and the Federal Principle

Yet there might have been one way in which the Judicial Committee did depart from the text of the Act. By accepting a "philosophy of federalism," it might have modified its construction to suit the federal principle of "co-ordinate and independent" authorities. This possibility has provoked Mr. MacDonald to raise another objection:

> This unconcern with the results of its role as a mere interpreter of a text comports ill with the fact that the Privy Council has in one very momentous matter been concerned with the Act as a Constitution. I refer to the fact that early in its career it formed a very definite view of *the nature of the Federal Union* effected by the Act and has persistently sought to make the Act square with that view. That view was that Canada is a true federation resulting from a "compact" between sovereign bodies the legislatures of which were intended to possess equal status and autonomy within their prescribed limits; and that it was the function of the courts to maintain this compact and make these legislative rivals hew to the line of division; and in particular to preserve provincial legislative "autonomy" from encroachment.

The first indication of such a concern for provincial autonomy was expressed by Sir Montague Smith, in *Citizens Insurance Company* v. *Parsons*,[72] 1881: "Notwithstanding this endeavour to give pre-eminence to the dominion parliament in cases of a conflict of powers, it is obvious that in some cases where this apparent conflict exists, the legislature could not have intended that the powers exclusively assigned to the provincial legislature should be absorbed in those given to the dominion

[70]As will be shown throughout the following discussion, but especially in chaps. 5, 7, and 10.
[71]Jennings, *Harvard Law Review*, LI (1937), 35: see also *LQR*, LII (1936), 182.
[72]7 A.C. 96, at 108. See also *Hodge* v. *The Queen* (1883), 9 A.C. 117, at 132.

parliament." In *Liquidators of the Maritime Bank of Canada* v. *Receiver-General of New Brunswick*,[73] 1892, Lord Watson added the following opinion:

The object of the Act was neither to weld the provinces into one, nor to subordinate provincial governments to a central authority, but to create a federal government in which they should all be represented, entrusted with the exclusive administration of affairs in which they had a common interest, each province retaining its independence and autonomy. That object was accomplished by distributing, between the Dominion and the provinces, all powers executive and legislative, and all public property and revenues which had previously belonged to the provinces; so that the Dominion Government should be vested with such of these powers, property, and revenues as were necessary for the due performance of its constitutional functions, and that the remainder should be retained by the provinces for the purposes of provincial government. But, in so far as regards those matters which, by sect. 92, are specially reserved for provincial legislation, the legislature of each province continues to be free from the control of the Dominion, and as supreme as it was before the passing of the Act.

In the *Local Prohibition* judgment[74] of 1896, Lord Watson reflected the same point of view:

These enactments [viz., the introductory words and the concluding paragraph of section 91] appear to their Lordships to indicate that the exercise of legislative power by the Parliament of Canada, in regard to all matters not enumerated in s. 91, ought to be strictly confined to such matters as are unquestionably of Canadian interest and importance, and ought not to trench upon provincial legislation with respect to any of the classes of subjects enumerated in s. 92. To attach any other construction to the general power which, in supplement of its enumerated powers, is conferred upon the Parliament of Canada by s. 91, would, in their Lordships' opinion, not only be contrary to the intendment of the Act, but would practically destroy the autonomy of the provinces. If it were once conceded that the Parliament of Canada has authority to make laws applicable to the whole Dominion, in relation to matters which in each province are substantially of local or private interest, upon the assumption that these matters also concern the peace, order, and good government of the Dominion, there is hardly a subject enumerated in s. 92 upon which it might not legislate, to the exclusion of the provincial legislatures.

During *In re the Initiative and Referendum Act*,[75] 1919, Lord Haldane agreed:

The scheme of the Act passed in 1867 was thus, not to weld the Provinces into one, nor to subordinate Provincial Governments to a central authority,

---

[73][1892] A.C. 437, at 441–42.

[74]*A.-G. Ont.* v. *A.-G. Can.*, [1896] A.C. 348, at 360–61.

[75][1919] A.C. 935, at 942. See also *John Deere Plow Co.* v. *Wharton*, [1915] A.C. 330, at 338.

but to establish a central government in which these Provinces should be represented, entrusted with exclusive authority only in affairs in which they had a common interest. Subject to this each Province was to retain its independence and autonomy and to be directly under the Crown as its head. Within these limits of area and subjects, its local Legislature, so long as the Imperial Parliament did not repeal its own Act conferring this status, was to be supreme, and had such powers as the Imperial Parliament possessed in the plenitude of its own freedom before it handed them over to the Dominion and the Provinces, in accordance with the scheme of distribution which it enacted in 1867.

In the *Labour Conventions* judgment[76] of 1937, Lord Atkin—stressing the "compact" and "provincial autonomy" arguments—concluded with this suggestion:

> It must not be thought that the result of this decision is that Canada is incompetent to legislate in performance of treaty obligations. In totality of legislative powers, Dominion and Provincial together, she is fully equipped. But the legislative powers remain distributed, and if in the exercise of her new functions derived from her new international status Canada incurs obligations they must, so far as legislation be concerned, when they deal with Provincial classes of subjects, be dealt with by the totality of powers, in other words by co-operation between the Dominion and the Provinces.

And in the *Unemployment Insurance* judgment,[77] also of 1937, Lord Atkin once more exhibited the Judicial Committee's concern for provincial legislative autonomy:

> In other words, Dominion legislation, even though it deals with Dominion property, may yet be so framed as to invade civil rights within the Province, or encroach upon the classes of subjects which are reserved to Provincial competence. It is not necessary that it should be a colourable device, or a pretence. If on the true view of the legislation it is found that in reality in pith and substance the legislation invades civil rights within the Province, or in respect of other classes of subjects otherwise encroaches upon the provincial field, the legislation will be invalid. To hold otherwise would afford the Dominion an easy passage into the Provincial domain.

It might seem inconsistent to criticize the Judicial Committee for adopting too literal an approach, and at the same time to complain that the Board was influenced by a consideration extraneous to the text of the British North America Act. On the other hand, since the constituent statute argument equates "liberal" with "federal" (and so "literal" with "provincial") it might be permissible to raise both objections simultaneously. But in either case, assuming that the Judicial Committee did

[76]*A.-G. Can.* v. *A.-G. Ont.*, [1937] A.C. 326, at 353–54.
[77]*A.-G. Can.* v. *A.-G. Ont.*, [1937] A.C. 355, at 366–67.

adopt the "federal principle" of co-ordinate and independent authorities, why did it do so? Mr. MacDonald's answer comes to this:

The truth is, also, that their Lordships never understood the kind of federalism intended to be given, and in terms given; and in revolt against contentions contrary to their own ideas, and against the pro-Dominion bias which underlay the distribution of powers, proceeded to establish a balance of jurisdiction more conformable to those ideas. "The only basic principle formulated by the Judicial Committee . . . concerns the retention and proper balancing of two equally sovereign legislatures. This principle is not expressed in the British North America Act and owes its origin to judicial sanction." In the result, as most competent writers have argued, it is incontestable that our Constitution, as it now exists in a text encrusted with decisions, is not what we sought or what the Imperial Parliament provided for us.[78]

However, that is not the only possible answer; for it is just as likely that the "federal principle" was not imposed on the British North America Act, but derived from it. In other words, the Judicial Committee might have concluded that the Canadian Constitution is "federal" in character, and should be maintained in this character, simply because of the manner in which legislative authority is distributed by the actual terms of the Act. And if some judges began with certain assumptions,[79] that does not preclude the framers of the Act from having held those same assumptions. In fact, as will now be shown, Mr. MacDonald's assertion that the federal principle "is not expressed in the British North America Act" is far from "incontestable."

[78]MacDonald, *CBR*, XXIX (1951), 1031. The enclosed quotation is from La Brie, *UTLJ*, VIII (1950), 346.

[79]Cf. Lord Haldane, in *A.-G. Australia v. Colonial Sugar Refining Co.*, [1914] A.C. 237, at 252-53 (cited in *John Deere Plow Co. v. Wharton*, [1915] A.C. 330, at 338), and Lord Wright, in *Cambridge Law Journal*, VIII (1944), 134–36.

Chapter Three

THE COMPARTMENT PROBLEM: I

1. The Exhaustion Theory

The distribution of legislative powers in a federal constitution is usually accomplished in two stages:[1] first, an "exhaustive" grant is made (so as to cover all the powers that are to be distributed); then the powers of either the central or the regional authority[2] are "enumerated" (and all "residuary" power left with the other authority). Disputes over legislative competence can thus be settled by means of a two-step procedure: if the impugned law concerns an enumerated subject, it is assigned to the authority with the enumerated powers; if that law does not concern an enumerated subject, it is assigned to the authority with the "residuary" power.

In the *Companies* judgment[3] of 1912, Lord Loreburn confirmed that the British North America Act exhausts the "area of self-government":

In 1867 the desire of Canada for a definite Constitution embracing the entire Dominion was embodied in the British North America Act. Now, there can be no doubt that under this organic instrument the powers distributed between the Dominion on the one hand and the provinces on the other hand cover the whole area of self-government within the whole area of Canada. It would be subversive of the entire scheme and policy of the Act to assume that any point of internal self-government was withheld from Canada. . . . Again, if the text says nothing expressly, then it is not to be presumed that the Constitution withholds the power altogether. On the contrary, it is to be taken for granted that the power is bestowed in some quarter unless it be extraneous to the statute itself (as, for example, a power to make laws for some part of His Majesty's Dominions outside of Canada) or otherwise is clearly repugnant to its sense. For whatever belongs to self-government in Canada belongs either to the Dominion or to the provinces, within the limits of the British North America Act.

---

[1]See Wheare, *Federal Government*, 11–15.
[2]Depending, normally, on which is to be the weaker.
[3]*A.-G. Ont* v. *A.-G. Can.*, [1912] A.C. 571, at 581 and 583.

33

This "Exhaustion Theory" was explicitly accepted in *Bank of Toronto* v. *Lambe*,[4] 1887, *Union Colliery Company* v. *Bryden*,[5] 1899, and *Attorney-General for Canada* v. *Attorney-General for Ontario*,[6] 1937. It was also implicitly acknowledged in *Citizens Insurance Company* v. *Parsons*,[7] 1881, *Ontario Mining Company* v. *Seybold*,[8] 1903, and *Great West Saddlery Company* v. *The King*,[9] 1921.

During the course of *Toronto Electric Commissioners* v. *Snider*,[10] 1925, however, Lord Haldane denied that "the whole legislative power is divided between the two" legislative authorities: "That is a popular expression, and even judges in the Judicial Committee are human; you must not strain casual expressions in connections where they are not applied. *It is not true*."[11] Whatever the cause or implication of this denial,[12] it is literally correct. For several provisions in the British North America Act do subtract from the combined legislative power of the federal parliament and the provincial legislatures: sections 51, 51A,[13] and 52 fix the representational features of the House of Commons; sections 55, 56, and 57 enable the imperial authorities to reserve and to disallow legislation passed by the federal parliament; sections 93, 99,[14] and 133 provide explicit guarantees concerning denominational schools, the tenure of judges, and the use of the English and French languages; sections 103, 104, and 105 impose limits on the power of the federal parliament to dispose of public monies; section 121 establishes the free admission of all articles of the growth, produce, or manufacture of any of the provinces into each of the other provinces; and section 125 prohibits the taxing of land or property belonging to Canada or to any province of Canada.

Moreover, the original grant of legislative power involved several omissions. Neither the federal parliament nor the provincial legislatures could change imperial legislation that extended to Canada by express word or necessary intendment.[15] Succession to the throne, as well as the

---

[4]12 A.C. 575, at 587.   [5][1899] A.C. 580, at 584–85.
[6][1937] A.C. 326, at 353–54.   [7]7 A.C. 96.   [8][1903] A.C. 73.
[9][1921] 2 A.C. 91. See also *Liquidators of the Maritime Bank of Canada* v. *Receiver-Gen. of N.B.*, [1892] A.C. 437—which is extraordinary not only for the implicit residuary assumption, but also for the explicit assignment of this residuary power to the provincial legislatures: see at 441–42.
[10][1925] A.C. 396.
[11]Quoted in the *O'Connor Report*, Annex 1, 16.
[12]And O'Connor seems to build rather a lot on what was only a fleeting exchange, made during the course of the argument, and not mentioned in the judgment itself: see *ibid.*, 16–18.
[13]As enacted by the British North America Act, 1915, 5–6 Geo. V, c. 45.
[14]Amended by the British North America Act, 1960, 9 Eliz. II, c. 2.
[15]Because of the Colonial Laws Validity Act, 1865, 28 and 29 Vict., c. 63.

royal style and titles, was likewise outside Canadian jurisdiction.[16] The office of Governor-General, while mentioned in sections 24, 55, 56, 57, and 105, was created through exercise of the Prerogative, rather than by the British North America Act.[17] The office of Lieutenant-Governor entailed appointment by the Governor-General-in-Council, tenure at the disposition of the Governor-General, and salary payments from the federal parliament.[18] The taxing power of the provincial legislatures was restricted to "direct taxation within the province in order to the raising of a revenue for provincial purposes" (which left open the question of indirect taxation, within the provinces, for provincial purposes[19]). The treaty-implementing power[20] was deficient in that no legislative body in Canada was able to enact extra-territorial legislation.[21] There was also no provision for the amendment of the British North America Act by effective action in Canada. And both the possibility of inter-delegation and the matter of civil liberties were incompletely covered.[22]

Some of these limitations—notably those concerned with the disabilities arising under the Colonial Laws Validity Act, the relationship between the law of Canada and the law of England, the possibility of imperial reservation and disallowance, the succession to the throne, the royal style and titles, and the office of Governor-General—were subsequently removed or altered.[23] Yet others—and most awkwardly, those concerning inter-delegation and civil liberties—remain. The "Exhaustion Theory" is therefore not strictly applicable to the constitution of Canada;[24] and the remark passed by Lord Haldane during the *Snider* case of 1925 is not so unintelligible as some critics suggest.[25]

[16]See Wheare, *Statute of Westminster*, 149–53.

[17]It was consequently dependent on the imperial, rather than the Canadian government, and so, presumably, was subject to the ultimate control of the imperial, rather than the Canadian parliament: see Laskin, *Constitutional Law*, 62.

[18]As per ss. 58, 59, and 60 of the B.N.A. Act of 1867: see Laskin, *Constitutional Law*, 64, and Saywell, *Lieutenant-Governor*, *passim*.

[19]This problem is discussed below, in chap. 8, sec. 2; see also Laskin, *Constitutional Law*, 64, chap. XII generally, and *UTLJ*, XIII (1959), 20.

[20]As later defined by the Judicial Committee through its restricted interpretation of s. 132: see below, chap. 8, sec. 3.

[21]See *Nadan* v. *The King*, [1926] A.C. 482.

[22]For a discussion of these questions, see Laskin, *Constitutional Law*, 35–37 and chap. xv.

[23]Both formally, by the Statute of Westminster, 1931, 22 Geo. V, c. 4, and informally, through the understandings reached at the Imperial Conferences of 1926 and 1930: see Wheare, *Statute of Westminster*, 24–40, and Laskin, *Constitutional Law*, 62–65.

[24]See Laskin, *Constitutional Law*, 35–37 and 938–44. The 20 major references to the Exhaustion Theory (or else to the closely related problem of extra-territorial powers) are marked in col. D of the Analytical Table: see below, 229–42.

[25]See *O'Connor Report*, 14–18.

2. The Compartment Question and the Three-Compartment View

The British North America Act is also unusual in its enumerative
character; for instead of the normal residuary statement and enumerated
list, it contains a "general" statement and two enumerated lists. Thus
in section 91, the federal parliament is given power "to make laws for
the Peace, Order, and good Government of Canada." Further on in
this section, however, there is a list of thirty-one[26] enumerated "classes
of subjects" (concerning which the federal parliament has "exclusive
legislative authority"). And then, in section 92, there is a list of sixteen
enumerated "classes of subjects" (concerning which the provincial legislatures may also "exclusively make laws"). The sections read as
follows:[27]

91. It shall be lawful for the Queen, by and with the Advice and Consent
of the Senate and House of Commons, to make Laws for the Peace, Order,
and good Government of Canada, in relation to all Matters not coming
within the Classes of Subjects by this Act assigned exclusively to the Legislatures of the Provinces; and for greater Certainty, but not so as to restrict
the Generality of the foregoing Terms of this Section, it is hereby declared
that (notwithstanding anything in this Act) the exclusive Legislative Authority of the Parliament of Canada extends to all Matters coming within the
Classes of Subjects next herein-after enumerated; that is to say. . . . [Here
thirty-one "Classes of Subjects" are enumerated. No 29—which is actually
the last—reads, "Such Classes of Subjects as are expressly excepted in the
Enumeration of the Classes of Subjects by this Act assigned exclusively to
the Legislatures of the Provinces."]
And any Matter coming within any of the Classes of Subjects enumerated
in this Section shall not be deemed to come within the Class of Matters of
a local or private Nature comprised in the Enumeration of the Classes of
Subjects by this Act assigned exclusively to the Legislatures of the Provinces.
92. In each Province the Legislature may exclusively make Laws in relation to Matters coming within the Classes of Subjects next herein-after
enumerated; that is to say. . . . [Here sixteen "Classes of Subjects" are enumerated. No. 16 reads, "Generally all Matters of a merely local or private
Nature in the Province."]

Section 91 accordingly consists of two "parts": the "Peace, Order,
and good Government" clause (up to the first semi-colon in the "intro-

[26]The original number of twenty-nine was increased through the addition of
heads 1 and 2a: the former (which caused the "Public Debt and Property" head
to be re-numbered as head 1a) was added by the British North America (No. 2)
Act, 1949, 13 Geo. VI, c. 81; the latter had been added earlier, by the British
North America Act, 1940, 3–4 Geo. VI, c. 36.
[27]For the complete Act and its amendments, see below, 189–225.

ductory words"); and the thirty-one "heads" (introduced by the phrase "and for greater Certainty," and rounded off by the "deeming" paragraph, beginning "And any Matter"). The first problem in the interpretation of the British North America Act concerns the relationship between these parts. Is the first supplementary to the second, or is the second illustrative of the first? If the heads are supplementary, sections 91 and 92 would contain three "compartments"—the Peace, Order, and good Government clause, the heads of section 91, and section 92. Alternatively, if the second part of section 91 is illustrative, there would be only two "compartments"—section 91 (as a whole) and section 92.

The three-compartment view is based on a pair of arguments: one derived from the introductory words of section 91, the other from the deeming paragraph. The legislative authority conferred on the federal parliament by the Peace, Order, and good Government clause is expressly confined to matters "not coming within the Classes of Subjects by this Act assigned exclusively to the Legislatures of the Provinces." But the federal parliament is also said to have an "exclusive" legislative authority, which "notwithstanding anything in this Act . . . extends to all Matters coming within the Classes of Subjects next herein-after enumerated." It follows that since these definitions would be incompatible unless they represented different "kinds" of powers, they must signify that the powers covered by the Peace, Order, and good Government clause are supplementary to those delimited by the heads—and that sections 91 and 92 contain three compartments.

As for the deeming paragraph, the question is whether the expression "Class of Matters of a local or private Nature" (which is "comprised in the Enumeration of the Classes of Subjects by this Act assigned exclusively to the Legislatures of the Provinces") refers to all the heads of section 92, or only to head 16 ("Generally all Matters of a merely local or private Nature in the Province"). If this expression refers to head 16 only, then the deeming paragraph would be no more than a safeguard against provincial "encroachments," under the authority of section 92(16), on the heads of section 91. On the other hand, if the expression "Class of Matters of a local or private Nature" refers to all the heads of section 92, then (because the deeming paragraph expressly applies to the heads of section 91 alone, and so excludes the Peace, Order, and good Government clause) three compartments must be entailed.

A supplementary interpretation of the heads of section 91 would involve an order of priority as well. Since the Peace, Order, and good Government clause is confined to matters "not coming within the

37

Classes of Subjects by this Act assigned exclusively to the Legislatures of the Provinces," section 92 must be "prior" to that clause. However, since the heads of section 91 are modified by the *non obstante* clause ("notwithstanding anything in this Act"), they must be prior to section 92. An order of priority—according to which the heads of section 91 outrank section 92, which in turn outranks the Peace, Order, and good Government clause—is the result. Furthermore, if the deeming paragraph ensures that any matter coming within the heads of section 91 does not come within section 92, then (because section 92 outranks the Peace, Order, and good Government clause) the same order of priority ensues.

The next effect would be a three-step procedure for settling disputes over legislative competence. If an impugned law were held to be, "in pith and substance," in relation to a matter coming within a subject enumerated in the heads of section 91, it would be assigned to the federal parliament. Similarly, if that law were held to be, "in pith and substance," in relation to a matter coming within a subject enumerated in section 92, it would be assigned to the provincial legislatures. But if the law were held not to be, "in pith and substance," in relation to a matter coming within a subject comprised in either the heads of section 91 or section 92, then (because of the Exhaustion Theory) it would come within the Peace, Order, and good Government clause, and so would be assigned to the federal parliament.[28]

Finally, in addition to imposing a three-compartment view, an order of priority among the three compartments, and a three-step procedure for settling disputes over legislative competence, a supplementary interpretation of the heads of section 91 would give the Peace, Order, and good Government clause a "residuary" character. For if that clause is supplementary to those heads, it would cover only the powers that were left over, or became "residuary," once the powers defined in the heads of section 91 and in section 92 had been distributed between the federal parliament and the provincial legislatures. In short, the Peace, Order, and good Government clause would be a mere catch-all for any legislative powers that were presumably included in the total grant of legislative authority, but which were not actually specified.

Such an interpretation could induce a tendency to regard the Peace, Order, and good Government clause in the light of a last resort—to be

[28]In practice, the three-step procedure is short-circuited by first asking whether s. 92 applies, and only then inquiring whether the heads of s. 91 are also applicable. This shortened procedure was used by Lord Haldane in *Toronto Electric Commissioners* v. *Snider*, [1925] A.C. 396, at 406. The question is treated more fully below, in chaps. 4 and 5.

invoked only when it proved impossible to consign a law to one of the enumerated lists. However, if the court of final appeal tried to fit as much legislation as possible into those lists, it could enlarge the ambit of the subjects comprised within them. Indeed, since the "subject" most susceptible to such enlarging is probably the one described in head 13 of section 92 ("Property and Civil Rights in the Province"),[29] the ultimate effect could be an enlargement of the legislative sphere of the provinces, at the expense of the federal parliament. Nor would this effect be lessened if the court were also determined to safeguard the "federal" character of the Canadian Constitution—or at any rate, to establish the principle of "co-ordinate and independent authorities."

3. The Two- and Four-Compartment Views

While the two-compartment view is also based on a pair of arguments, in this case both arguments are derived from the introductory words of section 91.[30] In the second part of those words, the thirty-one enumerated classes of subjects are listed "for greater Certainty, but not so as to restrict the Generality of the foregoing Terms of this Section." As if to underline that explanation, this second part is then expressed in declaratory, rather than enacting terms ("it is hereby declared" and "extends," as opposed to "shall extend"). It would seem to follow that the heads of section 91 illustrate the ambit of the Peace, Order, and good Government clause; that the two "parts" of section 91 are not separate, but conjoined; and that sections 91 and 92 contain only two compartments—section 91 (as a whole) and section 92.

If section 91 is read as a whole, however, the *non obstante* clause (which in the three-compartment view, refers to the heads of section 91 only) must refer to the Peace, Order, and good Government clause as well. Section 91 must therefore be "prior," as a whole, to section 92. On the other hand, this priority need not imply that the legislative authority of the federal parliament must outrank that of the provincial legislatures. For the notion of exclusive legislative spheres, and hence the federal principle of "co-ordinate and independent authorities," can still be preserved: by defining the word "matter" so as to distinguish between "subject" and "scope." In other words, the federal parliament

29For reasons that are shown below, in chap. 6, sec. 2 and chap. 7.
30The following account is based on O'Connor's *Report*, the thesis of which (see below, chap. 5, sec. 1) has been adopted almost universally, and sometimes literally: see Kennedy, *Cambridge Law Journal*, VIII (1943), 146–60.

must have exclusive power to make laws concerning any "subject," providing those laws are of national "scope." And the provincial legislatures must have exclusive power to make laws concerning the "subjects" enumerated in section 92, providing those laws are of provincial "scope."

Disputes over legislative competence can now be settled by means of a two-step procedure. If an impugned law were held to be, "in pith and substance," in relation to a matter coming within a "subject" comprised in section 92—and if it were also of provincial "scope"—it would be assigned to the provincial legislatures. However, if that law were held to be, "in pith and substance," in relation to any matter of national "scope," then—regardless of "subject"—it would come within the Peace, Order, and good Government clause, and so would be assigned to the federal parliament.

Finally, in addition to imposing a two-compartment view, the priority of section 91 (as a whole) over section 92, and a two-step procedure for settling disputes over legislative competence, an illustrative interpretation of the heads of section 91 would give the Peace, Order, and good Government clause a "general," rather than a "residuary" character. Instead of being a mere catch-all for residuary legislative powers, this clause would become the means of defining the legislative authority of the federal parliament. And this authority would enable that parliament to make laws concerning any "subject"—providing those laws were of national "scope."

Such an interpretation might well alarm the courts. The federal parliament would be able, and perhaps tempted, to infringe on the autonomy of the provincial legislatures. Moreover, the judiciary would be involved, not just in a particular political situation, but in the general political process. For the courts would be required to estimate both the intentions of the legislating bodies and the likely effects of their legislation. They would accordingly become the arbiters, if not the censors, of legislative actions. And they would probably tend to produce more "factual" decisions, which do not lend themselves easily to the establishment of precedents. The adoption of a two-compartment view could thus entail fundamental changes, not merely in the character of the judgments in appeal cases, but in the significance of the Rule of Precedent and the Theory of Judicial Restraint.

This is not to imply that the three-compartment procedure fails to allow for the consideration of "scope." On the contrary, the Dimensions and Emergency Doctrines[31] make it possible to accept the three-com-

[31]See below, chap. 9, sec. 3; chap. 11; chap. 12, sec. 1.

partment view, and at the same time to ensure that laws concerned with "subjects" enumerated in section 92 (and not concerned with any "subject" enumerated in the heads of section 91) are assigned to the federal parliament.[32] However, the classification step would now be determined by the ranking of the three compartments; for since the Peace, Order, and good Government clause is outranked by section 92, considerations of "subject" would normally carry more weight in the consignment process than those of "scope." In fact, given a concern for the principle of "co-ordinate and independent authorities," a solicitude for the legislative autonomy of the provinces, and an acceptance of the three-compartment view, the consideration of "scope" would probably require the presence of very exceptional circumstances.

Sections 91 and 92 have also been viewed as containing four compartments: the Peace, Order, and good Government clause; the heads of section 91; heads 1–15 (inclusive) of section 92; and section 92, head 16.[33] This view is derived from the general phrasing of section 92 (16). In the *Local Prohibition* judgment[34] of 1896, Lord Watson observed that head 16 appears to have "the same office which the general enactment with respect to matters concerning the peace, order, and good government of Canada, so far as supplementary of the enumerated subjects, fulfils in s. 91." Accordingly, in the *Manitoba Liquor Act* judgment[35] of 1902, Lord Macnaghten proposed a corresponding order of priority, together with a four-step procedure for settling disputes over legislative authority.

Unfortunately, however, this view distorts the third-compartment status of the Peace, Order, and good Government clause. Whereas the status of that clause is based on the overall structure of sections 91 and 92, the fourth-compartment status of section 92 (16) is derived from the phrasing of the head itself.[36] The latter reasoning is therefore basically different from the former, if not incompatible with it. Furthermore, since section 92(16) is on the same structural footing as the other heads of section 92, and since those heads (according to the supplementary

[32]For further discussion of this possibility, see below, chap. 4, sec. 2; chap. 5, secs. 2 and 3; chap. 6, sec. 1; chap. 7, sec. 1; chap. 9, secs. 1 and 2; chap. 11; chap. 12, sec. 1.

[33]See Clokie, *Canadian Government*, 210–16; also (though more implicitly) Clement, *Canadian Constitution*, passim.

[34]*A.-G. Ont.* v. *A.-G. Can.*, [1896] A.C. 348, at 365. See below, chap. 4, sec. 1.

[35]*A.-G. Man.* v. *Manitoba Licence Holders' Association*, [1902] A.C. 73, at 78. See below, 48 and 88.

[36]Compounded by the application of the "Paramountcy Doctrine," according to which federal legislation is said to "override" provincial legislation where neither is *ultra vires*.

interpretation of section 91) are all "prior" to the Peace, Order, and good Government clause, it is doubtful whether a fourth-compartment character can be ascribed to head 16 of section 92 at all. But in any case, it seems more meaningful to contrast the two- and three-compartment views. For the only explicit "authority" behind the four-compartment view is a construction proposed by Lord Macnaghten, on the basis of an observation made by Lord Watson, as to the "apparent" office of section 92(16). In contrast, both the determining feature of the Judicial Committee's interpretative scheme, and the burden of the textual debate over that scheme, are concerned with the interrelationship of the two "parts" of section 91.[37]

[37]The 32 major references to the introductory words of s.91, as well as the 16 to the deeming paragraph, are marked in col. D of the Analytical Table.

Chapter Four

THE COMPARTMENT PROBLEM: II

1. The Basis of the Three-Compartment View

The first incontestable precursor of the final solution to the Compartment Problem is Lord Watson's judgment in *Tennant* v. *Union Bank*,[1] 1894:

The question turns upon the construction of two clauses in the British North America Act, 1867. Sect. 91 gives the Parliament of Canada power to make laws in relation to all matters not coming within the classes of subjects by the Act exclusively assigned to the legislatures of the provinces, and also exclusive legislative authority in relation to certain enumerated subjects, the fifteenth of which is "Banking, Incorporation of Banks, and the Issue of Paper Money." Sect. 92 assigns to each provincial legislature the exclusive right to make laws in relation to the classes of subjects therein enumerated; and the thirteenth of the enumerated classes is "Property and Civil Rights in the Province."

Statutory regulations with respect to the form and legal effect, in Ontario, of warehouse receipts and other negotiable documents, which pass the property of goods without delivery, unquestionably relate to property and civil rights in that province; and the objection taken by the appellant to the provisions of the Bank Act would be unanswerable if it could be shewn that, by the Act of 1867, the Parliament of Canada is absolutely debarred from trenching to any extent upon the matters assigned to the provincial legislature by sect. 92. But sect. 91 expressly declares that, "notwithstanding anything in this Act," the exclusive legislative authority of the Parliament of Canada shall extend to all matters coming within the enumerated classes; which plainly indicates that the legislation of that Parliament, so long as it strictly relates to these matters, is to be of paramount authority. To refuse effect to the declaration would render nugatory some of the legislative powers specially assigned to the Canadian Parliament. For example, among the enumerated classes of subjects in sect. 91, are "Patents of Invention and Discovery," and "Copyrights." It would be practically impossible for the Dominion Parliament to legislate upon either of these subjects without affecting the property and civil rights of individuals in the provinces.

---

[1][1894] A.C. 31, at 44–45.

Lord Watson thus divided the legislative authority of the federal parliament into two "kinds": the Peace, Order, and good Government power; "*and also* exclusive legislative authority in relation to certain enumerated subjects." Reinforcing this division with the enacting tense "shall extend" (in place of the declaratory tense "extends"), he affixed the *non obstante* clause, "notwithstanding anything in this Act," to the heads of section 91 alone. He then concluded that federal legislation is paramount only when it "strictly relates" to matters coming within the classes of subjects mentioned in those heads. In brief, Lord Watson adopted the three-compartment view.

However, since it involved a conflict between one of the heads of section 91 (head 15) and one of the heads of section 92 (head 13), and so did not actually concern the Peace, Order, and good Government cause, the *Tennant* decision cannot be taken as an authority for that view. All it can be said to establish is that the heads of section 91 "outrank" section 92.[2] And as a matter of fact, that was all Lord Tomlin claimed for it in the *Fish Canneries* judgment[3] of 1930: "(1) The legislation of the Parliament of the Dominion, so long as it strictly relates to subjects of legislation expressly enumerated in s. 91, is of paramount authority, even though it trenches upon matters assigned to the provincial legislatures by s. 92: see *Tennant* v. *Union Bank of Canada*."

The full three-compartment view was established by the *Local Prohibition* judgment[4] of 1896. Faced with a conflict between the Peace, Order, and good Government clause and head 13 of section 92 ("Property and Civil Rights in the Province"), Lord Watson developed this argument:

> The general authority given to the Canadian Parliament by the introductory enactments of s. 91 is "to make laws for the peace, order, and good government of Canada, in relation to all matters not coming within the classes of subjects by this Act assigned exclusively to the legislatures of the provinces"; and it is declared, but not so as to restrict the generality of these words, that the exclusive authority of the Canadian Parliament extends to all matters coming within the classes of subjects which are enumerated in the clause. There may, therefore, be matters not included in the enumeration, upon which the Parliament of Canada has power to legislate, because they concern the peace, order, and good government of the Dominion. But to those matters which are not specified among the enumerated subjects of legislation, the exception from s. 92, which is enacted by the concluding words of s. 91, has no application; and, in legislating with regard to such matters, the Dominion Parliament has no authority to encroach upon any

---

[2]See Varcoe, *Legislative Power*, 73–74.

[3]*A.-G. Can.* v. *A.-G. B.C.*, [1930] A.C. 111, at 118.

[4]*A.-G. Ont.* v. *A.-G. Can.*, [1896] A.C. 348, at 360–61.

class of subject which is exclusively assigned to provincial legislatures by s. 92. These enactments appear to their Lordships to indicate that the exercise of legislative power by the Parliament of Canada, in regard to all matters not enumerated in s. 91, ought to be strictly confined to such matters as are unquestionably of Canadian interest and importance, and ought not to trench upon provincial legislation with respect to any of the classes of subjects enumerated in s. 92. To attach any other construction to the general power which, in supplement of its enumerated powers, is conferred upon the Parliament of Canada by s. 91, would, in their Lordships' opinion, not only be contrary to the intendment of the Act, but would practically destroy the autonomy of the provinces. If it were once conceded that the Parliament of Canada has authority to make laws applicable to the whole Dominion, in relation to matters which in each province are substantially of local or private interest, upon the assumption that these matters also concern the peace, order, and good government of the Dominion, there is hardly a subject enumerated in s. 92 upon which it might not legislate, to the exclusion of the provincial legislatures.

Lord Watson now underlined the stipulation that the legislative authority conferred on the federal parliament in the Peace, Order, and good Government clause is restricted to matters "not coming within the Classes of Subjects by this Act assigned exclusively to the Legislatures of the Provinces." As he put it, "in legislating with regard to such matters, the Dominion Parliament has no authority to encroach upon any class of subject which is exclusively assigned to the provincial legislatures." But this stricture was justified on different grounds from those suggested in the *Tennant* judgment. There, Lord Watson had emphasized the *non obstante* clause—which he referred to the heads of section 91 only, as distinct from the Peace, Order, and good Government clause. Here, he emphasized the concluding paragraph of section 91—which "enacts" that any matter apparently coming within both section 92 and the heads of section 91 should be deemed to lie within the exclusive legislative competence of the federal parliament. This new justification undercuts the argument that the second part of the introductory words of section 91 is in declaratory, rather than enacting form; that the *non obstante* clause, which is in this second part, refers back to the Peace, Order, and good Government clause; that the heads of section 91 illustrate the legislative authority conferred in the opening words of the section; and that sections 91 and 92 of the British North America Act contain only two compartments. It accordingly precludes the two-compartment view.

However, the deeming paragraph cannot be used to support the existence of a three-compartment view unless the expression "Class of Matters of a local or private Nature" refers to all the heads of section

92. And in the *Parsons* decision[5] of 1881, Sir Montague Smith had commented "that this paragraph applies in its grammatical construction only to No. 16 of sect. 92." In order to use his new justification, therefore, Lord Watson was forced to deny that earlier comment:[6]

It was apparently contemplated by the framers of the Imperial Act of 1867 that the due exercise of the enumerated powers conferred upon the Parliament of Canada by s. 91 might, occasionally and incidentally, involve legislation upon matters which are primâ facie committed exclusively to the provincial legislatures by s. 92. In order to provide against that contingency, the concluding part of s. 91 enacts that "any matter coming within any of the classes of subjects enumerated in this section shall not be deemed to come within the class of matters of a local or private nature comprised in the enumeration of the classes of subjects by this Act assigned exclusively to the legislatures of the provinces." It was observed by this Board in *Citizens' Insurance Co. of Canada* v. *Parsons* that the paragraph just quoted "applies in its gramatical construction only to No. 16 of s. 92." The observation was not material to the question arising in that case, and it does not appear to their Lordships to be strictly accurate. It appears to them that the language of the exception in s. 91 was meant to include and correctly describes all the matters enumerated in the sixteen heads of s. 92, as being, from a provincial point of view, of a local or private nature.

It will be seen later how this new justification was exploited by the critics of the Judicial Committee's interpretative scheme.[7]

Lord Watson also admitted that "there may, therefore, be matters not included in the enumeration, upon which the Parliament of Canada has power to legislate, because they concern the peace, order, and good government of the Domnion." But such matters could be of two types: concerning "subjects" that are not mentioned in either the heads of section 91 or section 92; and concerning "subjects" that are not mentioned in the heads of section 91, but that are mentioned in section 92. Was Lord Watson referring to the first type, and so merely asserting that the residuary legislative power rests with the federal parliament? Or was he referring to the second, and so implying that the legislative power conferred in the Peace, Order, and good Government clause is something more than residuary? In other words, was he suggesting that "subject," alone, is not a sufficient criterion for the classification of all laws, and that some laws must also be classified in terms of "scope"?

These questions were answered explicitly:[8]

Their Lordships do not doubt that some matters, in their origin local and provincial, might attain such dimensions as to affect the body politic of the

---

[5]*Citizens Insurance Co.* v. *Parsons* (1881), 7 A.C. 96, at 108.
[6]*A.-G. Ont.* v. *A.-G. Can.*, [1896] A.C. 348, at 359.
[7]See below, chap. 5 and chap. 12, sec. 2.
[8]*A.-G. Ont.* v. *A.-G. Can.*, [1896] A.C. 348, at 361.

Dominion, and to justify the Canadian Parliament in passing laws for their regulation or abolition in the interest of the Dominion. But great caution must be observed in distinguishing between that which is local and provincial, and therefore within the jurisdiction of the provincial legislatures, and that which has ceased to be merely local or provincial, and has become matter of national concern, in such sense as to bring it within the jurisdiction of the Parliament of Canada.

Thus, even in the first authority for the three-compartment view, the need to consider "scope," as well as "subject," was acknowledged. The circumstances required for such a consideration (whether they involve simply the "dimensions" of the proposed legislation, or whether some "emergency" must also exist) might be left until the discussion of the Dimensions and Emergency Doctrines.[9] But in either case, whenever the federal parliament makes laws under the authority of the Peace, Order, and good Government clause in relation to "matters" concerning the "subjects" enumerated in section 92, it does not "trench on" the exclusive legislative authority of the provinces. For such "matters," by definition, do not "come within" section 92. "Matters," that is to say, while normally synonymous with "subjects,"[10] become distinct when held to entail "scope" as well; and the use of the Peace, Order, and good Government clause in an extra-residuary capacity is consequently not incompatible with the three-compartment view.

2. The Affirmation of the Three-Compartment View

The approval given this view in the *Local Prohibition* judgment of 1896 was repeated in the *Fisheries* judgment[11] of 1898. Referring to the introductory words of section 91, Lord Herschell added the following statement:

The earlier part of this section read in connection with the words beginning "and for greater certainty" appears to amount to a legislative declaration that any legislation falling strictly within any of the classes specially enumerated in s. 91 is not within the legislative competence of the Provincial Legislatures under s. 92. In any view the enactment is express that laws in relation to matters falling within any of the classes enumerated in s. 91 are within the "exclusive" legislative authority of the Dominion Parliament.

[9]See below, chap. 11.

[10]Hence the term "subject-matter," which was commonly used by the Judicial Committee, but which is avoided in this study because of its ambiguity in relation to "scope."

[11]*A.-G. Can.* v. *A.'s-G. Ont., Que., N.S.,* [1898] A.C. 700, at 715.

Whenever, therefore, a matter is within one of these specified classes, legislation in relation to it by a Provincial Legislature is in their Lordships' opinion incompetent.

The same approval is apparent in the *Manitoba Liquor Act* judgment[12] of 1902; for Lord Macnaghten declared that if the Peace, Order, and good Government clause conflicts with head 13 of section 92, "it might be questionable whether the Dominion Legislature could have authority to interfere with the exclusive jurisdiction of the province in the matter." Similarly, in the *Companies* judgment[13] of 1912, Lord Loreburn assumed that "in the 91st section the Dominion Parliament is invested with the duty of making laws for the peace, order, and good government of Canada, *subject to expressed reservations.*" And in *John Deere Plow Company* v. *Wharton*,[14] 1915, Lord Haldane not only agreed, but ascribed the priority of the heads of section 91 to the deeming paragraph, rather than to the *non obstante* clause:

The general power conferred on the Dominion by s. 91 to make laws for the peace, order, and good government of Canada extends in terms only to matters not coming within the classes of subjects assigned by the Act exclusively to the Legislatures of the Provinces. But if the subject-matter falls within any of the heads of s. 92, it becomes necessary to see whether it also falls within any of the enumerated heads of s. 91, for if so, by the concluding words of that section it is excluded from the powers conferred by s. 92.

Moreover, in the *Insurance Act* judgment[15] of 1916, Lord Haldane repeated his acceptance of the three-compartment view:

It must be taken to be now settled that the general authority to make laws for the peace, order, and good government of Canada, which the initial part of s. 91 of the British North America Act confers, does not, unless the subject-matter of legislation falls within some one of the enumerated heads which follow, enable the Dominion Parliament to trench on the subject-matters entrusted to the provincial Legislatures by the enumeration in s. 92. There is only one case, outside the heads enumerated in s. 91, in which the Dominion Parliament can legislate effectively as regards a province, and that is where the subject-matter lies outside all of the subject-matters enumeratively entrusted to the province under s. 92.

Mr. F. P. Varcoe claims that during the twenty years following the *Local Prohibition* judgment of 1896 "no mention appears to have been made of this problem [i.e., the number of compartments]. . . . It is noteworthy that no authority was cited in the judgment of the Judicial

---

12*A.-G. Man.* v. *Manitoba Licence Holders' Association*, [1902] A.C. 73, at 78.
13*A.-G. Ont.* v. *A.-G. Can.*, [1912] A.C. 571, at 584. Italics mine.
14[1915] A.C. 330, at 337–38.
15*A.-G. Can.* v. *A.-G. Alta.*, [1916] 1 A.C. 588, at 595.

Committee [i.e., in the *Insurance Act* judgment of 1916] as supporting this proposition [i.e., that sections 91 and 92 contain three compartments]."[16] As was just demonstrated, however, a three-compartment view is evident in four judgments between 1896 and 1916: those of 1898, 1902, 1912, and 1915.[17] The effect of Mr. Varcoe's disregard of those judgments is to support the thesis, developed in the *O'Connor Report*, that the "fatal error" in the Judicial Committee's interpretative scheme can be traced to the Watson-Haldane "misdirection."[18] But even on the dubious assumption that the three-compartment view was an "error," and that this error was first committed in the *Tennant* and *Prohibition* judgments of 1894 and 1896, it would seem that three different judges[19] accepted the three-compartment view before Lord Haldane extended Lord Watson's reasoning.[20]

This extension was acomplished in four cases: *Great West Saddlery Company* v. *The King*,[21] 1921; *In re the Board of Commerce Act, 1919, and the Combines and Fair Prices Act, 1919*,[22] 1922; *Fort Frances Pulp and Power Company* v. *Manitoba Free Press Company*,[23] 1923; and *Toronto Electric Commissioners* v. *Snider*,[24] 1925. The first two indicate a change of "justification." In the *Great West Saddlery* judgment,[25] the argument was still based on the deeming paragraph: Lord Haldane repeated the opinion he expressed in *John Deere Plow Company* v. *Wharton*, 1915—that the words in this paragraph "apply, not only to the merely local or private matters in the Province referred to in head 16 of s. 92, but to the whole of the sixteen heads in that section." He thereby accepted Lord Watson's protest, in the *Local Prohibition* judgment of 1896, against the "grammatical construction" comment that Sir Montague Smith had made in the *Parsons* judgment of 1881. In contrast, during the *Board of Commerce* judgment,[26] Lord Haldane apparently reverted to Lord Watson's earlier reliance, in the *Tennant* judgment of 1894, on the introductory words of section 91. For he now

[16]Varcoe, *Legislative Power*, 61–62.
[17]Viz., *A.-G. Can.* v. *A.'s-G. Ont., Que., N.S.*, [1898] A.C. 700; *A.-G. Man.* v. *Manitoba Licence Holders' Association*, [1902] A.C. 73; *A.-G. Ont.* v. *A.-G. Can.*, [1912] A.C. 571; *John Deere Plow Co.* v. *Wharton*, [1915] A.C. 330.
[18]For a detailed criticism of this thesis, see below, chap. 5, secs. 1 and 2.
[19]Viz., Lords Herschell, Macnaghten, and Haldane. The judgment in *John Deere Plow Co.* v. *Wharton* was also delivered by Lord Haldane.
[20]On the other hand, in so far as it involved the first definite conflict, since the *Local Prohibition* case, between the Peace, Order, and good Government clause and s. 92(13), the *Insurance Act* judgment of 1916 was the first authoritative confirmation of Lord Watson's three-compartment view.
[21][1921] 2 A.C. 91.   [22][1922] 1 A.C. 191.
[23][1923] A.C. 695.   [24][1925] A.C. 396.
[25][1921] 2 A.C. 91, at 99–100.   [26][1922] 1 A.C. 191, at 197.

argued in terms of those words alone: "No doubt the initial words of s.91 of the British North America Act confer on the Parliament of Canada power to deal with subjects which concerned the Dominion generally, provided that they are not withheld from the powers of that Parliament to legislate, by any of the express heads in s. 92, untrammelled by the enumeration of special heads in s. 91." But this last argument is admittedly a very uncertain "reversion."

As for the other two judgments, in the *Fort Frances* case,[27] Lord Haldane not only upheld legislation passed by the federal parliament on the sole authority of the Peace, Order and good Government clause, but did so despite his awareness that the impugned law would interfere with property and civil rights in the province. However, this decision does not represent a departure from the three-compartment view; for it was justified on the basis of the Emergency Doctrine, which is quite compatible with, and even presumes that view.[28] Indeed, several statements in the *Fort Frances* judgment affirm the existence of three compartments: Lord Haldane insisted that "the general control of property and civil rights for normal purposes remains with the Provincial Legislatures"; that "as a general principle, the Dominion Parliament is to be excluded from trenching on property and civil rights in the Provinces of Canada"; and that "As the Dominion Parliament cannot ordinarily legislate so as to interfere with property and civil rights in the Provinces, it could not have done what the two statutes under consideration purport to do had the situation been normal." Furthermore, in the *Snider* judgment[29] of 1925, Lord Haldane (this time rejecting the Emergency Doctrine) unmistakably confirmed the three-compartment view:

The Dominion Parliament has, under the initial words of s. 91, a general power to make laws for Canada. But these laws are not to relate to the classes of subjects assigned to the Provinces by s. 92, unless their enactment falls under heads specifically assigned to the Dominion Parliament by the enumeration in s. 91. When there is a question as to which legislative authority has the power to pass an Act, the first question must therefore be whether the subject falls within s. 92. Even if it does, the further question must be answered, whether it falls also under an enumerated head in s. 91. If so, the Dominion has the paramount power of legislating in relation to it. If the subject falls within neither of the sets of enumerated heads, then the Dominion may have power to legislate under the general words at the beginning of s. 91.

---

[27][1923] A.C. 695, at 703–5.
[28]See above, 40–41, 46–47; also below, chap. 9, sec. 3 and chap. 11.
[29][1925] A.C. 396, at 406.

The next instance of the Judicial Committee's acceptance of that view is the *Fish Canneries* judgment[30] of 1930. Lord Tomlin developed these "propositions":

(1.) The legislation of the Parliament of the Dominion, so long as it strictly relates to subjects of legislation expressly enumerated in s. 91, is of paramount authority, even though it trenches upon matters assigned to the provincial legislatures by s. 92: see *Tennant* v. *Union Bank of Canada*.
(2.) The general power of legislation conferred upon the Parliament of the Dominion by s. 91 of the Act in supplement of the power to legislate upon the subjects expressly enumerated must be strictly confined to such matters as are unquestionably of national interest and importance, and must not trench on any of the subjects enumerated in s. 92 as within the scope of provincial legislation, unless these matters have attained such dimensions as to affect the body politic of the Dominion: see *Attorney-General for Ontario* v. *Attorney-General for the Dominion* [the *Local Prohibition* judgment of 1896].

It has already been noted that the *Tennant* judgment of 1894 can be taken as an authority only in so far as the heads of section 91 and section 92 are concerned. Yet even if it is confined to the latter part of section 91, Lord Tomlin's first proposition does separate that part from the general statement, and so lays a basis for the third-compartment character of the Peace, Order, and good Government clause. This character is then confirmed in the second proposition: deliberately employing the phrase "in supplement of," Lord Tomlin warned that the legislative power conferred in the clause "must be strictly confined to such matters as are unquestionably of national interest and importance," and "must not trench on any of the subjects enumerated in s. 92."

But that warning is phrased too loosely. For it implies that when a matter has attained "such dimensions as to affect the body politic of the Dominion," the federal parliament may "trench on" the exclusive sphere of the provincial legislatures; and this was not the implication of the *Local Prohibition* judgment of 1896. On the contrary, Lord Watson expressly stated that "in legislating with regard to such matters [as are not within the heads of section 91], the Dominion Parliament has no authority to encroach upon any class of subjects which is exclusively assigned to provincial legislatures by s. 92."[31] In other words, when acting on the authority of the Peace, Order, and good Government clause alone, the federal parliament may pass legislation concerned with a "subject" mentioned in section 92 only if that "subject" has become of

[30]*A.-G. Can.* v. *A.-G. B.C.*, [1930] A.C. 111, at 118.
[31]*A.-G. Ont.* v. *A.-G. Can.*, [1896] A.C. 348, at 360.

such "scope" as to place it, by definition, outside section 92, and for this reason, inside the Peace, Order, and good Government clause.[32]

Accordingly, the federal parliament simply cannot "trench on" the exclusive legislative sphere of the provinces, and in so far as it conveys a contrary impression, Lord Tomlin's second proposition is misleading. Lord Haldane's explanation, in the *Insurance Act* judgment of 1916, was not only sounder, but also more consistent with Lord Watson's original admission: "There is only one case, outside the heads enumerated in s. 91, in which the Dominion Parliament can legislate effectively as regards a province, and that is where the subject-matter lies outside all of the subject-matters enumeratively entrusted to the provinces under s. 92."[33] An even plainer version of this "correct" interpretation is found in the *Fort Frances* judgment[34] of 1923:

It is proprietary [*sic*] and civil rights in new relations, which they do not present in normal times, that have to be dealt with; and these relations, which affect Canada as an entirety, fall within s. 91, because in their fullness they extend beyond what s. 92 can really cover. The kind of power adequate for dealing with them is only to be found in that part of the constitution which establishes power in the State as a whole.

. . . The enumeration in s. 92 is not in any way repealed in the event of such an occurrence, but a new aspect of the business of Government is recognized as emerging, an aspect which is not covered or precluded by the general words in which powers are assigned to the Legislatures of the Provinces as individual units.

The Judicial Committee repeated its acceptance of the three-compartment view in several decisions subsequent to the *Fish Canneries* judgment of 1930. In the *Quebec Insurance* judgment[35] of 1932, for example, Lord Dunedin accepted the distinction Lord Haldane had drawn in the *Insurance Act* case[36] of 1916, between the Peace, Order, and good Government clause and the heads of section 91. Similarly, in the *Aeronautics* judgment[37] of 1932, Lord Sankey assumed that section 91 is divided into two unequal parts:

Sect. 91 tabulates the subjects to be dealt with by the Dominion, and s. 92 the subjects to be dealt with exclusively by the Provincial legislatures, but it will not be forgotten that s. 91, in addition, authorizes the King by and

---

[32]See Plaxton, *Canadian Constitutional Decisions*, xiv–xv.

[33]*A.-G. Can.* v. *A.-G. Alta.*, [1916] 1 A.C. 588, at 595.

[34]*Fort Frances Pulp and Power Co.* v. *Manitoba Free Press Co.*, [1923] A.C. 695, at 704 and 705.

[35]*In re the Insurance Act of Canada*, [1932] A.C. 41, at 50–51.

[36]*A.-G. Can.* v. *A.-G. Alta*, [1916] 1 A.C. 588.

[37]*In re the Regulation and Control of Aeronautics in Canada*, [1932] A.C. 54, at 64–65.

with the advice and consent of the Senate and House of Commons of Canada to make laws for the peace, order and good government of Canada in relation to all matters not coming within the classes of subjects by this Act assigned exclusively to the legislatures of the Provinces, and further provides that any matter coming within any of the classes of subjects enumerated in the section shall not be deemed to come within the classes of matters of a local and private nature comprised in the enumeration of classes of subjects assigned by s. 92 exclusively to the legislatures of the Provinces.

Again, in the *Radio* judgment[38] of 1932, Lord Dunedin spoke of "the preferential place enjoyed by the enumerated subjects of s. 91." In the *Natural Products Marketing Act* judgment[39] of 1937, Lord Atkin ruled that "it is therefore plain that the Act purports to affect property and civil rights in the Province, and if not brought within one of the enumerated classes of subjects in s. 91 must be beyond the competence of the Dominion Legislature." In the *Debt Adjustment Act* judgment[40] of 1943, Lord Maugham—justifying the priority of the heads of section 91 on both the introductory words and the deeming paragraph of that section (the latter being "inserted from abundant caution")—proceeded as follows:

In the view of their Lordships, there is no need, at any rate on this occasion, for any new statement as to the true construction of the British North America Act. The main propositions are now well established, and are re-stated here mainly as a matter of convenience. It is well settled that in case of conflict between the enumerated heads of s. 91 and heads of s. 92 the former must prevail. The words of s. 91, and particularly the emphatic sentence: "and for greater certainty, but not so as to restrict the generality of the foregoing terms of this section, it is hereby declared that (notwithstanding anything in this Act) the exclusive legislative authority of the Parliament of Canada extends to all matters coming within the classes of subjects next hereinafter enumerated" must be given their natural effect. The final words of the section inserted from abundant caution were these: "and any matter coming within any of the classes of subjects enumerated in this section shall not be deemed to come within the class of matters of a local or private nature comprised in the enumeration of the classes of subjects by this Act assigned exclusively to the legislatures of the provinces." It follows that legislation coming in pith and substance within one of the classes specially enumerated in s. 91 is beyond the legislative competence of the provincial legislatures under s. 92.

. . . It must not be forgotten that where the subject-matter of any legislation is not within any of the enumerated heads either of s. 91 or s. 92, the sole power rests with the Dominion under the preliminary words of s. 91, relative to "laws for the peace, order, and good government of Canada."

[38]*In re the Regulation and Control of Radio Communication in Canada*, [1932] A.C. 304, at 314.
[39]*A.-G. B.C.* v. *A.-G. Can.*, [1937] A.C. 377, at 386.
[40]*A.-G. Alta.* v. *A.-G. Can.*, [1943] A.C. 356, at 370 and 371.

And in the *Hours of Work Act* judgment[41] of 1950, Lord Reid—emphasizing the deeming paragraph, rather than the Peace, Order, and good Government clause—once more assumed the existence of three compartments:

Three matters are dealt with in ss. 91 and 92: first, the general power to make laws for the peace, order, and good government of Canada conferred on the Parliament of Canada by the first part of s. 91; secondly, the classes of subjects enumerated in the latter part of s. 91 as being within the exclusive legislative authority of the Parliament of Canada; and thirdly, the classes of subjects enumerated in s. 92 as being within the exclusive legislative authority of the provincial legislatures.

From at least 1894 onwards, then, the Judicial Committee definitely adopted a three-compartment view of sections 91 and 92 of the British North America Act. This view was explicitly approved in the judgments referred to in the foregoing discussion, but the same approval can be discerned, implicitly, in many other decisions. Since the Dimensions and Emergency Doctrines both presume the division of section 91 into two parts of unequal weight, any decision that involves the acceptance of either of those doctrines necessarily involves the acceptance of three compartments. It follows that such judgments as *Labour Conventions*,[42] 1937, *Unemployment Insurance*,[43] 1937, *Canada Temperance Act*,[44] 1946, *Japanese Canadians*,[45] 1946, and *Margarine*,[46] 1951, are also examples of three-compartment approval. Certain other judgments (*In re Silver Brothers*,[47] 1932, for instance) provide a similar indication by virtue of the assumptions involved in their reasoning. And then there are the eleven controversial decisions, usually held to represent a departure from the three-compartment view, but in some cases actually implying an acceptance of it, that will be analysed in the next chapter.[48]

[41]*C.P.R.* v. *A.-G. B.C.*, [1950] A.C. 122, at 136; see also at 140–41.
[42]*A.-G. Can.* v. *A.-G. Ont.*, [1937] A.C. 326, at 352–53.
[43]*A.-G. Can.* v. *A.-G. Ont.*, [1937] A.C. 355, at 365–66.
[44]*A.-G. Ont.* v. *Canada Temperance Federation*, [1946] A.C. 193, at 205–8.
[45]*Co-operative Committee on Japanese Canadians* v. *A.-G. Can.*, [1947] A.C. 87, at 101–2 and 108.
[46]*Canadian Federation of Agriculture* v. *A.-G. Que.*, [1951] A.C. 179, at 197–98.
[47][1932] A.C. 514.
[48]The 18 references in which the three-compartment view was explicitly confirmed are marked in col. D of the Analytical Table.

Chapter Five

THE COMPARTMENT PROBLEM: III

1. The O'Connor Analysis

Since 1939, accounts of the Judicial Committee's interpretative scheme have been practically defined by W. F. O'Connor's Senate *Report*. This *Report* was the first acount to be based on the Compartment Problem, and so, in this respect at least, is an undeniable landmark. If O'Connor had finally demonstrated the determining characteristic of the scheme, however, his analysis of the judgments which produced it was not so conclusive. The purpose of this chapter is to show the weakness of that analysis.[1]

O'Connor begins his argument like this:

The so-called Fathers of Confederation thought that there could not possibly be any doubt or difficulty as between sections 91 and 92 of the B.N.A. Act. They had in mind two grand divisions into one or the other of which any enacted law (for they thought in terms of enacted law) must fall. It must necessarily be a law of either a general or a local character, that is, it must needs be of a Dominion character or a provincial character. They had also (*a*) carefully identified, so far as possible, the kinds of local laws that the provinces might enact, leaving all non-local law making to the Dominion, and (*b*) stipulated, in addition, certain *local laws* that the provinces were to be *deemed* incapable of enacting. Neither the Dominion nor the provinces were given any authority or jurisdiction, exclusive or otherwise, over any *field of law*. Each, instead, was given legislative authority to enact statutes *in relation to matters coming within* certain classifications some whereof might be called fields of law but, even if so, by far the most whereof certainly could not. Sections 91 and 92 classify, to a large extent, *government utilities and services*. The law-making authority, however, was not over the "field" or classification, but over the matter (arising in the shape of concrete legislation) which "came within" and was assignable by the court to the class, or, if you prefer it so, to the field, whether of service or of law, as the case might be. The court, so the Fathers thought, could and would, as each statute, Dominion or provincial, came before it for

---

[1] O'Connor's evaluation is not commented on until chap. 12, sec. 2.

judgment, ascertain to what class in section 91 or 92 the legislation in pith and substance belonged (i.e., came within) and could and would assign that statute to its proper class, if necessary, for it might not be necessary in the case of a matter other than local. The plan did not fail. It worked well for over twenty years and then was repealed, not by the Imperial Parliament but by an Imperial judicial tribunal.[2]

Having developed this version of the two-compartment view—and indicated his evalution of the Judicial Committee's interpretative scheme —O'Connor examines each of the "critical" decisions reached before 1894. He discovers the genesis of the Board's "repeal" in the *Parsons* judgment[3] of 1881:

An error in construction of the terms of section 91 of the B.N.A. Act was stated in this decision at this point. It is my belief that to that error—quite immaterial so far as the case in which it was made is concerned—may be traced what is now said to be the failure of the scheme of distribution of legislative authority under the B.N.A. Act to achieve its intended purpose. The error was this—The Board failed to notice (the case for decision not being affected by such failure) that the office of the *declaratory* part of section 91—that part which contains the *non obstante* provision—was *to declare an extension to the enumerated provisions of section 91 of that exclusiveness which was already, necessarily, present in that residuum which necessarily under the scheme of distribution of legislative authority that the B.N.A. Act provides, represents the full legislative authority of Canada and is enacted by the opening words of section 91*, wherefore the declaratory part of the section does not exclude, but *borrows from*, the general opening words of the section, whereas the concluding, non-declaratory, "deeming" enactment of section 91 has a different office—to prevent provincial enactment as local or private law of any matter, however local or private, that comes within any of the enumerated provisions of section 91 and to make it clear that Dominion enactment in relation to such matters *although* in a private or local aspect, is valid.[4]

Despite all the "slips" and "errors" in the *Parsons* judgment, however, "no primacy had yet been attached to the enumerated provisions of that section." This "fatal error in construction"—because of which "almost all cases decided since early in the nineties and involving sections 91 and 92 deviate from the text of the Act"—must be attributed, rather, to Lord Watson:

The decision in the Parsons Case (No. 5) had no immediate effect, nor was there any real reason why it ever should have any effect, in causing the misconstruction of section 91. It contained some loose expression, but that can be said of many excellent decisions, and the Parsons Case is after all, an

[2]*O'Connor Report*, Annex 1, 25.
[3]*Citizens Insurance Co.* v. *Parsons* (1881), 7 A.C. 96.
[4]*O'Connor Report*, Annex 1, 30–31.

excellent decision. It was twelve years later when some of the things said in the Parsons Case, severed from their setting, served to divert from its bed the stream of true interpretation of sections 91 and 92 of the B.N.A. Act. . . .[5]

Up to this stage, fourteen years after confederation had been accomplished, judicial interpretation had proceeded in consonance with the London resolutions [of 1866] as embodied in a legislative text which had been intended to express the spirit of those resolutions and had, so far, been found to have done so. Matters of a general character, that is matters concerning in fact the whole Dominion or more than one province had not been denied subjection to Dominion legislative authority and matters local or private in a province had been held, subject to the final paragraph of section 91, to be within the exclusive legislative authority of the province. Nor does Citizens Insurance Company v Parsons itself, *qua* what was decided by it, make any real inroad upon intended Dominion powers. . . .[6]

No primacy had yet been attached to the enumerated provisions of section 91 over the unenumerated provisions of that section. The blow is struck in the next case to be discussed[7] [viz., *Tennant* v. *Union Bank*, 1894]. It is done, and the same process is repeated in a later decision[8] [viz., *Voluntary Assignments*, 1894] by, in the first instance, mere unnecessary mention, without elaboration or argument. Subsequently[9] [i.e., in the *Local Prohibition* judgment of 1896] there ensues a reference back to the case wherein the mention was made, as to an authority.[10]

O'Connor then analyses the nature of the "blow struck in the *Tennant* judgment of 1894, and repeated in the *Local Prohibition* judgment of 1896:

First appears the misquotation "shall extend" for "extends." Then follows the *mere mention* of "*matters* coming within the enumerated classes." Lastly comes the unnecessary injection of the emphatic words (as to the legislation of the Dominion Parliament) "*so long as it strictly relates to these matters,*" meaning matters coming within *enumerated* classes. Here we have an unreasoned exclusion of the residuary clause—a subjection of it to enumerations which really proceed from and depend on it—and an "authority" to which, two years later, in the next case to be reviewed [viz., the *Local Prohibition* judgment], Lord Watson can refer back, cite it, as he does, along with Cushing v Dupuy, and thus firmly and enduringly impose upon future Boards and Canadian courts a new and erroneous construction of section 91 of the B.N.A. Act of so serious a character that it has paralysed many essential law making activities of the Dominion. The construction of section 91 that I am at the moment attacking as a deviation from the text of section 91 of the B.N.A. Act—a construction that restricts the *paramountcy* of the provisions of section 91 to the *enumerated* provisions thereof, is thus founded by Lord Watson upon Cushing v Dupuy (Case No. 4) which, if in point at all, is authority contra, and upon an *obiter dictum* of Lord Watson himself in

---

[5]*Ibid.*, 33.
[7]See *ibid.*, 35–38.
[9]See *ibid.*, 39–50.

[6]*Ibid.*, 31.
[8]See *ibid.*, 46.
[10]*Ibid.*, 35.

Tennant v Union Bank (Case No. 11), which proceeded upon a recited *alteration* of the text.[11]

Finally, the perpetuation of this "fatal error" is blamed, above all, on Lord Haldane:

I am thus led to express the opinion that the present day Judicial Committee of the Privy Council is not to be blamed for certain recently delivered decisions which have not found favour in Canada. These decisions are based on previous decisions of the Board and upon arguments before the Board made upon the basis that such previous decisions represent "the law." If, in 1896, while the iron was hot, when Lord Watson had just delivered the opinion in the Prohibition case (No. 13) or, later, when Lord Haldane had begun to deliver a series of decisions, which exceeded those of Lord Watson in their emasculatory effect upon the Dominion's legislative authority, protest had been raised, pressure exerted and, above all, the right argument presented, based on the text of the Act, in support of Dominion rights, *non constat* but that present day decisions of the Judicial Committee would be precisely the reverse of what they are to-day, and the provinces might now be the complainants.[12]

In short, O'Connor bases his analysis on a division of the Judicial Committee's decisions into two groups: those before, and those after, the *Tennant* and *Prohibition* judgments of 1894 and 1896. In the former group, he argues, the two-compartment view was invariably adopted; in the latter, almost as invariably, preference was shown for the three. But this new interpretation was contrary to both the intentions of the Fathers of Confederation and the terms of the British North America Act. The Judicial Committee, and especially Lords Watson and Haldane, were thus responsible for encumbering Canada with an incorrect, as well as an unpractical constitution.

2. Criticism of O'Connor's Analysis

(a) The Pre-1894 Judgments

O'Connor's analysis is not supported by the judgments before 1894. In *L'Union St. Jacques de Montréal v. Bélisle*,[13] 1874, Lord Selborne construed sections 91 and 92 as follows:

The scheme of the 91st and 92nd sections is this. By the 91st section some matters—and their Lordships may do well to assume, for the argument's sake,

---

[11]*Ibid.*, 37–38.   [12]*Ibid.*, 68–69; see also at 64, 70, and 72–75.
[13]6 A.C. 31, at 35–36. This is O'Connor's "Case No. 1": see his *Report*, Annex 1, 25–27, and Annex 3, 5–6.

that they are all matters except those afterwards dealt with by the 92nd section—their Lordships do not decide it, but for the argument's sake they will assume it; certain matters being upon that assumption all those which are not mentioned in the 92nd section are reserved for the exclusive legislation of the Parliament of *Canada*, called the Dominion Parliament; but beyond controversy there are certain other matters, not only reserved for the Dominion Parliament, but assigned to the exclusive power and competency of the provincial legislature in each province. Among those the last is thus expressed: "Generally all matters of a merely local or private nature in the province." If there is nothing to control that in the 91st section, it would seem manifest that the subject matter of this Act, the 33 Vict. c.58, is a matter of a merely local or private nature in the province, because it relates to a benevolent or benefit society incorporated in the city of *Montreal* within the province, which appears to consist exclusively of members who would be subject *primâ facie* to the control of the provincial legislature. This Act deals solely with the affairs of that particular society, and in this manner: —taking notice of a certain state of embarrassment resulting from what it describes in substance as improvident regulations of the society, it imposes a forced commutation of their existing rights upon two widows, who at the time when that Act was passed were annuitants of the society under its rules, reserving to them the rights so cut down in the future possible event of the improvement up to a certain point of the affairs of the association. Clearly this matter is private; clearly it is local, so far as locality is to be considered, because it is in the province and in the city of *Montreal*; and unless, therefore, the general effect of that head of sect. 92 is for this purpose qualified by something in sect. 91, it is a matter not only within the competency, but within the exclusive competency of the provincial legislature. Now sect. 91 qualifies it undoubtedly, if it be within any one of the different classes of subjects where specially enumerated; because the last and concluding words of sect. 91 are: "And any matter coming within any of the classes of subjects enumerated in this section shall not be deemed to come within the class of matters of a local or private nature comprised in the enumeration of the classes of subjects by this Act assigned exclusively to the Legislatures of the provinces." But the *onus* is on the Respondent to shew, that this, being of itself of a local or private nature, does also come within one or more of the classes of subjects specially enumerated in the 91st section.

Lord Selborne thus assumed not only that the deeming paragraph must refer to head 16 of section 92 alone, but that "all those [matters] which are not mentioned in the 92nd section are reserved for the exclusive legislation of the Parliament of Canada." However, since the three-compartment view does not require the deeming paragraph to refer to all the heads of section 92,[14] and since the reservation comment need amount to no more than a recognition of the Exhaustion Theory,[15] neither of these assumptions is incompatible with an acceptance of three

[14]See above, chap. 3, sec. 2.
[15]See above, chap. 3, sec. 1.

compartments. Indeed, the judgment seems to imply that number; for Lord Selborne drew a distinction between the heads of section 91 and the Peace, Order, and good Government clause. But at least the *L'Union St. Jacques* decision does not establish, either explicitly or implicitly, a two-compartment presumption.

The judgment in *Dow* v. *Black*,[16] 1875, is similarly inconclusive. Sir James Colville, began with the following principle: "Sects. 91 and 92 purport to make a distribution of legislative powers between the Parliament of *Canada* and the provincial legislatures, sect. 91 giving a general power of legislation to the Parliament of *Canada*, subject only to the exception of such matters as by sect. 92 were made subjects upon which the provincial legislatures were exclusively to legislate." He then characterized the provincial Act in question:

Their Lordships are further of opinion, with Mr. Justice *Fisher*, the dissentient Judge in the Supreme Court, that the Act in question, even if it did not fall within the 2nd article [i.e., section 92(2)], would clearly be a law relating to a matter of a merely local or private nature within the meaning of the 9th article of sect. 92 of the Imperial Statute; and therefore one which the provincial legislature was competent to pass, unless its subject-matter could be distinctly shewn to fall within one or other of the classes of subjects specially enumerated in the 91st section. This view is in accordance with the ruling of this tribunal in the recent case of the *L'Union St. Jacques de Montréal* v. *Dame Julie Bélisle*, decided on the 8th of July, 1874.

Describing the legislative authority of the federal parliament as "general," Sir James decided that it must cover all the "subject-matters" not enumerated in section 92. Again, however, neither this description, nor even this decision, prevents section 91 from being divided into two parts of unequal weight. On the contrary, by reasoning that if the Act in question were in relation to head 9 of section 92, the provincial legislature would be competent "unless its subject-matter could be distinctly shewn to fall within one or other of the classes of subjects specially enumerated in the 91st section," Sir James appears to have drawn a qualitative distinction between the heads of section 91 and the Peace, Order, and good Government clause. Moreover, by referring to head 9 of section 92 as a "matter of a merely local or private nature," he seems to have implied that the deeming paragraph could refer to any of the heads of section 92. And here O'Connor is not simply mistaken, but disingenuous; for in quoting Sir James' characterization, he omits the words "within the meaning of the 9th article of section 92

[16] A.C. 272, at 280 and 282. This is O'Connor's "Case No. 2": see *Report*, Annex 1, 27–28, and Annex 3, 6.

of the Imperial Statute"[17]—and so gives the impression that the phrase "matter of a merely local or private nature" referred to section 92(16), rather than to section 92(9).

It is also impossible to accept O'Connor's citation of *Valin* v. *Langlois*,[18] 1879. It is true that Lord Selborne made these remarks:

If the subject-matter is within the jurisdiction of the Dominion Parliament, it is not within the jurisdiction of the Provincial Parliament, and that which is excluded by the 91st section from the jurisdiction of the Dominion Parliament is not anything else than matters coming within the classes of subjects assigned exclusively to the Legislatures of the provinces. The only material class of subjects relates to the administration of justice in the provinces, which, read with the 41st section, cannot be reasonably taken to have anything to do with election petitions. There is therefore nothing here to raise a doubt about the power of the Dominion Parliament to impose new duties upon the existing Provincial Courts, or to give them new powers, as to matters which do not come within the classes of subjects assigned exclusively to the Legislatures of the provinces.

Nevertheless, it is not easy to appreciate O'Connor's commentary: "Note that no *enumerated* Dominion power *re* this head of jurisdiction appears in section 91. Legislative authority, therefore, must have been related to the introductory words of section 91. Section 41 does not expressly authorize the altering legislation. It assumes that when enacted it will be enacted under section 91. Neither does the Board raise any question *re* enumerated or residuary powers, or supplementary powers."[19] But neither was it necessary to raise this question; that need would occur only if the disputed legislation seemed to come within section 92.[20] Lord Selborne's remarks might merely imply an acknowledgment of the Exhaustion Theory, and consequently do not entail either an acceptance of the two-compartment view, or a rejection of the three.

The judgment in *Cushing* v. *Dupuy*,[21] 1880, likewise fails to prove O'Connor's analysis. Actually, since the conflict here was between one head of section 91 (head 21) and two heads of section 92 (heads 13 and 14), the Peace, Order, and good Government clause was not involved at all. Granted that Sir Montague Smith said this:

It would be impossible to advance a step in the construction of a scheme for the administration of insolvent estates without interfering with and

---

[17]See the *O'Connor Report*, Annex 1, 27.

[18]5 A.C. 115, at 119–20. This is O'Connor's "Case No. 3": see his *Report*, Annex 1, 28, and Annex 3, 7. See also Jackett, in Corry, *et. al.*, eds., *Legal Essays*, 157.

[19]*O'Connor Report*, Annex 3, 7.   [20]See above, chap. 3, sec. 2.

[21]5 A.C. 409, at 415–16. This is O'Connor's "Case No. 4": see his *Report*, Annex 1, 28, and Annex 3, 8–9. See also Jackett, in Corry, *et al.*, eds., *Legal Essays*, 157.

modifying some of the ordinary rights of property, and other civil rights, nor without providing some mode of special procedure for the vesting, realisation, and distribution of the estate, and the settlement of the liabilities of the insolvent. Procedure must necessarily form an essential part of any law dealing with insolvency. It is therefore to be presumed, indeed it is a necessary implication, that the Imperial statute, in assigning to the Dominion Parliament the subjects of bankruptcy and insolvency, intended to confer on it legislative power to interfere with property, civil rights, and procedure within the Provinces, so far as a general law relating to those subjects might affect them.

Granted, too, that something might be made of the word "general": thus, while it could be simply a synonym for "federal," it could also indicate a willingness to consign legislation on the basis of "scope." Yet even if this rather tenuous interpretation were accepted, *Cushing* v. *Dupuy* can hardly be said to establish the thesis that before 1894 the Judicial Committee favoured the two-compartment view.

And the *Parsons* judgment[22] of 1881 seems almost an authority to the contrary. Sir Montague Smith began his analysis of the distribution of legislative power with the following statement:

The scheme of this legislation, as expressed in the first branch of sect. 91, is to give to the dominion parliament authority to make laws for the good government of Canada in all matters not coming within the classes of subjects assigned exclusively to the provincial legislature. If the 91st section had stopped here, and if the classes of subjects enumerated in sect. 92 had been altogether distinct and different from those in sect. 91, no conflict of legislative authority could have arisen. The provincial legislatures would have had exclusive legislative power over the sixteen classes of subjects assigned to them, and the dominion parliament exclusive power over all other matters relating to the good government of Canada. But it must have been foreseen that this sharp and definite distinction had not been and could not be attained, and that some of the classes of subjects assigned to the provincial legislatures unavoidably ran into and were embraced by some of the enumerated classes of subjects in sect. 91; hence an endeavour appears to have been made to provide for cases of apparent conflict; and it would seem that with this object it was declared in the second branch of the 91st section, "for greater certainty, but not so as to restrict the generality of the foregoing terms of this section" that (notwithstanding anything in the Act) the exclusive legislative authority of the parliament of Canada should extend to all matters coming within the classes of subjects enumerated in that section. With the same object, apparently, the paragraph at the end of sect. 91 was introduced, though it may be observed that this paragraph applies in its grammatical construction only to No. 16 of sect. 92.

O'Connor breaks this statement into two parts, pausing after the words "some of the classes of subjects assigned to the provincial legis-

[22]*Citizens Insurance C*o. v. *Parsons* (1881), 7 A.C. 96, at 107–8. This is O'Connor's "Case No. 5": see his *Report*, Annex 1, 29–33, and Annex 3, 9–13.

latures unavoidably ran into and were embraced by some of the enumerated classes of subjects in sect. 91." He then comments on these words: "There is a slip here. How could this occur upon the stated hypothesis? 'If the 91st section had *stopped*' before any of the enumerations of section 91 were written, which is the hypothesis, the enumerations of section 92 *could not* 'run into' any enumerations of section 91 for none would have existed."[23] But is there a slip here? Is that even the stated hypothesis? What Sir Montague Smith surely meant by "if the 91st section had stopped" was "if there were no second branch to the introductory words of section 91" (or if there were no "and for greater certainty" annotation between the Peace, Order, and good Government clause and the heads of section 91). For he went on to say, in the same sentence, "and if the classes of subjects enumerated in sect. 92 had been altogether distinct and different from those [meaning those enumerated] in sect. 91, no conflict of legislative authority could have arisen." Accordingly, since some of the classes of subjects enumerated in section 92 "ran into and were embraced by" some of the classes of subjects enumerated in section 91, the latter were given priority, in cases of apparent conflict, by inserting the "and for greater certainty" annotation (which included a *non obstante* clause). But if Sir Montague Smith's statement were interpreted in that way, the priority of the heads of section 91 over section 92 would be derived from both the *non obstante* clause and the deeming paragraph (which has "the same object, apparently"); and O'Connor would have been forced to admit not only that the three-compartment view is independent of the argument derived from the deeming paragraph, but that the Judicial Committee accepted this view well before Lord Watson committed his "fatal error."

In any case, Sir Montague Smith's procedural account is almost certainly based on the three-compartment view. For he argued that the legislative authority of the provinces can be "overborne" only if the "subject" of the disputed Act "primâ facie falls within" one of the heads of section 91:

The first question to be decided is, whether the Act impeached in the present appeal falls within any of the classes of subjects enumerated in sect. 92, and assigned exclusively to the legislatures of the provinces; for if it does not, it can be of no validity, and no other question would then arise. It is only when an Act of the provincial legislature primâ facie falls within one of these classes of subjects that the further questions arise, viz., whether, notwithstanding this is so, the subject of the Act does not also fall within one of the enumerated classes of subjects in sect. 91, and whether the power of the provincial legislature is or is not thereby overborne.[24]

---

[23]*O'Connor Report*, Annex 1, 30.   [24]7 A.C. 91, at 109.

In the light of this argument, it is difficult to see how O'Connor can maintain his interpretation of sections 91 and 92, and simultaneously assert that "the Parsons Case is, after all, an excellent decision."[25] And it is still more difficult to see how he can insist that until the *Tennant* and *Local Prohibition* judgments of 1894 and 1896, the Judicial Committee invariably adopted a·two-compartment view.

This insistence is also at odds with the three-compartment procedure followed by Lord Watson in *Dobie* v. *Temporalities Board*,[26] 1881:

> According to the principles established by the judgment of this Board in the cases already referred to [notably, *Citizens Insurance Company* v. *Parsons*], the first step to be taken, with a view to test the validity of an Act of the provincial Legislature is to consider whether the subject-matter of the Act falls within any of the classes of subjects enumerated in sect. 92. If it does not then the Act is of no validity. If it does then these further questions may arise viz., "whether notwithstanding that it is so the subject of the Act does not also fall within one of the enumerated classes of subjects in sect. 91, and whether the power of the provincial Legislature is or is not thereby overborne."

The last judgment in O'Connor's pre-1894 group—*Russell* v. *The Queen*,[27] 1882—has been distinguished so often that its very nature is open to debate.[28] But at least one feature is undeniable—Sir Montague Smith accepted the three-compartment procedure:

> The general scheme of the British North America Act with regard to the distribution of legislative powers, and the general scope and effect of sects. 91 and 92, and their relation to each other, were fully considered and commented on by this Board in the case of the *Citizens Insurance Company* v. *Parsons*. According to the principle of construction there pointed out, the first question to be determined is, whether the Act now in question falls within any of the classes of subjects enumerated in sect. 92, and assigned exclusively to the Legislatures of the Provinces. If it does, then the further question would arise, viz., whether the subject of the Act does not also fall within one of the enumerated classes of subjects in sect. 91, and so does not still belong to the Dominion Parliament. But if the Act does not fall within any of the classes of subjects in sect. 92, no further question will remain, for it cannot be contended, and indeed was not contended at their Lordships' bar, that, if the Act does not come within one of the classes of subjects assigned to the Provincial Legislatures, the Parliament of Canada had not, by its general power "to make laws for the peace, order, and good government of Canada," full legislative authority to pass it.

---

[25] *O'Connor Report*, Annex 1, 33.

[26] 7 A.C. 136, at 149. O'Connor does not mention this judgment.

[27] 7 A.C. 829, at 836 and 842. This is O'Connor's "Case No. 6": see his *Report*, Annex 1, 33–35, and Annex 3, 14–18.

[28] See below, 143–46; 150; 154–55.

The Canada Temperance Act of 1878 was then judged to lie within the legislative authority of the federal parliament. It is not clear whether the consignment was to the Peace, Order, and good Government clause, or to head 2 of section 91:

Their Lordships having come to the conclusion that the Act in question does not fall within any of the classes of subjects assigned exclusively to the Provincial Legislatures, it becomes unnecessary to discuss the further question whether its provisions also fall within any of the classes of subjects enumerated in sect. 91. In abstaining from this discussion, they must not be understood as intimating any dissent from the opinion of the Chief Justice of the Supreme Court of Canada and the other Judges, who held that the Act, as a general regulation of the traffic in intoxicating liquors throughout the Dominion, fell within the class of subject, "the regulation of trade and commerce," enumerated in that section, and was, on that ground, a valid exercise of the legislative power of the Parliament of Canada.

But in either case, the Canada Temperance Act was judged to lie within the legislative authority of the federal parliament because it was held not to be a law in relation to a matter coming within any of the classes of "subjects" enumerated in section 92. The reason why it was not so held may be left until the discussion on the Dimensions and Emergency Doctrines;[29] the point at issue is that it was held to fall outside section 92.

O'Connor claims something quite different: "Note well that in this case the contest was one between the 'peace, order and good government clause' of section 91 and the 'Property and Civil Rights' and other specific classifications of section 92 and that *the general, unenumerated* clause of section 91 'overbore' or 'overrode' (as the cases express it) the 'exclusive' provincial provisions of section 92."[30] But that was not the "contest." Far from considering whether the Canada Temperance Act fell within the Peace, Order, and good Government clause or section 92, Sir Montague Smith held that it did not fall within section 92, and that it was therefore unnecessary to decide whether it fell within the Peace, Order, and good Government clause or the heads of section 91. Moreover the difference is vital: O'Connor implies that if the Judicial Committee held the Canada Temperance Act to be of national rather than provincial "scope," it must have rejected any priority distinction between the Peace, Order, and good Government clause and the heads of section 91.

This argument is intrinsically deficient. Since "scope" considerations are not incompatible with the three-compartment view,[31] even if the

29See below, chap. 11.
30*O'Connor Report*, Annex 1, 33.   31See above, chap. 3, sec. 3.

Russell judgment were based on the "scope" of the Canada Temperance Act, a two-compartment view need not have been adopted. But if Sir Montague Smith's words are read as they stand—and if they are, they would accord with his remarks in the *McCarthy Act Reference*[32] of 1885—it seems questionable whether his decision had anything to do with "scope." For the Canada Temperance Act might have been consigned to the Peace, Order, and good Government clause (assuming that this, and not section 91(2), applied) purely because of its "subject": because it was a prohibitory, and not a regulatory Act, and so was not in relation to a matter coming within any of the classes of "subjects" comprised in section 92.[33] And if the Act were consigned to the Peace, Order, and good Government clause simply by default (as provided for in the Exhaustion Theory), the contest would have involved the size, and not the priority of section 92(13), and the decision would concern the Ambit, rather than the Compartment Problem.[34] At most, though, the *Russell* judgment establishes nothing more than the limited proposition stated by Lord Haldane in his *Insurance Act* judgment[35] of 1916: "There is only one case, outside the heads enumerated in s. 91, in which

[32]No judgment was delivered in this reference, which is not recorded in the *Appeal Cases*. A transcript of the proceedings, taken from shorthand notes and printed separately (see Bibliography, under Dominion Liquor License Acts, 1883-4, *Report of Proceedings*), was found in the Privy Council Office, London, and the remarks referred to occur on pp. 44 and 64 of this *Report*. Although counsel for the Dominion (Sir Farrer Herschell) advocated an "O'Connor interpretation" of both *Russell* v. *The Queen* and the two-compartment view (at 93–95), his arguments failed to impress a Board which included three of the five judges who had heard the *Russell* appeal: viz., Smith, Peacock, and Couch. (The other judges in this reference were Halsbury, FitzGerald, and Monkswell, the others in the *Russell* appeal being Collier and Hannen). O'Connor's followers might note Sir Montague Smith's own reaction: "It is only the enumerated things that are declared to override the exclusive power given to the Provinces under section 92" (at 167). See also the comments at 28, 42, 44, 51, 62–63, 79–80, 84, 93–95, 98–99, 103–4, 106, 116–19, and 167.

[33]During the *McCarthy Act Reference*, Sir Montague made a point of contrasting the prohibitory character of the Canada Temperance Act with the regulatory character of the McCarthy Act (see *Report of Proceedings*, at 44 and 64). His argument, presumably, was that if the former Act had been regulatory, it might have been consigned to one of the more particular heads of s. 92 (perhaps head 15?), rather than to the general "subject" of "Property and Civil Rights in the Province." It might have then come within s. 92, and so, like the McCarthy Act, been *ultra vires* the federal parliament.

[34]See below, chap. 6 and chap. 7, sec. 3.

[35]*A.-G. Can.* v. *A.-G. Alta.*, [1916] 1 A.C. 588, at 595. Cf. *Hodge* v. *The Queen* (1883), 7 A.C. 117, at 129, where Sir Barnes Peacock interpreted the *Russell* judgment in three-compartment terms; also the *McCarthy Act Reference*, where Sir Montague Smith affirmed that "the decision in *Russell* v. *The Queen* did not proceed upon section 91 overriding section 92, but upon the power not being within section 92" (*Report of Proceedings*, 116; see also at 44 and 80).

the Dominion Parliament can legislate effectively as regards a province, and that is where the subject-matter lies outside all of the subject-matters enumeratively entrusted to the province under s. 92. *Russell v. The Queen* is an instance of such a case."

(b) The Post-1896 Judgments

The first intimation of a departure from the three-compartment view after 1896 was given by Sir Arthur Wilson in *La Compagnie Hydraulique de St. François* v. *Continental Heat and Light Company*,[36] 1909: "where, as here, a given field of legislation is within the competence both of the Parliament of Canada and of the provincial Legislature, and both have legislated, the enactment of the Dominion Parliament must prevail over that of the province if the two are in conflict, as they clearly are in the present case." As it stands, this remark is inconsistent with the reasoning of the *Tennant* and *Local Prohibition* judgments. Admittedly, only a small qualification would secure a fit; if a phrase like "under one of the heads of section 91"[37] were inserted, for example, the remark would read as follows: "where, as here, a given field of legislation is within the competence both of the Parliament of Canada, *under one of the heads of section 91*, and of the provincial Legislature, and both have legislated, the enactment of the Dominion Parliament must prevail over that of the province if the two are in conflict, as they clearly are in this case." Still, without such an insertion, Sir Arthur Wilson's remark might indicate a two-compartment assumption, and E. R. Cameron accordingly concludes that the judgment represents a departure from the three-compartment view.[38] However, since this conclusion is dependent on the assumption that "the jurisdiction of the Dominion Parliament must be rested in this case solely upon the power to make laws for the peace, order and good government of Canada,"[39] and since it is uncertain whether the impugned law was justified under that clause or under one of the heads of section 91,[40]

[36][1909] A.C. 194, at 198.
[37]As suggested in Cameron, *Canadian Constitution*, I, 73–74.
[38]Viz., head 29, by virtue of the exceptions specified in s. 92(10). Sir Arthur did not explain why the "given field of legislation is within the competence both of the Parliament of Canada and of the provincial Legislature." However, counsel for the appellants presumed a conflict between s. 92(11) and s. 91(29), and so argued that the federal law was not justified under the latter because its objects were "very different" from those that might be carried into that head by virtue of the exceptions in s. 92(10): see [1909] A.C. 194, at 196–97.
[39]Cameron, *Canadian Constitution*, I, 73.
[40]*Ibid.*, 73–74.

it is doubtful whether too much should be made of the judgment in *La Compagnie Hydraulique de St. François* v. *Continental Heat and Light Company*.

Anyway, O'Connor's first instance of two-compartment reasoning after 1896 is the following observation, made by Lord Birkenhead in *Canadian Pacific Wine Company* v. *Tuley*,[41] 1921:

It was contended at the Bar that this statute [viz., the Summary Convictions Act, passed by the Legislature of British Columbia in 1915] was ultra vires of the provincial Legislature, on the ground that it was an attempt to enact provincial legislation for "criminal law," including procedure in criminal matters, within the words of s. 91, head 27, of the British North America Act. But that section only declared that it is to be lawful for the Sovereign, with the advice of the Dominion Parliament, to make laws for the peace, order and good government of Canada generally, in relation to all matters not coming within the classes of subjects by the Act exclusively assigned to the Legislatures of the provinces, and the enumeration of matters which follows in s. 91 to which the exclusive authority of the Dominion Parliament extends is only a declaration that certain subjects fall under this description.

On this basis, O'Connor contrives an extensive argument:

It will have been noticed that Viscount Birkenhead's construction of the enumerated provisions of section 91 as *"certain subjects"* *which are declared by that section to "fall under the description" of "laws for the peace, order and good government of Canada generally"* etc. is one that I have been supporting as a true construction of the text of the Act. I submit that from that construction it must follow, in reason, that any *exclusive* character, as against the provisions of section 92, and any incidental paramountcy, that appertains to the enumerated provisions which "fall under this description" appertains as fully to the unenumerated provisions whose exclusive character, by the text, *extends* to the enumerated provisions.[42]

But the *Canadian Pacific Wine Company* judgment cannot be used as the basis for this argument. Even if the words "declaration" and "extends" were given the semi-technical denotation O'Connor presumes, both the context in which they were employed and the decision that was finally reached have a very different bearing from the one he imputes. For Lord Birkenhead went on like this:

When the language of s. 92, which defines the matters to which the exclusive legislative authority of the province extends, is scrutinized, this definition is found to include the administration of justice in the provinces embracing the constitution, maintenance and organization of provincial Courts, both

---

[41][1921] 2 A.C. 417, at 422–23. This is O'Connor's "Case No. 13": see his *Report*, Annex 1, 50–51 and Annex 3, 96.

[42]*O'Connor Report*, Annex 1, 50–51.

civil and criminal, and procedure in civil matters in these Courts. Head 15 of s. 92 expressly adds the imposition of punishment by fine, penalty or imprisonment, for enforcing any law of a province, made in relation to any of the classes of subject enumerated in the section; and head 16 gives exclusive legislative power to the provincial Legislatures in all matters of a merely local character. Reading ss. 91 and 92 together, their Lordships entertain no doubt that the Summary Convictions Act was within the competence of the Legislature of British Columbia. It relates only to punishment for offences against the provisions of the statutes of the province, and is to be read as if the provisions to this end were expressly declared in some such statute. No other conclusion would appear to be in harmony with the principle of construction laid down by the Judicial Committee in *Attorney-General for Ontario* v. *Attorney-General for the Dominion* [i.e., the *Local Prohibition* judgment of 1896].

By first taking a statement out of context, and then subjecting it to a microscopic examination, O'Connor creates a totally false impression. It is extremely dubious whether *Canadian Pacific Wine Company* v. *Tuley*, 1921, represents a departure from the three-compartment view.[43]

The next possible instance of a two-compartment decision is the *Proprietary Articles Trade Association* judgment[44] of 1931. Underlining Lord Atkin's description of the heads of section 91 as "particular instances of the general powers assigned to the Dominion," O'Connor asserts that "for the second time in recent years . . . the Board showed signs of a trend backwards to the text of the Act."[45] But this really is excessive; for O'Connor has again disregarded the context of his quotation:

. . . the general powers of legislation for the peace, order and good government of Canada are committed to the Dominion Parliament, though they are subject to the exclusive powers of legislation committed to the Provincial legislatures and enumerated in s. 92. But the Provincial powers are themselves qualified in respect of the classes of subjects enumerated in s. 91, as particular instances of the general powers assigned to the Dominion. Any matter coming within any of those particular classes of subjects is not to be deemed to come within the classes of matters assigned to the Provincial legislatures. This almost reproduces the express words of the sections, and this rule is well settled.

Since Lord Atkin accepted the three-compartment procedure for settling disputes over legislative competence (as he did six years later, in the *Natural Products Marketing Act* judgment[46] of 1937), his description

[43]See Gray's criticism in *CBR*, XVII (1939), 314.
[44]*Proprietary Articles Trade Association* v. *A.-G. Can.*, [1931] A.C. 310, at 316. This is O'Connor's "Case No. 54": see his *Report*, Annex 1, 51 and 75–76, and Annex 3, 128–31.
[45]*O'Connor Report*, Annex 1, 75.
[46]*A.-G. B.C.* v. *A.-G. Can.*, [1937] A.C. 377, at 386. See above, 53.

"particular instances of the general powers assigned to the Dominion" must have been nothing more than loose expression. The *Proprietary Articles Trade Association* judgment of 1931 does not represent a departure from the three-compartment view either.

As for *Attorney-General for Ontario* v. *Canada Temperance Federation*,[47] 1946, Lord Simon began by noting that "the object of the appeal is to challenge the decision of the Board in the case of *Russell* v. *The Queen*, or at any rate .to deny its applicability to the Act now in question."[48] He then decided that "their Lordships are not prepared to hold either that *Russell* v. *The Queen* was wrongly decided or that it has ceased to be a binding authority by reason that the Act of 1878 has been re-enacted in 1927."[49] Between these statements, however, he made the following comment:

In their Lordships' opinion, the true test must be found in the real subject matter of the legislation: if it is such that it goes beyond local or provincial concern or interests and must from its inherent nature be the concern of the Dominion as a whole (as, for example, in the *Aeronautics* case and the *Radio* case), then it will fall within the competence of the Dominion Parliament as a matter affecting the peace, order and good government of Canada, though it may in another aspect touch on matters specially reserved to the provincial legislatures.[50]

If this comment were taken to imply that the ultimate test of competence is whether a law is of national or provincial "scope," it would be compatible with the two-compartment view. At the same time, since it could also imply that resort must be had to the Peace, Order, and good Government clause when a law is of such "scope" as to make it unclassifiable as "a law in relation to matters coming within the classes of subjects" enumerated in section 92, it would not be incompatible with the existence of three compartments. In other words, the comment could be merely one more acknowledgment of the Dimensions Doctrine, as outlined by Lord Watson in the *Local Prohibition* judgment[51] of 1896. Indeed, Lord Simon's citation of the *Aeronautics*[52] and *Radio*[53] judgments, if not his upholding of *Russell* v. *The Queen*, tends to support the latter interpretation; for the first two judgments seem to presume three compartments,[54] and even the last could have involved that con-

---

[47][1946] A.C. 193. [48]*Ibid.*, at 202.
[49]*Ibid.*, at 208. [50]*Ibid.*, at 205.
[51]*A.-G. Ont.* v. *A.G. Can.*, [1896] A.C. 348, at 360–61. See above, 46–47.
[52]*In re the Regulation and Control of Aeronautics in Canada*, [1932] A.C. 54.
[53]*In re the Regulation and Control of Radio Communication in Canada*, [1932] A.C. 304.
[54]See above, 52–53.

struction.[55] On the other hand, the *Canada Temperance Act* judgment of 1946 might be considered sufficiently ambiguous to warrant its being described as a departure from the three-compartment view.

In general, though, O'Connor's analysis would seem to be controvertible. It cannot be claimed that in the period before the *Tennant*[56] and *Local Prohibition*[57] judgments of 1894 and 1896, the Judicial Committee invariably adopted the two-compartment view. On the contrary, the judgments in this period not only accord with, but in some cases depend on, an acceptance of the three. And that is true even of *Russell* v. *The Queen.*[58] Nor do the two decisions cited as departures after 1896—that is, the *Canadian Pacific Wine Company* judgment[59] of 1921, and the *Proprietary Articles Trade Association* judgment[60] of 1931— reveal a two-compartment inclination. It must be concluded that O'Connor's analysis, together with the blame he imputed to Lords Watson and Haldane, is at best not proven.

But the question of whether the Judicial Committee ever departed from the three-compartment view is really undebatable. There are only two possible instances of such a departure: Sir Arthur Wilson's judgment in *La Compagnie Hydraulique de St. François* v. *Continental Heat and Light Company,*[61] 1909, and Lord Simon's judgment in *Attorney-General of Ontario* v. *Canada Temperance Federation,*[62] 1946. And since the former could have involved only an inadvertent omission, while the latter could have entailed three compartments just as easily as two, even these instances are indeterminate. The remarkable consistency of the Judicial Committee's interpretative scheme is perhaps nowhere so obvious as in the judgments concerning the basic "Compartment Problem" of the British North America Act.

The eleven "instances" of two-compartment judgments (the eight cited by O'Connor, plus the three not mentioned in his *Report*) were delivered in these cases:[63]

---

[55]See above, 64–67.
[56]*Tennant* v. *Union Bank*, [1894] A.C. 31.
[57]*A.-G. Ont.* v. *A.-G. Can.*, [1896] A.C. 348.
[58][1882], 7 A.C. 829.
[59]*Canadian Pacific Wine Co.* v. *Tuley*, [1921] 2 A.C. 417.
[60]*Proprietary Articles Trade Association* v. *A.-G. Can.*, [1931] A.C. 310.
[61][1909] A.C. 194.
[62][1946] A.C. 193.
[63]The cases preceded by asterisks actually read more like three- than two-compartment decisions; nos. 3 and 4 could be either; and nos. 8 and 11 just might be two. Ironically, there is no mention of the last pair (or of no. 6) in the *O'Connor Report*. All these references are marked in col. D of the Analytical Table.

*1. *L'Union St. Jacques de Montréal* v. *Bélisle* (1874), 6 A.C. 31.

*2. *Dow* v. *Black* (1875), 6 A.C. 272.

 3. *Valin* v. *Langlois* (1879), 5 A.C. 115.

 4. *Cushing* v. *Dupuy* (1880), 5 A.C. 409.

*5. *Citizens Insurance Company* v. *Parsons* (1881), 7 A.C. 96.

*6. *Dobie* v. *Temporalities Board* (1881), 7 A.C. 136.

*7. *Russell* v. *The Queen* (1882), 7 A.C. 829.

 8. *La Compagnie Hydraulique de St. François* v. *Continental Heat and Light Company*, [1909] A.C. 194.

*9. *Canadian Pacific Wine Company* v. *Tuley*, [1921] 2 A.C. 417.

*10. *Proprietary Articles Trade Association* v. *Attorney-General for Canada*, [1931] A.C. 310.

 11. *Attorney-General for Ontario* v. *Canada Temperance Federation*, [1946] A.C. 193.

Chapter Six

THE AMBIT PROBLEM: I

1. Delimitation Difficulties in the B.N.A. Act

The spheres of legislative authority in a federal constitution can be delimited either by means of a general description of the nature of those spheres, or else through a detailed specification of their size, or ambit. The effect of the first method is to leave the original compromise relatively unprotected, but to establish a more flexible, or "organic," constitution. The effect of the second is to safeguard the compromise, but to limit the means of adjusting it to new conditions.

The proponents of the "constituent statute argument" contend that the British North America Act reflects the former method. The original intention was to ensure the consignment of legislation on the basis of "scope," rather than "subject." If a law were of national "scope," it would come within federal jurisdiction; if it were of provincial scope, it would come within provincial jurisdiction. The vital parts of sections 91 and 92 are consequently the Peace, Order, and good Government clause (by which the federal parliament is given power to legislate in relation to all matters of national "scope"), and head 16 of section 92 (which, as the Judicial Committee itself admitted, "has the same office"[1] as the Peace, Order, and good Government clause). It follows that the heads enumerated in sections 91 and 92 indicate the "kind" of laws that could be of national, or provincial "scope"—and that Canada has an organic constitution, which must be continuously correlated with the contemporary situation. O'Connor puts the argument like this:

I think that the scheme of distribution of legislative powers under the Act is

---

[1] *A.-G. Ont.* v. *A.-G. Can.*, [1896] A.C. 348, at 365. The use made of this reference in the above argument is possibly unwarranted; for although Lord Watson's qualification—"so far as [the Peace, Order, and good Government clause is] supplementary of the enumerated subjects"—might make s. 92(16) "residuary," it would not make the Peace, Order, and good Government clause "general": see the previous discussion of the four-compartment view, in chap. 3, sec. 3.

one so flexible, so well fitted to keep in step with time, that those who framed it might justifiably have hoped that such a simple and efficient scheme in relation to legislative authority could not be misunderstood and might always endure. What they thought of as a general Act—one enacted by and for the Dominion with Dominion purposes—that is one enacted in a Dominion "aspect"—would, as they conceived, come within Dominion jurisdiction. What they thought of as a provincial or "local" Act—one enacted by and for a province with provincial or "local" purposes—that is one enacted in a provincial "aspect"—would, as they conceived, come within provincial jurisdiction. If either Dominion or province were to enact the wrong *kind* of an Act it would be *ultra vires*, on the ground that the enacting legislature was not authorized to enact that *kind* of an Act. They did not anticipate—they could not foresee—any possibility of clashing of jurisdiction. Macdonald said so. They had even gone so far (after identifying in the Dominion an exhaustive residuary power), as to enumerate for the convenience of Dominion and provinces alike, a "sample" list of classes of subjects in relation to which the Dominion might legislate. They had also indicated, as they thought, *some things* in relation to which the Dominion might *not* legislate. But laws, and not *things* ere uppermost in their minds. They thought of *kinds, sorts, species, of laws.*[2]

If disputes over legislative competence were directed by considerations of "scope," however, they would be primarily concerned with the intent and effect of the law in question; and the efforts to interpret the terms of sections 91 and 92 would be governed by an illustrative purpose. Nonetheless, resort to those heads would still occur, if only as a means of settling doubts as to "scope"; such resort would in turn require some definition of the terms of those heads; and this definition would eventually become one, if not the principal means of consigning impugned legislation. It is doubtful, in other words, whether even the most general view of the delimitation of legislative spheres in the British North America Act would obviate attempts to construe the heads of sections 91 and 92.

But in any case, the Judicial Committee decided that the Act reveals a more particular intention. The framers must have been more concerned with "subject" than with "scope"; for above all, they tried to ensure that the federal authorities were excluded from certain areas of activity. And the heads of sections 91 and 92 must represent not merely the kind of laws that could be of national, or provincial "scope," but the "subjects" concerning which, under normal conditions, only the provincial authorities may legislate. That is why the Act contains not only a Peace, Order, and good Government clause, but also two lists of specific "subjects"—and why Canada has a constitution which, however inflexible, provides a crucial reassurance for certain elements of the

[2]*O'Connor Report*, 12–13.

population. In *Re Companies Incorporation*,[3] 1913, Duff J. summed up this argument as follows:

> The division of powers (under the general scheme of the Act) is according to the subject matter of the legislation, not according to the persons to be affected by the legislation. Care was taken to specify those cases in which it was thought necessary that the rights of a particular class of persons as such or a particular class of institutions as such should be exclusively committed to the control of one legislature or of the other.

Since certain heads appear to overlap, or "conflict," the attempts to construe sections 91 and 92 are also logically necessary. Thus, heads 1, 3, and 4 of section 91, and heads 2, 3, and 5 of section 92, deal with "concerns of government property and finance." Heads 2, 2A, 5–15 inclusive, 17, 26, 27, and 28 of section 91, and heads 4, 6–9 inclusive, 11, 12, 14, and 15 of section 92 deal with "public services." Heads 24 and 25 of section 91 deal with "specific classes of persons." Heads 9 and 24 of section 91, the exceptions carried over to that section (by force of head 29) from head 10 of section 92, and heads 10 and 13 of section 92 deal with "physical objects." Heads 10, 15, and 16 of section 91, and heads 11 and 12 of section 92, deal with "rights and obligations as between individuals." And heads 2, 18–23 inclusive, 26, and 27 of section 91, as well as heads 13 and 14 of section 92, deal with "divisions of jurisprudence."

However, some of the "subjects" mentioned in these heads "cross-section" others. Indeed, this "cross-sectioning" effect is the defining characteristic of the "subjects" coming within the category "divisions of jurisprudence"; and that is especially evident in the case of head 2 of section 91 ("The Regulation of Trade and Commerce"), head 27 of section 91 ("The Criminal Law, except the Constitution of Courts of Criminal Jurisdiction, but including the Procedure in Criminal Matters"), and head 13 of section 92 ("Property and Civil Rights in the Province"). Regardless of other factors, the conflicts among such heads would necessitate a construction of sections 91 and 92.

Similarly, there could be conflicts involving the "general provisions" of those sections, or even other sections in the Act. A law might seem consignable to one or more of the heads of section 91, and also to head 16 of section 92; or to one or more of the heads of section 92, and also to head 16 of that section. Or else a law might seem consignable to one or more of the heads of section 91 or 92, and also, say, to section 41,[4]

---

[3]48 S.C.R. 331, at 410.
[4]See *A.-G. Ont.* v. *A.-G. Can.*, [1925] A.C. 750, at 752–53.

93,[5] 94,[6] 96,[7] or 132.[8] Or a law might seem consignable to both of the general provisions in sections 91 and 92 (the Peace, Order, and good Government clause and head 16 of section 92); or to either of those provisions, and also to another section, or sections, of the Act.

Such conflicts can obviously be resolved only by redefining the terms that are not mutually exclusive (or from another standpoint, by restricting the ambits of the overlapping parts of the Act). It is debatable, however, whether these redefinings should be reduced to a set of principles. In the *Parsons* judgment[9] of 1881, Sir Montague Smith—while stressing the need "to arrive at a reasonable and practical construction of the language of the sections, so as to reconcile the respective powers they contain, and give effect to all of them"—offered this advice: "In performing this difficult duty, it will be a wise course for those on whom it is thrown, to decide each case which arises as best they can, without entering more largely upon an interpretation of the statute than is necessary for the decision of the particular question in hand." And in *John Deere Plow Company* v. *Wharton*,[10] 1915, Lord Haldane agreed:

The structure of ss. 91 and 92, and the degree to which the connotation of the expressions used overlaps, render it, in their Lordships' opinion, unwise on this or any other occasion to attempt exhaustive definitions of the meaning and scope of these expressions. Such definitions, in the case of language used under the conditions in which a constitution such as that under consideration was framed, must almost certainly miscarry. It is in many cases only by confining decisions to concrete questions which have actually arisen in circumstances the whole of which are before the tribunal that injustice to future suitors can be avoided. . . . It must be borne in mind in construing the two sections that matters which in a special aspect and for a particular purpose may fall within one of them may in another aspect and for a different purpose fall within the other. In such cases the nature and scope of the legislative attempt of the Dominion or the Province, as the case may be, have to be examined with reference to the actual facts if it is to be possible to determine under which set of powers it falls in substance and in

---

[5]See *Ottawa Roman Catholic Separate Schools Trustees* v. *Ottawa*, [1917] A.C. 76, at 80.
[6]See *Citizens Insurance Co.* v. *Parsons* (1881), 7 A.C. 96, at 110–11.
[7]See *Valin* v. *Langlois* (1879), 5 A.C. 115, at 119–20.
[8]See *A.-G. Can.* v. *A.-G. Ont.*, [1937] A.C. 326, at 342 and 349–50.
[9]*Citizens Insurance Co.* v. *Parsons* (1881), 7 A.C. 96, at 109.
[10][1915] A.C. 330, at 338–39. See also *A.-G. Man.* v. *Manitoba Licence Holders' Association*, [1902] A.C. 73, at 77; *Proprietary Articles Trade Association* v. *A.-G. Can.*, [1931] A.C. 310, at 316–17; *A.-G. Alta.* v. *A.-G. Can.*, [1939] A.C. 117, at 129. This inclination to abstain from arguments concerning constitutional doctrine was accompanied by a similar disinclination to decide abstract or general questions: see *A.-G. B.C.* v. *A.-G. Can.*, [1914] A.C. 153, at 161–62, and *A.-G. Ont.* v. *A.-G. Can.*, [1916] 1 A.C. 598, at 601–2.

reality. This may not be difficult to determine in actual and concrete cases. But it may well be impossible to give abstract answers to general questions as to the meaning of the words, or to lay down any interpretation based on their literal scope apart from their context.

Even so, the judgments delivered by the Judicial Committee have made the ambits of the conflicting parts of the British North America Act both clearer, and more certain, than they were in 1867.

2. The General "Causes" of the Ambit Solutions

This study is principally concerned with the parts of the Act that had a critical effect on the distribution of legislative powers.[11] These are the Peace, Order, and good Government clause; head 16 of section 92; head 2 of section 91 ("The Regulation of Trade and Commerce"); head 27 of section 91 (the "Criminal Law" head)—which involves head 15 of section 92; head 3 of section 91 and head 2 of section 92 (the "Taxing Power" heads)—which involve heads 1A and 8 of section 91, heads 4 and 9 of section 92, and sections 100, 118, 121, 122, and 125; head 13 of section 92 ("Property and Civil Rights in the Province"); and section 132 (the "Treaty Obligations" section).

On the whole, the most important "federal" parts (heads 2, 3, and 27 of section 91, section 132, and the Peace, Order, and good Government clause) were given a restrictive interpretation. In contrast, the contending provincial parts (heads 2, 13, and 15—though not head 16—of section 92) were viewed expansively. It may therefore be concluded that the over-all effect of the solutions devised for the Ambit Problem was to safeguard, or perhaps to expand, the provincial legislative sphere. But it may not be concluded that the Judicial Committee displayed a predilection for the provincial side. For such a conclusion not only confuses cause and effect, but suggests that the Committee had a provincial bias. This suggestion is usually expressed in a less overt form: the general effect of the solutions to the Ambit Problem is attributed to the Judicial Committee's "philosophy of Canadian federalism."[12] While the Board might have sympathized with this "philosophy,"[13] however,

---

[11]However, all the parts are listed in col. C of the Analytical Table. W. R. Jackett's *Chart of Privy Council Decisions* was a useful aid in the preparation of this column.

[12]See Laskin, *Constitutional Law*, 150.

[13]See above, chap. 2, sec. 3.

that sympathy need not have been the main, let alone the sole "cause" of its solutions.

In fact, those solutions were directly obtained by applying the Rules of Statutory Interpretation.[14] Some of these applications involved a "resort to extrinsic aids."[15] Thus, references were made to earlier laws in the *Parsons* case[16] of 1881, in the *Voluntary Assignments* case[17] of 1894, and in the *Marriage Reference* case[18] of 1912. The legislative history of an Act was surveyed in the *Proprietary Articles Trade Association* case[19] of 1931. In *Croft* v. *Dunphy*,[20] 1933, the power conferred to legislate on a particular topic was gauged in relation to "what is ordinarily treated as embraced within that topic in the legislative practice of the State which has conferred the power." Even the work of scholars, while normally suspect, has not been utterly ignored: one of the Judicial Committee's most far-reaching definitions (of "Direct Taxation," as used in head 2 of section 92) was based on a formula recommended by John Stuart Mill.[21]

In general, though, the Board tended to rely on "internal" evidence, derived from the terms of the Act itself. As Sir Montague Smith noted, in the *Parsons* judgment[22] of 1881, those terms had to be mutually reconciled: "It could not have been the intention that a conflict should exist; and, in order to prevent such a result, the two sections must be read together, and the language of one interpreted, and, where necessary, modified, by that of the other. In this way it may, in most cases, be found possible to arrive at a reasonable and practical construction of the language of the sections, so as to reconcile the respective powers they contain, and give effect to all of them." This reconciliation has been achieved in different types of conflict: involving the parts of each section,

[14]See above, chap. 1, sec. 2, and chap. 2, sec. 2.

[15]See above, 9–12.

[16]*Citizens Insurance Co.* v. *Parsons* (1881), 7 A.C. 96, at 110 and 111; i.e., with respect to ss. 91(2) and 92(13).

[17]*A.-G. Ont.* v. *A.-G. Can.*, [1894] A.C. 189, at 196–200; i.e., with respect to s. 91(21).

[18]*In re Marriage Reference to Supreme Court*, [1912] A.C. 880, at 887; i.e., with respect to s. 91(26).

[19]*Proprietary Articles Trade Association* v. *A.-G. Can.*, [1931] A.C. 310, at 317–25; i.e., with respect to s. 91(27).

[20][1933] A.C. 156, at 165; i.e., with respect to s. 91(27). See also Lord Cave, in *Royal Bank of Canada* v. *Larne*, [1928] A.C. 187, at 197; i.e., with respect to s. 91(21).

[21]See *Bank of Toronto* v. *Lambe* (1887), 12 A.C. 575, at 582–83; *Brewers and Maltsters' Association* v. *A.-G. Ont.*, [1897] A.C. 231, at 236; *Cotton* v. *The King*, [1914] A.C. 176, at 191–93. Cf. *Halifax* v. *Fairbanks' Estate*, [1928] A.C. 117, at 125.

[22]*Citizens Insurance Co.* v. *Parsons* (1881), 7 A.C. 96, at 108–9.

considered independently; involving the parts of section 91, as opposed to either the parts, or the whole, of section 92; involving section 91 or section 92, as against different sections of the Act; and involving sections other than sections 91 and 92. Thus, in section 91,[23] heads 2, 15, 17, 18, 19, and 21 have all been reconciled, while in section 92,[24] heads 11, 13, and 16 have also been fitted together. In the same way, section 91(3) has been made consistent with section 92(4);[25] section 91(10) with section 92(13);[26] section 91(26) with section 92(12);[27] section 92(13) with any case of property and civil rights;[28] section 92(14) with sections 41,[29] 96, 99, and 100;[30] section 92, as a whole, with the Peace, Order, and good Government clause;[31] and the Peace, Order, and good Government clause with section 93.[32]

Most of these reconciliations were achieved by applying the linguistic principle, that general language yields to particular expression.[33] This principle—recognized by Sir Montague Smith in the *Parsons* judgment[34] of 1881, and affirmed by Lord Caldecote in *Lethbridge Northern Irrigation District Board of Trustees* v. *Independent Order of Foresters,*[35] 1940—was outlined by Lord Haldane (though with reference to sections 91 and 92 only) in *Great West Saddlery Company* v. *The King,*[36] 1921:

The rule of construction is that general language in the heads of s. 92 yields to particular expressions in s. 91, where the latter are unambiguous. The rule may also apply in favour of the Province in construing merely general words in the enumerated heads in s. 91. . . . Whether an exception is to be read in either case depends on the application of the principle that language which is merely general is, as a rule, to be harmonized with expressions which are at once precise and particular by treating the latter as operating by way of exception. The two sections must be read together, and the whole of the

[23]See *ibid.*, at 112.
[24]See *John Deere Plow Co.* v. *Wharton*, [1915] A.C. 330, at 339–40, and *A.-G. Ont.* v. *A.-G. Can.*, [1896] A.C. 348, at 365.
[25]See *Citizens Insurance Co.* v. *Parsons* (1881), 7 A.C. 96, at 108; *Bank of Toronto* v. *Lambe* (1887), 12 A.C. 575, at 585; *Caron* v. *The King*, [1924] A.C. 999, at 1003–4.
[26]See *Paquet* v. *Quebec Pilots' Corporation*, [1920] A.C. 1029, at 1031.
[27]See *Citizens Insurance Co.* v. *Parsons* (1881), 7 A.C. 96, at 108.
[28]See *John Deere Plow Co.* v. *Wharton*, [1915] A.C. 330, at 339–40, and *Great West Saddlery Co.* v. *The King*, [1921] 2 A.C. 91, at 105.
[29]See *Valin* v. *Langlois* (1879), 5 A.C. 115, at 118–20.
[30]See *A.-G. Ont.* v. *A.-G. Can.*, [1925] A.C. 750, at 752–53.
[31]See *Citizens Insurance Co.* v. *Parsons* (1881), 7 A.C. 96, at 108.
[32]See *Ottawa Roman Catholic Separate Schools Trustees* v. *Mackell*, [1917] A.C. 62, at 68.
[33]See above, 12–13.
[34]See *Citizens Insurance Co.* v. *Parsons* (1881), 7 A.C. 96, at 110.
[35][1940] A.C. 513, at 528–29.
[36][1921] 2 A.C. 91, at 116.

scheme for distribution of legislative powers set forth in their language must be taken into account in determining what is merely general and what is particular in applying the rule of construction.

To begin with conflicts involving the parts of each section, since the other heads of section 91 are worded more particularly than head 2 ("The Regulation of Trade and Commerce"), the latter has been confined to general trade and commerce: as Sir Montague Smith pointed out in the *Parsons* judgment, "if the words had been intended to have the full scope of which in their literal meaning they are susceptible, the specific mention of such of the other classes of subjects enumerated in sect. 91 would have been unnecessary; as, 15, banking; 17, weights and measures; 18, bills of exchange and promissory notes; 19, interest; and even 21, bankruptcy and insolvency".[37] For the same reason, head 13 of section 92 ("Property and Civil Rights in the Province") has been held not to include the "subjects expressly dealt with in the other heads of that section—and so, for example, does not extend to "The Incorporation of Companies with Provincial Objects" because of the more particular wording of head 11.[38] The general wording of head 16 of section 92 has likewise been held to exclude the "subjects" mentioned in all the other heads of that section.[39] And the separation of the Peace, Order, and good Government clause from the heads of section 91 is at least compatible with the same linguistic principle.[40]

As for conflicts between section 91 and section 92, head 26 of section 91 ("Marriage and Divorce") has been held not to include "The Solemnization of Marriage in the Province" because this "subject" is included in head 12 of section 92.[41] Head 3 of section 91 ("The raising of Money by any Mode or System of Taxation") has been held not to include "Direct Taxation within the Province in order to the raising of a Revenue for Provincial Purposes" because this "subject" is included in head 3 of section 91.[42] Head 13 of section 92 ("Property and Civil Rights in the Province") has been held not to include "Navigation and Shipping" because this "subject" is included in head 10 of section 91.[43] The expression "civil rights," as found in head 13 of section 92, has been held not to cover cases more expressly dealt

[37]*Citizens Insurance Co.* v. *Parsons* (1881), 7 A.C. 96, at 112.

[38]*John Deere Plow Co.* v. *Wharton*, [1915] A.C. 330, at 339–40.

[39]See above, 41–42 and below, 87–88.

[40]Though it is usually supported by different arguments: see above, chap. 3, sec. 2, and chap. 4.

[41]See *Citizens Insurance Co.* v. *Parsons* (1881), 7 A.C. 96, at 108.

[42]See *ibid.*; *Bank of Toronto* v. *Lambe* (1887), 12 A.C. 575, at 585; *Caron* v. *The King*, [1924] A.C. 999, at 1003–4.

[43]See *Paquet* v. *Quebec Pilots' Corporation*, [1920] A.C. 1029, at 1031.

with in either section 91 or the other heads of section 92.[44] And if the linguistic principle has not been used to separate the heads of section 91 from the Peace, Order, and good Government clause, it has been invoked to justify the exclusion of the powers conferred in the heads of section 92 from the residuary power of the federal parliament.[45]

Finally, the resolution of conflicts involving other sections of the Act can be illustrated by two cases. In *Valin* v. *Langlois*,[46] 1879, Lord Selborne decided that head 14 of section 92 ("The Administration of Justice in the Province . . .") did not concern election petitions because section 41 required the continuance of existing election laws until the Parliament of Canada made other provision. Then in *Ottawa Roman Catholic Separate Schools Trustees* v. *Mackell*,[47] 1917, Lord Buckmaster settled a conflict between the Peace, Order, and good Government clause and section 93 by reasoning that since the latter section covers education arrangements, this "subject" is "excluded from the powers conferred on the Parliament of Canada, and is placed wholly within the competence of the provincial legislatures. . . ."

The various parts of the British North America Act—and particularly the deeming paragraph of section 91[48]—have also been reconciled by means of grammatical construction. During the *Parsons* judgment[49] of 1881, Sir Montague Smith observed that "this paragraph applies in its grammatical construction only to No. 16 of sect. 92." In the *Local Prohibition* judgment[50] of 1896, however, Lord Watson repudiated that view: "The observation was not material to the question arising in that case, and it does not appear to their Lordships to be strictly accurate.

[44]See *John Deere Plow Co.* v. *Wharton*, [1915] A.C. 330, at 339–40, and *Great West Saddlery Co.* v. *The King*, [1921] 2 A.C. 91, at 105.

[45]See *Citizens Insurance Co.* v. *Parsons* (1881), 7 A.C. 96, at 108. "Heads," in this last statement, should be read as meaning "heads 1–15 inclusive"—even though Sir Montague Smith did not expressly exclude head 16 from his argument, at 108 (cf. Lord Watson, in *A.-G. Ont.* v. *A.-G. Can.*, [1896] A.C. 348, at 365). But if s. 92(16) were excluded, the relationship between it and the Peace, Order, and good Government clause might be considered another type of conflict between ss. 91 and 92; and if so, then since the federal power is generally held to override the provincial (see Lord Watson, *ibid.*), this relationship might be claimed as an exception to the "linguistic principle." Alternatively, it might be argued that if the Peace, Order, and good Government clause and s. 92(16) are both "residuary," neither need be considered "particular"; so that head 16 would not be relevant to the present argument—and there would be no "exception" to the "linguistic principle."

[46]5 A.C. 115, at 119.

[47][1917] A.C. 62, at 68.

[48]For the different interpretations given this paragraph, see above, chaps. 3, 4, and 5; for the resulting controversy, see below, chap. 12, sec. 2.

[49]*Citizens Insurance Co.* v. *Parsons* (1881), 7 A.C. 96, at 108.

[50]*A.-G. Ont.* v. *A.-G. Can.*, [1896] A.C. 348, at 359.

It appears to them that the language of the exception in s. 91 was meant to include and correctly describes all the matters enumerated in the sixteen heads of s. 92, as being, from a provincial point of view, of a local or private nature." The implications of this new grammatical construction were later developed (so far as the relative ambits of section 92 and the heads of section 91 were concerned) in *John Deere Plow Company* v. *Wharton*,[51] 1915, and *Great West Saddlery Company* v. *The King*,[52] 1921. In the latter judgment, for instance, Lord Haldane argued as follows:

As is now well settled the words quoted [viz., the deeming paragraph] apply, not only to the merely local or private matters in the Province referred to in head 16 of s. 92, but to the whole of the sixteen heads in that section: *A.-G. for Ontario* v. *A.-G. for Canada* [i.e., the *Local Prohibition* judgment of 1896]. The effect, as was pointed out in the decision just cited, is to effect a derogation from what might otherwise have been literally the authority of the Provincial Legislatures, to the extent of enabling the Parliament of Canada to deal with matters local and private where, though only where, such legislation is necessarily incidental to the exercise of the enumerated powers conferred on it by s. 91.

The construction suggested by Lord Watson for the deeming paragraph was accordingly used to restrict the ambits of heads 13 and 14 of section 92 (relative to heads 3, 22, and 27 of section 91),[53] heads 13, 14, and 16 of section 92 (relative to head 21 of section 91),[54] and head 13 of section 92 (relative to head 15 of section 91).[55] However, Lord Watson did not apply the deeming paragraph that way. Since he was not so concerned with conflicts between section 92 and the heads of section 91, as with conflicts between section 92 and the Peace, Order, and good Government clause, his application was somewhat different:

There may, therefore, be matters not included in the enumeration, upon which the Parliament of Canada has power to legislate, because they concern the peace, order, and good government of the Dominion. But to those matters which are not specified among the enumerated subjects of legislation, the exception from s. 92, which is enacted by the concluding words of s. 91, has no application; and, in legislating with regard to such matters, the Dominion Parliament has no authority to encroach upon any class of subjects which is exclusively assigned to provincial legislatures by s. 92.[56]

---

[51][1915] A.C. 330, at 337–38.

[52][1921] 2 A.C. 91, at 99–100.

[53]See *Proprietary Articles Trade Association* v. *A.-G. Can.*, [1931] A.C. 310, at 316 and 323–27.

[54]See *A.-G. Alta.* v. *A.-G. Can.*, [1943] A.C. 356, at 369–71 and 374–75.

[55]See *A.-G. Can.* v. *A.-G. Que.*, [1947] A.C. 33, at 42–43.

[56] *A.-G. Ont.* v. *A.-G. Can.*, [1896] A.C. 348, at 360.

The grammatical construction eventually accepted for the deeming paragraph of section 91 was therefore used to restrict both the ambit of section 92 (relative to the heads of section 91), and the ambit of the Peace, Order, and good Government clause (relative to section 92 in general, and head 13 in particular).

The resolution of the Ambit Problem was also affected by the solutions designed for the Compartment Problem. Thus the residuary character accorded the Peace, Order, and good Government clause[57] encouraged the tendency to fit as many laws as possible into the heads of sections 91 and 92, and so to expand the ambits of those heads. Because of its historical antecedents, cross-sectioning character, and comparative immunity to the onslaughts of the linguistic principle, however, the head most susceptible to such expansion is head 13 of section 92 ("Property and Civil Rights in the Province").[58] And so the ultimate effect of accepting the three-compartment view was to establish an expansive, as well as exclusive sphere of provincial legislative authority.

This argument is not the same as the previous one, concerning the deeming paragraph. Since the three-compartment view can be supported independently of that paragraph (simply by reference to the statement "and for greater certainty"), the connection between this view and the Ambit Problem must be treated separately from the connection between the deeming paragraph and that problem. At the same time, these connections are alike in that neither is of a logical nature. While it may not be concluded, then, that the solution to the Compartment Problem logically required the solution to the Ambit Problem, it might be suspected that the connection between those solutions is more than coincidental. And it might be noticed that the solutions are not merely compatible, but congruous.

The solutions to the Consignment Problem had a similar impact. Thus the ambit of head 2 of section 91 was affected by the Ancillary Doctrine, while the ambit of the Peace, Order, and good Government clause was first expanded by the Dimensions Doctrine, and then restricted by the Doctrine of Emergency Powers.[59] The results of this impact—especially in the case of the Peace, Order, and good Government clause—will be traced in the next chapter; but again, the congruity of the solutions might be noticed here.

As far as jurisprudential assumptions are concerned, the acceptance

---

[57]See above, chap. 3, sec. 2.
[58]See below, chap. 7, sec. 3.
[59]See below, chap. 12.

of a particular "philosophy of federalism" could have influenced the resolution of the Ambit Problem. But so could the acceptance of the Rule of Precedent and the Theory of Judicial Restraint. For if the Peace, Order, and good Government clause were expanded so as to require a predominant emphasis on "scope," the court of final appeal would be more concerned with intentions and conditions than if it were simply required to identify the "subject" concerned. Since precedents would then be more involved with particular facts (and so less comprehensive of general principles), judgments would become more susceptible to the distinguishing process, and less conducive to certainty and stability. Moreover, since the courts would have to consider not only the "subject" of an impugned law, but also the purposes and effects of such legislation, the judiciary would become not merely the arbiter, but the critic of the legislature's actions. Is it surprising that the Judicial Committee favoured a restricted interpretation of the Peace, Order, and good Government clause—especially when this interpretation was also indicated by both the linguistic principle and the three-compartment view?

To summarize, the resolution of the Ambit Problem was directly achieved through an occasional resort to extrinsic aids, some grammatical construction, and the employment of the "linguistic principle." No doubt the solutions to the Compartment and Consignment Problems, as well as the Judicial Committee's jurisprudential assumptions, exerted some influence; and the Board's "federal philosophy" cannot be discounted. However, such possibilities are more easily raised than established; and the latter hypothesis, in particular, needs to be treated cautiously. For since it carries the same insinuation as the charge of provincial bias—that the "cause" of the Judicial Committee's interpretative scheme was extraneous to the British North America Act itself—this hypothesis could be prejudicial. Yet even if it were shown that the Judicial Committee did accept a certain federal philosophy, it would not follow that this acceptance must have been anterior to the Board's interpretation of the Act.[60] Indeed, if the terms of the Act are construed in a three-compartment way, the result might well be a scheme that would entail, when generalized, the same "philosophy."

But the above emphasis on congruity is not meant to imply that the particular solutions to the Ambit Problem were invariably consistent. The definition given section 91(2) in the *Parsons* judgment[61] of 1881

[60]See above, chap. 2, sec. 3.
[61]*Citizens Insurance Co.* v. *Parsons* (1881), 7 A.C. 96, at 112–13.

was progressively restricted[62] until, in the *Proprietary Articles Trade Association* judgment[63] of 1931, Lord Atkin rejected the more extreme constructions.[64] Similarly, despite its confined interpretation in the *Board of Commerce* judgment[65] of 1922, section 91(27) eventually became an "expanding field."[66] And the ambit of the Peace, Order, and good Government clause oscillated between the "Dimensions" and "Emergency" interpretations.[67] Such inconsistencies will be better appreciated, however, when the ambit of each part of the British North America Act is considered separately.

[62]See *In re the Board of Commerce Act, 1919, and the Combines and Fair Prices Act, 1919*, [1922] 1 A.C. 191, at 198, and *Toronto Electric Commissioners v. Snider*, [1925] A.C. 396, at 410.

[63]*Proprietary Articles Trade Association v. A.-G. Can.*, [1931] A.C. 310, at 326.

[64]For a fuller discussion of this development, see below, chap. 7, sec. 2.

[65]*In re the Board of Commerce Act, 1919, and the Combines and Fair Prices Act, 1919*, [1922] 1 A.C. 191, at 198–99.

[66]See *Proprietary Articles Trade Association v. A.-G. Can.*, [1931] A.C. 310, at 323–25, and *A.-G. B.C. v. A.-G. Can.*, [1937] A.C. 368, at 375–76. Cf. these two judgments of the Supreme Court of Canada: *Provincial Secretary of Prince Edward Island v. Egan*, [1941] S.C.R. 396, and *Lord's Day Alliance v. A.-G. B.C.*, [1959] S.C.R. 497. For a fuller discussion, see below, chap. 8, sec. 1.

[67]See below, chap. 7, sec. 1, and chap. 11.

Chapter Seven

THE AMBIT PROBLEM: II

1. The Ambits of the Peace, Order, and Good Government Clause and Section 92(16)

The fact that the three-compartment view gives a "residuary" character to the Peace, Order, and good Government clause[1] probably accounts for the failure of this clause to become an "expansible federal provision." Legislation was normally consigned to the "third compartment" only when it was held not to be in relation to a matter coming within the classes of "subjects" enumerated in either section 91 or section 92. Thus in *Great West Saddlery Company* v. *The King*,[2] 1921, Lord Haldane argued that since "the power of a Province to legislate for the incorporation of companies is limited to companies with Provincial objects, and there is no express power conferred to incorporate companies with powers to carry on business throughout the Dominion and in every Province . . . such a power is covered by the general enabling words of s. 91, which, because of the gap, confer it exclusively on the Dominion." In the same way, the residuary character of the Peace, Order, and good Government clause enabled the passage of laws authorizing the Crown to deport aliens,[3] and to obtain answers to legal and factual questions from the Supreme Court of Canada.[4]

Since it is not solely residuary, however, the Peace, Order, and good Government clause is not completely inelastic. And legislation that would normally be classified as in relation to a "subject" enumerated in section 92 has been considered, because of various exceptional conditions, to fall within the legislative authority of the federal parliament. In other

[1]See above, chap. 3, sec. 2.
[2][1921] 2 A.C. 91, at 114. See also *John Deere Plow Co.* v. *Wharton*, [1915] A.C. 330, and *A.-G. Man.* v. *A.-G. Can.*, [1929] A.C. 260.
[3]See *A.-G. Can.* v. *Cain*, [1906] A.C. 542, at 547, and *British Coal Corporation* v. *The King*, [1935] A.C. 500, at 518–19.
[4]See *A.-G. Ont.* v. *A.-G. Can.*, [1912] A.C. 571, at 583–84.

words, while legislation is consigned primarily on the basis of "subject," the Peace, Order, and good Government clause provides some opportunity for the consideration of "scope" as well.[5] For if a law affected a "subject" enumerated in section 92, and yet was of such "scope" as to make it a "law of national concern," it would no longer be "in relation to" a matter coming within section 92, and so would be consigned to the federal parliament under the authority of the Peace, Order, and good Government clause. This clause has a greater ambit, therefore, than a strictly residuary construction would imply.

The question of how much greater must be left till the discussion of the Consignment Problem;[6] for this ambit was determined on the basis of "scope," rather than "subject"—and so was defined indirectly, rather than directly (that is, by means of the doctrines devised for the consignment of legislation to the Peace, Order, and good Government clause). In general, though, since the ambit of this third compartment is largely a matter of residuary legislative authority, the Peace, Order, and good Government clause, if not completely inelastic, has been almost completely neglected.

Head 16 of section 92 ("Generally all Matters of a merely local or private Nature in the Province") did not become an expansible provision either. In fact, although frequently cited in addition to a more particular head, section 92(16) was held to govern a judgment in only two,[7] or possibly three,[8] cases. During the *Local Prohibition* judgment[9] of 1896, Lord Watson suggested a reason for this neglect:

> It is not necessary for the purposes of the present appeal to determine whether provincial legislation for the suppression of the liquor traffic, confined to matters which are provincial or local within the meaning of Nos. 13 and 16, is authorized by the one or by the other of these heads. It cannot, in their Lordships' opinion, be logically held to fall within both of them. In s. 92, No. 16 appears to them to have the same office which the general enactment with respect to matters concerning the peace, order, and good government of Canada, so far as supplementary of the enumerated subjects, fulfils in s. 91. It assigns to the provincial legislature all matters in a provincial sense local or private which have been omitted from the preceding enumeration, and, although its terms are wide enough to cover, they were obviously not meant to include, provincial legislation in relation to the classes of subjects already enumerated.

---

[5]See above, 40–41, and below, chap. 11.   [6]See below, chap. 11.

[7]Viz., *L'Union St. Jacques de Montréal* v. *Bélisle* (1874), 6 A.C. 31, and *A.-G. Man.* v. *Manitoba Licence Holders' Association*, [1902] A.C. 73.

[8]*A.-G. Ont.* v. *A.-G. Can.*, [1896] A.C. 348 might be added—providing one accepts Lord Macnaghten's interpretation, in the *Manitoba Liquor Act* judgment ([1902] A.C. 73, at 78; see below, 88).

[9]*A.-G. Ont.* v. *A.-G. Can.*, [1896] A.C. 348, at 365.

And in the *Manitoba Liquor Act* judgment[10] of 1902, Lord Macnaghten extended the argument:

Although this particular question [viz., whether the provincial legislation for the suppression of the liquor traffic was supported under head 13 or head 16] was thus left apparently undecided, a careful perusal of the judgment leads to the conclusion that, in the opinion of the Board, the case fell under No. 16 rather than under No. 13. And that seems to their Lordships to be the better opinion. In legislating for the suppression of the liquor traffic the object in view is the abatement or prevention of a local evil, rather than the regulation of property and civil rights—though, of course, no such legislation can be carried into effect without interfering more or less with "property and civil rights in the province." Indeed, if the case is to be regarded as dealing with matters within the class of subjects enumerated in No. 13, it might be questionable whether the Dominion Legislature could have authority to interfere with the exclusive jurisdiction of the province in the matter.

The last sentence probably explains not only why head 16 was neglected by the Judicial Committee, but also why it has been promoted by critics of the Judicial Committee's interpretative scheme.[11] If Lord Watson's comment on "the same office" were taken to imply that section 92(16) occupies a position analogous to that of the Peace, Order, and good Government clause,[12] it might be argued, on the basis of the Paramountcy Doctrine,[13] that any legislation supported by head 16 alone must be "subordinate" to any legislation supported by the Peace, Order, and good Government clause. That was the doubt raised by Lord Macnaghten's comment—and the probable reason why section 92(16) became a controversial means of defining the sphere of provincial legislative authority.[14]

2. The Ambit of Section 91(2)

The Judicial Committee also confined head 2 of section 91 ("The Regulation of Trade and Commerce"). In the *Parsons* judgment[15] of

[10]*A.-G. Man.* v. *Manitoba Licence Holders' Association*, [1902] A.C. 73, at 78.
[11]See Rand J., in *Reference re Farm Products Marketing Act, R.S.O. 1950, c. 131, as Amended*, [1957] S.C.R. 198; Kennedy and Wells, *Taxing Power*, 152; Laskin, *Constitutional Law*, 430–32 and 658.
[12]Vis-à-vis both the heads of s. 91 and the other heads of s. 92.
[13]See above, 41–42.
[14]See *L'Union St. Jacques de Montréal* v. *Bélisle* (1874), 6 A.C. 31, at 35–36; *Dow* v. *Black* (1875), 6 A.C. 272, at 280–82; *Hodge* v. *The Queen* (1883), 9 A.C. 117, at 131–32. The 27 major references to s. 92(16) are marked in col. D of the Analytical Table.
[15]*Citizens Insurance Co.* v. *Parsons* (1881), 7 A.C. 96, at 112–13.

1881, Sir Montague Smith—after deciding that "the words 'property' and 'civil rights' [in the conflicting class, head 13 of section 92] are plainly used in their largest sense"—made this statement:

The words "regulation of trade and commerce," in their unlimited sense are sufficiently wide, if uncontrolled by the context and other parts of the Act, to include every regulation of trade ranging from political arrangements in regard to trade with foreign governments, requiring the sanction of parliament, down to minute rules for regulating particular trades. But a consideration of the Act shews that the words were not used in this unlimited sense. In the first place the collocation of No. 2 with classes of subjects of national and general concern affords an indication that regulations relating to general trade and commerce were in the mind of the legislature, when conferring this power on the dominion parliament. If the words had been intended to have the full scope of which in their literal meaning they are susceptible, the specific mention of several of the other classes of subjects enumerated in sect. 91 would have been unnecessary; as, 15, banking; 17, weights and measures; 18, bills of exchange and promissory notes; 19, interest; and even 21, bankruptcy and insolvency.

"Regulation of trade and commerce" may have been used in some such sense as the words "regulations of trade" in the Act of Union between England and Scotland (6 Anne, c. 11), and as these words have been used in Acts of State relating to trade and commerce. Article V. of the Act of Union enacted that all the subjects of the United Kingdom should have "full freedom and intercourse of trade and navigation" to and from all places in the United Kingdom and the colonies; and Article VI. enacted that all parts of the United Kingdom from and after the Union should be under the *same* "prohibitions, restrictions, and *regulations of trade*." Parliament has at various times since the Union passed laws affecting and regulating specific trades in one part of the United Kingdom only, without its being supposed that it thereby infringed the Articles of Union. Thus the Acts for regulating the sale of intoxicating liquors notoriously vary in the two kingdoms. So with regard to Acts relating to bankruptcy, and various other matters.

Construing therefore the words "regulation of trade and commerce" by the various aids to their interpretation above suggested, they would include political arrangements in regard to trade requiring the sanction of parliament, regulation of trade in matters of interprovincial concern, and it may be that they would include general regulation of trade affecting the whole dominion. Their Lordships abstain on the present occasion from any attempt to define the limits of the authority of the dominion parliament in this direction. It is enough for the decision of the present case to say that, in their view, its authority to legislate for the regulation of trade and commerce does not comprehend the power to regulate by legislation the contracts of a particular business or trade, such as the business of fire insurance in a single province, and therefore that its legislative authority does not in the present case conflict or compete with the power over property and civil rights assigned to the legislature of Ontario by No. 13 of sect. 92.

And in *Bank of Toronto* v. *Lambe*,[16] 1887, Lord Hobhouse agreed:

It has been earnestly contended that the taxation of banks would unduly cut down the powers of the parliament in relation to matters falling within class 2, viz., the regulation of trade and commerce; and within class 15, viz., banking, and the incorporation of banks. Their Lordships think that this contention gives far too wide an extent to the classes in question. They cannot see how the power of making banks contribute to the public objects of the provinces where they carry on business can interfere at all with the power of making laws on the subject of banking, or with the power of incorporating banks. The words "regulation of trade and commerce" are indeed very wide, and in *Severn's Case* it was the view of the Supreme Court that they operated to invalidate the licence duty which was there in question. But since that case was decided the question has been more completely sifted before the Committee in *Parson's Case*, and it was found absolutely necessary that the literal meaning of the words should be restricted, in order to afford scope for powers which are given exclusively to the provincial legislatures. It was there thrown out that the power of regulation given to the parliament meant some general or interprovincial regulations. No further attempt to define the subject need now be made, because their Lordships are clear that if they were to hold that this power of regulation prohibited any provincial taxation on the persons or things regulated, so far from restricting the expressions, as was found necessary in *Parson's Case*, they would be straining them to their widest conceivable extent.

In *Toronto* v. *Virgo*,[17] 1896, Lord Davey proposed a further restriction: section 91(2) should not be used in a prohibitory, as opposed to regulatory, manner. This restriction was accordingly applied by Lord Watson, in the *Local Prohibition* judgment[18] of 1896:

The scope and effect of No. 2 of s. 91 were discussed by this Board at some length in *Citizens' Insurance Co.* v. *Parsons*, where it was decided that, in the absence of legislation upon the subject by the Canadian Parliament, the Legislature of Ontario had authority to impose conditions, as being matters of civil right, upon the business of fire insurance, which was admitted to be a trade, so long as those conditions only affected provincial trade. Their Lordships do not find it necessary to reopen that discussion in the present case. The object of the Canada Temperance Act of 1886 is, not to regulate retail transactions between those who trade in liquor and their customers, but to abolish all such transactions within every provincial area in which its enactments have been adopted by a majority of the local electors. A power

---

[16]12 A.C. 575, at 585–86. Meanwhile, s. 91(2) had been referred to, but not defined, in *Russell* v. *The Queen* (1882), 7 A.C. 829, at 842, and *Hodge* v. *The Queen* (1883), 9 A.C. 117, at 128–29. The Supreme Court of Canada considered the head—and took a wider view—in *Severn* v. *The Queen* (1878), 2 S.C.R. 70, *Fredericton* v. *The Queen* (1880), 3 S.C.R. 505, and *In re Prohibitory Liquor Laws* (1894), 24 S.C.R. 170.

[17][1896] A.C. 88, at 93.

[18]*A.-G. Ont.* v. *A.-G. Can.*, [1896] A.C. 348, at 362–63.

to regulate, naturally, if not necessarily, assumes, unless it is enlarged by the context, the conservation of the thing which is to be made the subject of regulation. In that view, their Lordships are unable to regard the prohibitive enactments of the Canadian statute of 1886 as regulations of trade and commerce. They see no reason to modify the opinion which was recently expressed on their behalf by Lord Davey in *Municipal Corporation of the City of Toronto* v. *Virgo* in these terms: "Their Lordships think there is a marked distinction to be drawn between the prohibition or prevention of a trade and the regulation or governance of it, and indeed a power to regulate and govern seems to imply the continued existence of that which is to be regulated or governed."

In *Montreal* v. *Montreal Street Railway*,[19] 1912, Lord Atkinson discovered another reason for confining "The Regulation of Trade and Commerce": "taken in their widest sense these words would authorize legislation by the Parliament of Canada in respect of several of the matters specifically enumerated in s. 92, and would seriously encroach upon the local autonomy of the province." This reasoning has been characterized as the "provincial autonomy" argument, and so contrasted with the "collocation" argument of the *Parsons* case.[20] However, that characterization again confuses cause and effect;[21] for even if Lord Atkinson did assume that the legislative authority of the provinces should be safeguarded, this assumption need not have been anterior, or extraneous, to his construction of the British North America Act.

Besides, the contrast leaves an impression that the "collocation" and "provincial autonomy" arguments are not merely distinct, but opposed. Yet these arguments are not mutually incompatible, and could well be connected. For Lord Atkinson's statement might simply mean that if head 2 of section 91 is not collocated with the heads of section 92, an "encroachment" on provincial autonomy would result. And in any case, it may not be presumed that a concern for provincial autonomy precludes a genuine collocation argument.

At this point, in *John Deere Plow Company* v. *Wharton*,[22] 1915, Lord Haldane decided that section 91(2) enables the federal parliament to delimit the powers of any company whose "objects" extend to the entire country. Further, he denied that the status and powers of such a company could be destroyed by a provincial legislature:

Their Lordships find themselves in agreement with the interpretation put by the Judicial Committee in *Citizens Insurance Co.* v. *Parsons* on head 2 of s. 91, which confers exclusive power on the Dominion Parliament to make laws regulating trade. This head must, like the expression, "Property

---

[19][1912] A.C. 333, at 344.
[20]See Laskin, *Constitutional Law*, 314.
[21]See above 77–78.   [22][1915] A.C. 330, at 340–41.

and Civil Rights in the Province," in s. 92, receive a limited interpretation. But they think that the power to regulate trade and commerce at all events enables the Parliament of Canada to prescribe to what extent the powers of companies the objects of which extend to the entire Dominion should be exercisable, and what limitations should be placed on such powers. For if it be established that the Dominion Parliament can create such companies, then it becomes a question of general interest throughout the Dominion in what fashion they should be permitted to trade. Their Lordships are therefore of opinion that the Parliament of Canada had power to enact the sections relied on in this case in the Dominion Companies Act and the Interpretation Act. They do not desire to be understood as suggesting that because the status of a Dominion company enables it to trade in a province and thereby confers on it civil rights to some extent, the power to regulate trade and commerce can be exercised in such a way as to trench, in the case of such companies, on the exclusive jurisdiction of the provincial Legislatures over civil rights in general. No doubt this jurisdiction would conflict with that of the Province if civil rights were to be read as an expression of unlimited scope. But, as has already been pointed out, the expression must be construed consistently with various powers conferred by ss. 91 and 92, which restrict its literal scope. It is enough for present purposes to say that the Province cannot legislate so as to deprive a Dominion company of its status and powers. This does not mean that these powers can be exercised in contravention of the laws of the Province restricting the rights of the public in the Province generally. What it does mean is that the status and powers of a Dominion company as such cannot be destroyed by provincial legislation.

But the *John Deere Plow Company* decision was not intended to enlarge the ambit of section 91(2). On the contrary, during the *Insurance Act* judgment[23] of 1916, Lord Haldane extended the *Parsons* argument —to hold that the head was inapplicable not merely to the "contracts of a particular business or trade," but to the business or trade itself:

There was a good deal in the Ontario Liquor Licence Act, and the powers of regulation which it entrusted to local authorities in the province, which seems to cover part of the field of legislation recognized as belonging to the Dominion in *Russell* v. *The Queen*. But in *Hodge* v. *The Queen* the Judicial Committee had no difficulty in coming to the conclusion that the local licensing system which the Ontario statute sought to set up was within provincial powers. It was only the converse of this proposition to hold, as was done subsequently by this Board, though without giving reasons, that the Dominion licensing statute known as the McCarthy Act, which sought to establish a local licensing system for the liquor traffic throughout Canada, was beyond the powers conferred on the Dominion Parliament by s. 91. Their Lordships think that as a result of these decisions it must now be taken that the authority to legislate for the regulation of trade and commerce does not extend to the regulation by a licensing system of a particular trade in which Canadians would otherwise be free to engage in the provinces.

---

[23]*A.-G. Can.* v. *A.-G. Alta.*, [1916] 1 A.C. 588, at 596.

Moreover, in the *Board of Commerce* judgment[24] of 1922, Lord Haldane not only distinguished his *John Deere Plow Company* decision, but reiterated the additional restriction he had imposed in the *Insurance Act* case:

In the case of Dominion companies their Lordships in deciding the case of *John Deere Plow Co.* v. *Wharton*, expressed the opinion that the language of s. 91, head 2, could have the effect of aiding Dominion powers conferred by the general language of s. 91. But that was because the regulation of the trading of Dominion companies was sought to be invoked only in furtherance of a general power which the Dominion Parliament possessed independently of it. Where there was no such power in Parliament, as in the case of the Dominion Insurance Act, it was held otherwise, and that the authority of the Dominion Parliament to legislate for the regulation of trade and commerce did not, by itself, enable interference with particular trades in which Canadians would, apart from any right of interference conferred by these words above, be free to engage in the provinces.

In fact, Lord Haldane practically reversed *John Deere Plow Company* v. *Wharton*. This decision had implied that the federal parliament may make laws concerning the regulation of trade and commerce in a province—providing those laws were "necessarily incidental" to legislation concerning a "subject" that comes within the exclusive jurisdiction of the parliament of Canada. In contrast, Lord Haldane now seemed to suggest that the federal parliament may not make laws concerning the regulation of trade and commerce in a province—unless those laws are "necessarily incidental" to legislation concerning a "subject" that comes within the exclusive jurisdiction of the parliament of Canada. Since the regulation of trade and commerce in a province would entail legislation concerning head 13 of section 92 ("Property and Civil Rights in the Province"), and since the only "subjects" that come within the exclusive jurisdiction of the parliament of Canada are those that are enumerated in section 91, this suggestion would mean that head 2 of section 91 may be invoked only in aid of a power conferred on the federal parliament by one of the other heads of section 91.

After repeating the suggestion in *Great West Saddlery Company* v. *The King*,[25] 1921, Lord Haldane developed its implications in *Toronto Electric Commissioners* v. *Snider*,[26] 1925:

Nor does the invocation of the specific power in s. 91 to regulate trade and commerce assist the Dominion contention. In *Citizens Insurance Co.* v. *Parsons* it was laid down that the collocation of this head (No. 2 of s. 91),

24*In re the Board of Commerce Act, 1919, and the Combines and Fair Prices Act, 1919*, [1922] 1 A.C. 191, at 198.
25[1921] 2 A.C. 91, at 118–19. 26[1925] A.C. 396, at 409–10.

with classes of subjects enumerated of national and general concern, indicates that what was in the mind of the Imperial Legislature when this power was conferred in 1867 was regulation relating to general trade and commerce. Any other construction would, it was pointed out, have rendered unnecessary the specific mention of certain other heads dealing with banking, bills of exchange and promissory notes, as to which it had been significantly deemed necessary to insert a specific mention. The contracts of a particular trade or business could not, therefore, be dealt with by Dominion legislation so as to conflict with the powers assigned to the Provinces over property and civil rights relating to the regulation of trade and commerce. The Dominion power has a really definite effect when applied in aid of what the Dominion Government are specifically enabled to do independently of the general regulation of trade and commerce, for instance, in the creation of Dominion companies with power to trade throughout the whole of Canada. This was shown in *John Deere Plow Co.* v. *Wharton.* The same thing is true of the exercise of the emergency power required, as on the occasion of war, in the interest of Canada as a whole, a power which may operate outside the specific enumerations in both ss. 91 and 92. And it was observed in *Attorney-General for Canada* v. *Attorney-General for Alberta* [viz., the *Insurance Act* judgment of 1916], in reference to attempted dominion legislation about insurance, that it must now be taken that the authority to legislate for the regulation of trade and commerce does not extend to the regulation, for instance, by a licensing system, of a particular trade in which Canadians would otherwise be free to engage in the Provinces. It is, in their Lordships' opinion, now clear that, excepting so far as the power can be invoked in aid of capacity conferred independently under other words in s. 91, the power to regulate trade and commerce cannot be relied on as enabling the Dominion Parliament to regulate civil rights in the Provinces.

On the other hand, during the *Proprietary Articles Trade Association* judgment[27] of 1931, Lord Atkin disassociated himself (though only in *obiter dicta*) from Lord Haldane's reasoning:

> The view that their Lordships have expressed makes it unnecessary to discuss the further ground upon which the legislation has been supported by reference to the power to legislate under s. 91, head 2, for "The regulation of trade and commerce." Their Lordships merely propose to disassociate themselves from the construction suggested in argument of a passage in the judgment in the *Board of Commerce* case under which it was contended that the power to regulate trade and commerce could be invoked only in further-ance of a general power which Parliament possessed independently of it. No such restriction is properly to be inferred from that judgment. The words of the statute must receive their proper construction where they stand as giving an independent authority to Parliament over the particular subject-matter. But following the second principle noticed in the beginning of this

[27]*Proprietary Articles Trade Association* v. *A.-G. Can.*, [1931] A.C. 310, at 316. Since the legislation in question was apparently upheld under ss. 91(3), 91(22), and 91(27), rather than s. 91(2), this disassociation was only *dicta*: see at 323–26.

judgment their Lordships in the present case forbear from defining the extent of that authority. They desire, however, to guard themselves from being supposed to lay down that the present legislation could not be supported on that ground.

Lord Atkin's judgment in the *Dominion Trade and Industry Commission Act* case[28] of 1937 has also been held to show "that the Regulation of Trade and Commerce must be treated as having full independent status as one of the enumerated heads of section 91."[29] *The King* v. *Nat Bell Liquors*,[30] 1922, and *Attorney-General for British Columbia* v. *McDonald Murphy Lumber Company*,[31] 1930, are examples of cases where "provincial legislation (absent any federal legislation) has been struck down where it avowedly, or as construed, embraced export or import control as a matter of interprovincial or foreign trade movement."[32] And the Supreme Court of Canada has conducted a steady retreat from the position adopted by Lord Haldane in the *Snider* judgment of 1925.[33]

Nevertheless, as Mr. Justice Laskin says, "one could not confidently assert, up to the time appeals to the Privy Council were abolished, that federal legislation could embrace regulation of a product as a whole even where the principal market was outside of the province of production; or that federal legislation would embrace regulation of a trade as a whole where it was carried on throughout the country by transactions that ignored provincial boundaries."[34] In the *Natural Products Marketing Act* judgment[35] of 1937, for instance, Lord Atkin himself ruled that "the regulation of trade and commerce does not permit the regulation of individual forms of trade or commerce confined to the Province." Furthermore, in *Shannon* v. *Lower Mainland Dairy Products Board*,[36] 1938, he made this statement:

It is now well settled that the enumeration in s. 91 of "the regulation of trade and commerce" as a class of subject over which the Dominion has exclusive legislative powers does not give the power to regulate for legitimate Provincial purposes particular trades or businesses so far as the trade or business is confined to the Province: *Citizens Insurance Co. of Canada* v. *Parsons*;

---

[28]*A.-G. Ont.* v. *A.-G. Can.*, [1937] A.C. 405.
[29]*Re Alberta Legislation*, [1938] S.C.R. 100, at 121 (per Duff J.).
[30][1922] 2 A.C. 128.
[31][1930] A.C. 357.
[32]Laskin, *Constitutional Law*, 316.
[33]See *Reference re Farm Products Marketing Act, R.S.O. 1950, c. 131, as Amended*, [1957] S.C.R. 198, and *Murphy* v. *C.P.R.*, [1958] S.C.R. 626. Cf. Laskin, *Constitutional Law*, 318–54 (particularly, 316–18).
[34]Laskin, *Constitutional Law*, 316.
[35]*A.-G. B.C.* v. *A.-G. Can.*, [1937] A.C. 377, at 386.
[36][1938] A.C. 708, at 719.

Reference re The Natural Products Marketing Act, 1934, *and Its Amending Act,* 1935. And it follows that to the extent that the Dominion is forbidden to regulate within the Province, the Province itself has the right under its legislative powers over property and civil rights within the Province.

Indeed, as late as 1951—in *Canadian Federation of Agriculture* v. *Attorney-General for Quebec*[37]—Lord Morton of Henryton repeated the "provincial autonomy" argument of *Montreal* v. *Montreal Street Railway*,[38] 1912:

The truth is that the present case is typical of the many cases in which the Board has felt bound to put some limit on the scope of the wide words used in head 2 of s. 91 "in order to preserve from serious curtailment, if not from virtual extinction, the degree of autonomy which, as appears from the scheme of the Act as a whole, the provinces were intended to possess" —see per Duff, J., in *Lawson* v. *Interior Tree Fruit and Vegetable Committee of Direction.* The necessity for putting such a limit leads to the rejection of counsel's first argument.

3. The Ambit of Section 92(13)

The most expansible part in the British North America Act was accordingly shown to be head 13 of section 92 ("Property and Civil Rights in the Province"). This part therefore became not only the gauge by which the ambits of the other parts of the Act were usually determined, but the principal means by which those other parts have been confined. In the *Parsons* judgment[39] of 1881, Sir Montague Smith explained the basis of the Judicial Committee's construction:

The main contention on the part of the respondent was that the Ontario Act in question had relation to matters coming within the class of subjects described in No. 13 of sect. 92, viz., "Property and civil rights in the province." The Act deals with policies of insurance entered into or in force in the province of Ontario for insuring property situate therein against fire, and prescribes certain conditions which are to form part of such contracts. These contracts, and the rights arising from them, it was argued, came legitimately within the class of subject, "Property and civil rights." The appellants, on the other hand, contended that civil rights meant only such rights as flowed from the law, and gave as an instance the status of persons. Their Lordships cannot think that the latter construction is the correct one. They find no sufficient reason in the language itself, nor in the other

[37][1951] A.C. 179, at 194–95. Note the other considerations mentioned at 193–94.

[38][1912] A.C. 333. The 26 major references to s. 91(2) are marked in col. D of the Analytical Table. For specific illustrations of the inter-action of economic activity, see Laskin, *Constitutional Law,* 318–430.

[39]*Citizens Insurance Co.* v. *Parsons* (1881), 7 A.C. 96, at 109–11.

parts of the Act, for giving so narrow an interpretation to the words "civil rights." The words are sufficiently large to embrace, in their fair and ordinary meaning, rights arising from contract, and such rights are not included in express terms in any of the enumerated classes of subjects in sect. 91. . . .

The provision found in sect. 94 of the British North America Act, which is one of the sections relating to the distribution of legislative powers, was referred to by the learned counsel on both sides as throwing light upon the sense in which the words "property and civil rights" are used. By that section the parliament of Canada is empowered to make provision for the uniformity of any laws relative to "property and civil rights" in Ontario, Nova Scotia, and New Brunswick, and to the procedure of the Courts in these three provinces, if the provincial legislatures choose to adopt the provision so made. The province of Quebec is omitted from this section for the obvious reason that the law which governs property and civil rights in Quebec is in the main the French law as it existed at the time of the cession of Canada, and not the English law which prevails in the other provinces. The words "property and civil rights" are, obviously, used in the same sense in this section as in No. 13 of sect. 92, and there seems no reason for presuming that contracts and the rights arising from them were not intended to be included in this provision for uniformity. If, however, the narrow construction of the words "civil rights," contended for by the appellants were to prevail, the dominion parliament could, under its general power, legislate in regard to contracts in all and each of the provinces and as a consequence of this the province of Quebec, though now governed by its own Civil Code, founded on the French law, as regards contracts and their incidents, would be subject to have its law on that subject altered by the dominion legislature, and brought into uniformity with the English law prevailing in the other three provinces, notwithstanding that Quebec has been carefully left out of the uniformity section of the Act.

It is to be observed that the same words, "civil rights," are employed in the Act of 14 Geo.3, c.83, which made provision for the Government of the Province of Quebec. Sect. 8 of that Act enacted that His Majesty's Canadian subjects within the province of Quebec should enjoy their property, usages, and other civil rights, as they had before done, and that in all matters of controversy relative to property and civil rights resort should be had to the laws of Canada, and be determined agreeably to the said laws. In this statute the words "property" and "civil rights" are plainly used in their largest sense; and there is no reason for holding that in the statute under discussion they are used in a different and narrower one.

This does not mean that the Judicial Committee always took a liberal view of section 92(13). In the earliest judgments, for example, the head seems to have been less of a bar to federal legislation than it came to be later on.[40] And in *John Deere Plow Company* v. *Wharton*,[41] 1915,

---

[40]Cf. *Citizens Insurance Co.* v. *Parsons* (1881), 7 A.C. 96, and *Russell* v. *The Queen* (1882), 7 A.C. 829. See also Laskin, *Constitutional Law*, 432.

[41][1915] A.C. 330, at 340.

Lord Haldane admitted this much: "The expression 'civil rights in the Province,' is a very wide one, extending, if interpreted literally, to much of the field of the other heads of s. 92 and also to much of the field of s. 91. But the expression cannot be so interpreted, and it must be regarded as excluding cases expressly dealt with elsewhere in the two sections, notwithstanding the generality of the words."

At the same time, Lord Haldane is also said to have remarked that "without expressing a final opinion about it, I should say 'civil rights' was a residuary expression."[42] And that was the ascription underlying both the normal construction of head 13 of section 92, and the basic delimitation of the legislative spheres of the provincial and the federal authorities.[43]

[42]Quoted from Lefroy, *Constitutional Law of Canada*, 426, in Laskin, *Constitutional Law*, 432.

[43]The 66 major references to s. 92(13) are marked in col. D of the Analytical Table.

Chapter Eight

THE AMBIT PROBLEM: III

1. The Ambits of Sections 91(27) and 92(15)

The Judicial Committee generally[1] gave a liberal interpretation to head 27 of section 91 ("The Criminal Law, except the Constitution of Courts of Criminal Jurisdiction, but including the Procedure in Criminal Matters"). Thus in *Russell* v. *The Queen*,[2] 1882, Sir Montague Smith made the following statement:

> Next, their Lordships cannot think that the Temperance Act in question properly belongs to the class of subjects, "Property and Civil Rights." It has in its legal aspect an obvious and close similarity to laws which place restrictions on the sale or custody of poisonous drugs, or of dangerously explosive substances. These things, as well as intoxicating liquors, can, of course, be held as property, but a law placing restrictions on their sale, custody, or removal, on the ground that the free sale or use of them is dangerous to public safety, and making it a criminal offence punishable by fine or imprisonment to violate these restrictions, cannot properly be deemed a law in relation to property in the sense in which those words are used in the 92nd section. What Parliament is dealing with in legislation of this kind is not a matter in relation to property and its rights, but one relating to public order and safety. That is the primary matter dealt with, and though incidentally the free use of things in which men may have property is interfered with, that incidental interference does not alter the character of the law. Upon the same considerations, the Act in question cannot be regarded as legislation in relation to civil rights. In however large a sense these words are used, it could not have been intended to prevent the Parliament of Canada from declaring and enacting certain uses of property, and certain acts in relation to property, to be criminal and wrongful. . . . Laws of this nature designed for the promotion of public order, safety, or morals, and which subject those who contravene them to criminal procedure and punishment, belong to the subject of public wrongs rather than to that of civil rights. They are of a nature which fall within the general authority of Parliament to make

---

[1]The most notable exceptions are Lord Haldane's judgments in the *Board of Commerce* and *Snider* cases of 1922 and 1925: see below, 100–01.

[2]7 A.C. 829, at 838–39.

laws for the order and good government of Canada, and have direct relation to criminal law, which is one of the enumerated classes of subjects assigned exclusively to the Parliament of Canada.

And the same reasoning was adopted by Lord Halsbury, in *Attorney-General for Ontario* v. *Hamilton Street Railway*,[3] 1903:

The question turns upon a very simple consideration. The reservation of the criminal law for the Dominion of Canada is given in clear and intelligible words which must be construed according to their natural and ordinary signification. Those words seem to their Lordships to require, and indeed to admit, of no plainer exposition than the language itself affords. Sect. 91, sub-s. 27, of the British North America Act, 1867, reserves for the exclusive legislative authority of the Parliament of Canada "the criminal law, except the constitution of Courts of criminal jurisdiction." It is, therefore, the criminal law in its widest sense that is reserved, and it is impossible, notwithstanding the very protracted argument to which their Lordships have listened, to doubt that an infraction of the Act, which in its original form, without the amendment afterwards introduced, was in operation at the time of confederation, is an offence against the criminal law. The fact that from the criminal law generally there is one exception, namely, "the constitution of Courts of criminal jurisdiction," renders it more clear, if anything were necessary to render it more clear, that with that exception (which obviously does not include what has been contended for in this case) the criminal law, in its widest sense, is reserved for the exclusive authority of the Dominion Parliament.

In the *Board of Commerce* judgment[4] of 1922, however, Lord Haldane appears to have favoured some restriction:

For analogous reasons the words of head 27 of s. 91 do not assist the argument for the Dominion. It is one thing to construe the words "the criminal law, except the constitution of courts in criminal jurisdiction, but including the procedure in criminal matters," as enabling the Dominion Parliament to exercise exclusive legislative power where the subject matter is one which by its very nature belongs to the domain of criminal jurisprudence. A general law, to take an example, making incest a crime, belongs to this class. It is quite another thing, first to attempt to interfere with a class of subject committed exclusively to the Provincial Legislature, and then to justify this by enacting ancillary provisions, designated as new phases of Dominion criminal law which require a title to so interfere as basis of their application.

In other words, Lord Haldane presumed the existence of an *a priori* "domain of criminal jurisdiction": because "criminal laws" have an "essential character," there must be predetermined limits to the federal parliament's sphere of legislative authority.

[3][1903] A.C. 524, at 528–29.
[4]*In re the Board of Commerce Act, 1919, and the Combines and Fair Prices Act, 1919*, [1922] 1 A.C. 191, at 198–99. See also *Toronto Electric Commissioners* v. *Snider*, [1925] A.C. 396, at 407.

As Lord Atkin complained in *Proprietary Articles Trade Association* v. *Attorney-General for Canada,*[5] 1931, such a definition would be difficult to apply:

"Criminal law" means "the criminal law in its widest sense": *Attorney-General for Ontario* v. *Hamilton Street Ry. Co.* It certainly is not confined to what was criminal by the law of England or of any Province in 1867. The Power must extend to legislation to make new crimes. Criminal law connotes only the quality of such acts or omissions as are prohibited under appropriate penal provisions by authority of the State. The criminal quality of an act cannot be discerned by intuition; nor can it be discovered by reference to any standard but one: Is the act prohibited with penal consequences? Morality and criminality are far from co-extensive; nor is the sphere of criminality necessarily part of a more extensive field covered by morality—unless the moral code necessarily disapproves all acts prohibited by the State, in which case the argument moves in a circle. It appears to their Lordships to be of little value to seek to confine crimes to a category of acts which by their very nature belong to the domain of "criminal jurisprudence"; for the domain of criminal jurisprudence can only be ascertained by examining what acts at any particular period are declared by the State to be crimes, and the only common nature they will be found to possess is that they are prohibited by the State and that those who commit them are punished.

Lord Haldane's decision in the *Board of Commerce* case was consequently distinguished as follows:

Their Lordships agree with the view expressed in the judgment of Newcombe J. that the passage in the judgment of the Board in the *Board of Commerce* case to which allusion has been made, was not intended as a definition. In that case their Lordships appear to have been contrasting two matters—one obviously within the line, the other obviously outside it. For this purpose it was clearly legitimate to point to matters which are such serious breaches of any accepted code of morality as to be obviously crimes when they are prohibited under penalties. The contrast is with matters which are merely attempts to interfere with Provincial rights, and are sought to be justified under the head of "criminal law" colourably and merely in aid of what is in substance an encroachment. The Board considered that the Combines and Fair Prices Act of 1919 came within the latter class, and was in substance an encroachment on the exclusive power of the Provinces to legislate on property and civil rights.

The original interpretation of section 91(27) was then reconfirmed, again by Lord Atkin, in the *Criminal Code* judgment[6] of 1937:

Their Lordships agree with the Chief Justice that this case is covered by the decision of the Judicial Committee in the *Proprietary Articles* case. The decision in that case seems to be inconsistent with the ground of dissent of Crocket J. that sub-s. (*a*) lacks "the characteristic feature of crime, viz., the

5[1931] A.C. 310, at 324–25.
6*A.-G. B.C.* v. *A.-G. Can.,* [1937] A.C. 368, at 375–76.

101

intent to do wrong." The basis of that decision is that there is no other criterion of "wrongness" than the intention of the Legislature in the public interest to prohibit the act or admission made criminal. Cannon J. was of opinion that the prohibition cannot have been made in the public interest because it has in view only the protection of the individual competitors of the vendor. This appears to narrow unduly the discretion of the Dominion Legislature in considering the public interest. The only limitation on the plenary power of the Dominion to determine what shall or shall not be criminal is the condition that Parliament shall not in the guise of enacting criminal legislation in truth and in substance encroach on any of the classes of subjects enumerated in s. 92. It is no objection that it does in fact affect them. If a genuine attempt to amend the criminal law, it may obviously affect previously existing civil rights. The object of an amendment of the criminal law as a rule is to deprive the citizen of the right to do that which, apart from the amendment, he could lawfully do. No doubt the plenary power given by s. 91(27) does not deprive the Provinces of their right under s. 92(15) of affixing penal sanctions to their own competent legislation. On the other hand, there seems to be nothing to prevent the Dominion, if it thinks fit in the public interest, from applying the criminal law generally to acts and omissions which so far are only covered by provincial enactments. In the present case there seems to be no reason for supposing that the Dominion are using the criminal law as a pretence or pretext, or that the legislature is in pith and substance only interfering with civil rights in the Province.

This general interpretation has been applied in several instances. In *Proprietary Articles Trade Association* v. *Attorney-General for Canada*,[7] 1931, Lord Atkin declared that the term "criminal law," as found in section 91(27), "certainly is not confined to what was criminal law by the law of England or of any of the Provinces in 1867. The power must extend to legislation to make new crimes." Similarly, the Supreme Court of Canada has held that a provincial legislature may neither relax prohibitions (whether absolute or qualified) that have been enacted by the federal parliament,[8] nor supplement (in order merely to strengthen) a punishment prescribed by that parliament.[9] And the authority of the federal parliament in relation to criminal procedure, as well as substantive criminal law, has received special recognition.[10]

[7][1931] A.C. 310, at 324. See also *Toronto Railway* v. *The King*, [1917] A.C. 630, at 639; *R.* v. *Superior Publishers and Zimmermann*, [1954] O.R. 981; *R. ex rel. Barrie* v. *Stelzer* (1959), 15 D.L.R. (2d) 280; *Brusch* v. *The Queen*, [1953] 1 S.C.R. 373; *R.* v. *Neil*, [1957] S.C.R. 685; *Re Race-Tracks and Betting* (1921), 49 O.L.R. 339.

[8]See *Re Morrison and Kingston*, [1938] O.R. 21; *R.* v. *Stanley* (1952), 104 C.C.C. 31; *A.-G. Can.* v. *Prince Albert*, [1952] 1 D.L.R. 195.

[9]See *Provincial Secretary of Prince Edward Island* v. *Egan*, [1941] S.C.R. 396; cf. *Boyce* v. *The Queen* (1959), 22 D.L.R. (2d) 255.

[10]See *Toronto* v. *The King*, [1932] A.C. 98; *A.-G. Que.* v. *A.-G. Can.*, [1945] S.C.R. 600; *Re Bence*, [1954] 2 D.L.R. 460.

On the other hand, although "Criminal Law" means "the criminal law in its widest sense,"[11] and also "connotes only the quality of such acts or omissions as are prohibited under appropriate penal provisions by authority of the State,"[12] section 91(27) does not confer a completely untrammelled power. For as Lord Haldane and Lord Atkin both warned, this head may not be used "colourably"—to bring within the legislative authority of the federal parliament a matter that really comes within a "subject" assigned exclusively to the provincial legislatures. Section 91(27) must therefore be related to section 92(15), "The Imposition of Punishment by Fine, Penalty, or Imprisonment for enforcing any Law of the Province made in relation to any Matter coming within any of the Classes of Subjects enumerated in this Section"—as well as to section 92(13), "Property and Civil Rights in the Province."[13]

Accordingly, in *Toronto Railway Company* v. *Toronto*,[14] 1920, Lord Cave relied on section 92(15) to deny "that the Act of 1918 (8 Geo.5, c.30), if it is to be construed as authorizing the imposition of a penalty for a past offence, deals with a criminal matter and was therefore beyond the powers of the provincial Legislature. . . ." In *Canadian Pacific Wine Company* v. *Tuley*,[15] 1921, Lord Birkenhead decided, despite section 91(27), that the Summary Convictions Act[16] of the legislature of British Columbia should be upheld on the basis of heads 15 and 16 of section 92. In *The King* v. *Nat Bell Liquors*,[17] 1922, Lord Sumner—interpreting the term "penalty" in section 92(15) to include "forfeitures"—concluded that since the word "criminal" is employed in contradistinction to "civil," it cannot be limited to the sense in which "criminal" legislation is reserved exclusively to the federal parliament by head 27 of section 91. And in the *Criminal Code* judgment[18] of 1937, Lord Atkin admitted that "the plenary power given by s. 91(27) does not deprive the Provinces of their right under s. 92(15) of affixing penal sanctions to their own competent legislation."

[11]*A.-G. Ont.* v. *Hamilton Street Railway*, [1903] A.C. 524, at 529.
[12]*Proprietary Articles Trade Association* v. *A.-G. Can.*, [1931] A.C. 310, at 324.
[13]There was also a relatively minor conflict with s. 92(14): see *Russell* v. *The Queen* (1882), 7 A.C. 829; *Canadian Pacific Wine Co.* v. *Tuley*, [1921] 2 A.C. 417; *A.-G. Ont.* v. *Reciprocal Insurers*, [1924] A.C. 328; *Lord's Day Alliance* v. *A.-G. Man.*, [1925] A.C. 384; *Toronto Electric Commissioners* v. *Snider*, [1925] A.C. 396; *Proprietary Articles Trade Association* v. *A.-G. Can.*, [1931] A.C. 310; *British Coal Corporation* v. *The King*, [1935] A.C. 500; *A.-G. Ont.* v. *A.-G. Can.*, [1937] A.C. 405; *A.-G. Ont.* v. *A.-G. Can.*, [1947] A.C. 127.
[14][1920] A.C. 446, at 452.
[15][1921] 2 A.C. 417, at 423.
[16]R.S.B.C. 1915, c. 59.
[17][1922] 2 A.C. 128, at 138.
[18]*A.-G. B.C.* v. *A.-G. Can.*, [1937] A.C. 368, at 376.

As in the case of section 91(2), however, the most critical conflict for section 91(27) was with section 92(13). In the *Reciprocal Insurers* judgment[19] of 1924, Duff J. explained the outcome like this:

In accordance with the principle inherent in these decisions [viz., *In re Board of Commerce Act*, 1922, *Russell* v. *The Queen*, 1882, and *Local Prohibition*, 1896] their Lordships think it is no longer open to dispute that the Parliament of Canada cannot, by purporting to create penal sanctions under s. 91, head 27, appropriate to itself exclusively a field of jurisdiction in which, apart from such a procedure, it could exert no legal authority, and that if, when examined as a whole, legislation in form criminal is found, in aspects and for purposes exclusively within the Provincial sphere, to deal with matters committed to the Provinces, it cannot be upheld as valid. And indeed, to hold otherwise would be incompatible with an essential principle of the Confederation scheme, the object of which, as Lord Watson said in *Maritime Bank of Canada* v. *Receiver-General of New Brunswick*, was "not to weld the Provinces into one or to subordinate the Provincial Governments to a central authority." "Within the spheres allotted to them by the Act the Dominion and the Provinces are," as Lord Haldane said in *Great West Saddlery Co.* v. *The King*, "rendered in general principle co-ordinate Governments."

Their Lordships think it undesirable to attempt to define, however generally, the limits of Dominion jurisdiction under head 27 of s. 91; but they think it proper to observe, that what has been said above does not involve any denial of the authority of the Dominion Parliament to create offences merely because the legislation deals with matters which, in another aspect, may fall under one or more of the sub-divisions of the jurisdiction entrusted to the Provinces. It is one thing, for example, to declare corruption in municipal elections, or negligence of a given order in the management of railway trains, to be a criminal offence and punishable under the Criminal Code; it is another thing to make use of the machinery of the criminal law for the purpose of assuming control of municipal corporations or of Provincial railways.

The ambit of section 91(27) was also restricted, because of section 92(13), in these judgments:[20]

1. *In re the Board of Commerce Act, 1919, and the Combines and Fair Prices Act, 1919*, [1922] 1 A.C. 191, at 199.

2. *Lord's Day Alliance* v. *Attorney-General for Manitoba*, [1925] A.C. 384, at 390–95.

3. *Toronto Electric Commissioners* v. *Snider*, [1925] A.C. 396, at 407–8.

[19]*A.-G. Ont.* v. *Reciprocal Insurers*, [1924] A.C. 328, at 342–43.

[20]For further discussion of the ambit of s. 91(27), see *University of Toronto Faculty of Law Review*, XV (1957). For an account of Canadian Supreme Court trends, see Laskin, *Constitutional Law*, 825 and 827–69. The 22 major references to s. 91(27), as well as the 10 to s. 92(15), are marked in col. D of the Analytical Table.

4. *Proprietary Articles Trade Association* v. *Attorney-General for Canada*, [1931] A.C. 310, at 324–25.

5. *In re the Insurance Act of Canada*, [1932] A.C. 41, at 53.

6. *Attorney-General for British Columbia* v. *Attorney-General for Canada*, [1937] A.C. 368, at 375–76.

7. *Attorney-General for British Columbia* v. *Attorney-General for Canada*, [1937] A.C. 377, at 389.

8. *Canadian Federation of Agriculture* v. *Attorney-General for Quebec*, [1951] A.C. 179, at 195–97.

2. The Ambits of Sections 91(3) and 92(2)

The "taxing power" provisions include not only head 3 of section 91 ("The raising of Money by any Mode or System of Taxation") and head 2 of section 92 ("Direct Taxation within the Provinces in order to the raising of a Revenue for Provincial Purposes"), but also sections 91 (1A and 8), 92 (4 and 9), 100, 118, 121, 122, and 125. To judge solely by the words of section 91(3), the federal parliament would seem to enjoy almost total taxing authority. And in one respect, this authority is even larger than those words suggest: during the Judicial Committee's last taxation case, *British Columbia Electric Railway* v. *The King*,[21] 1946, Lord Simon decided that "the effect of the Statute of Westminster upon s. 91 of the British North America Act, head 3, is to make that head read: 'the raising of money by any mode or system of taxation, even though such laws have an extra-territorial operation'."

Yet if section 91(3) covered all possible taxing powers, section 92(2) would be meaningless. This difficulty was resolved by means of the linguistic principle: the taxing power conferred by the more particularly worded section 92(2) was subtracted from that conferred by section 91(3).[22] Before this principle could be fully applied, however, the ambit of the provincial head (or effectively, the definition of the term "direct taxation") had to be decided. Thus in *Bank of Toronto* v. *Lambe*,[23]

[21][1946] A.C. 527, at 542.
[22]In the earliest judgments the term "Direct Taxation" was defined implicitly, through a series of concrete decisions: see *Dow* v. *Black* (1875), 6 A.C. 272; *A.-G. Que.* v. *Queen Insurance Co.* (1878), 3 A.C. 1090; *Citizens Insurance Co.* v. *Parsons* (1881), 7 A.C. 96; *Dobie* v. *Temporalities Board* (1881), 7 A.C. 136. The first attempt at an abstract definition was made in *A.-G. Que.* v. *Reed* (1884), 10 A.C. 141, at 143–44—a judgment that was later distinguished in *A.-G. B.C.* v. *Kingcome Navigation Co.*, [1934] A.C. 45, at 52.
[23]12 A.C. 575, at 581–83.

1887, Lord Hobhouse accepted the definition of John Stuart Mill, and so developed the following argument:

First, is the tax a direct tax? For the argument of this question the opinions of a great many writers on political economy have been cited, and it is proper, or rather necessary, to have careful regard to such opinions, as has been said in previous cases before this Board. But it must not be forgotten that the question is a legal one, viz., what the words mean, as used in this statute; whereas the economists are always seeking to trace the effect of taxation throughout the community, and are apt to use the words "direct," and "indirect," according as they find that the burden of the tax abides more or less with the person who first pays it. This distinction is illustrated very clearly by the quotations from a very able and clear thinker, the late Mr. Fawcett, who, after giving his tests of direct and indirect taxation, makes remarks to the effect that a tax may be made direct or indirect by the position of the tax-payers or by private bargains about its payment. Doubtless, such remarks have their value in an economical discussion. Probably it is true of every indirect tax that some persons are both the first and the final payers of it; and of every direct tax that it affects persons other than the first payers; and the excellence of an economist's definition will be measured by the accuracy with which it contemplates and embraces every incident of the thing defined. But that very excellence impairs its value for the purposes of the lawyer. The legislature cannot possibly have meant to give a power of taxation valid or invalid according to its actual results in particular cases. It must have contemplated some tangible dividing line referable to and ascertainable by the general tendencies of the tax and the common understanding of men as to those tendencies.

After some consideration Mr. Kerr chose the definition of John Stuart Mill as the one he would prefer to abide by. That definition is as follows:

"Taxes are either direct or indirect. A direct tax is one which is demanded from the very persons who it is intended or desired should pay it. Indirect taxes are those which are demanded from one person in the expectation and intention that he shall indemnify himself at the expense of another; such are the excise or customs.

"The producer or importer of a commodity is called upon to pay a tax on it, not with the intention to levy a peculiar contribution upon him, but to tax through him the consumers of the commodity, from whom it is supposed that he will recover the amount by means of an advance in price."

It is said that Mill adds a term—that to be strictly direct a tax must be general; and this condition was much pressed at the Bar. Their Lordships have not thought it necessary to examine Mill's works for the purpose of ascertaining precisely what he does say on this point; nor would they presume to say whether for economical purposes such a condition is sound or unsound; but they have no hesitation in rejecting it for legal purposes. It would deny the character of a direct tax to the income tax of this country, which is always spoken of as such, and is generally looked upon as a direct tax of the most obvious kind; and it would run counter to the common understanding of men on this subject, which is one main clue to the meaning of the legislature.

Their Lordships then take Mill's definition above quoted as a fair basis for testing the character of the tax in question, not only because it is chosen by the Appellant's counsel, nor only because it is that of an eminent writer, nor with the intention that it should be considered a binding legal definition, but because it seems to them to embody with sufficient accuracy for this purpose an understanding of the most obvious indicia of direct and indirect taxation, which is a common understanding, and is likely to have been present to the minds of those who passed the Federation Act.

Further glosses on the term "direct taxation" were provided by Lord Herschell, in *Brewers and Maltsters' Association* v. *Attorney-General for Ontario*,[24] 1897; by Lord Moulton, in *Cotton* v. *The King*,[25] 1914; by Lord Cave, in *Halifax* v. *Fairbanks' Estate*,[26] 1928; by Lord Macmillan, in *Attorney-General for British Columbia* v. *McDonald Murphy Lumber Company*,[27] 1930; by Lord Thankerton, in *Attorney-General for British Columbia* v. *Kingcome Navigation Company*,[28] 1934; by Lord Haldane, in *Attorney-General for Manitoba* v. *Attorney-General for Canada*,[29] 1925, and in *Attorney-General for British Columbia* v. *Canadian Pacific Railway*,[30] 1927; by Lord Warrington of Clyffe, in *The King* v. *Caledonian Collieries*,[31] 1928; by Lord Thankerton, again, in *Lower Mainland Dairy Products Sales Adjustment Committee* v. *Crystal Dairy*,[32] 1933; and by Lord Simon, in *Atlantic Smoke Shops* v. *Conlon*,[33] 1943. Finally, in *Attorney-General for British Columbia* v. *Esquimalt and Nanaimo Railway*,[34] 1950, Lord Greene drew the distinction between a "direct" and an "indirect" tax along these lines:

It is argued, however, that the tax, whatever name be given to it, is an indirect tax because the natural tendency for the person who is to be assessed to it will be to pass it to others and thus indemnify himself against it. This operation of passing, it is said, would take one or other or both of two forms—a "passing back" to the railway company by means of a lowering of the purchase price, and a "passing on" to purchasers of the cut timber. It is probably true of many forms of tax which are indisputably direct that the assessee will desire, if he can, to pass the burden of the tax on to the shoulders of another. But this is only an economic tendency. The assessee's efforts may be conscious or unconscious, successful or unsuccessful; they may be defeated in whole or in part by other economic forces. This type of tendency appears to their Lordships to be something fundamentally different from the "passing on" which is regarded as the hallmark of an indirect tax. Moreover, in all the cases where various forms of tax have been discussed not one instance has been found of what in the present case is described as

---

24[1897] A.C. 231, at 235–37.
25[1914] A.C. 176, at 191–93. 26[1928] A.C. 117, at 124–25.
27[1930] A.C. 357, at 363–65. 28[1934] A.C. 45, at 54–59.
29[1925] A.C. 561, at 566–68. 30[1927] A.C. 934, at 937–38.
31[1928] A.C. 358, at 361–63. 32[1933] A.C. 168, at 176–77.
33[1943] A.C. 550, at 563–70. 34[1950] A.C. 87, at 118–20.

107

"passing back." Their Lordships are not prepared to hold that this tendency in the present case produces, or helps to produce, an indirect quality in the tax. Moreover, the tax is assessed after and not before a sale, and may not become payable for a considerable time thereafter. Whatever is "passed back" in the form of economic consequence by way of reduction of purchase price, it cannot be the *tax*. Mill's well-known formula is that a direct tax is one which is demanded from the very persons who it is intended and desired should pay it, while indirect taxes are those which are demanded from one person in the expectation and intention that he shall indemnify himself at the expense of another. In *City of Halifax* v. *Fairbanks' Estate*, Lord Cave, in delivering the judgment of the Board, used expressions which, if not correctly understood, might appear to lay down too rigid a test for the classification of taxes; but, as is pointed out by Lord Simon L.C. in the judgment of the Board in the latter case of *Atlantic Smoke Shops, Ld.* v. *Conlon*, those expressions "should not be understood as relieving the courts from the obligation of examining the real nature and effect of the particular tax in the present instance, or as justifying the classification of the tax as indirect merely because it is in some sense associated with the purchase of an article." In the latter case a somewhat complicated method of taxing the consumption of tobacco was adopted. It was held to be a direct tax because it was imposed on the actual consumer on the occasion of a purchase by him. A similar result from the revenue point of view could no doubt have been secured by imposing the tax on the manufacturer or on the vendor. But such a tax would have been an indirect tax since the operation of passing the burden of the tax to the consumer in the shape of an increase of price would have been in practice almost automatic. This case, in their Lordships' view, affords a good example of the caution with which the "pith and substance" principle ought to be applied. The object of that principle is to discover what the tax really is; it must not be used for the purpose of holding that what is really a direct tax is an indirect tax on the ground that an equivalent result could have been obtained by using the technique of indirect taxation.

Meanwhile, in the *Parsons* judgment[35] of 1882, Sir Montague Smith had tried to adapt the linguistic principle to the "taxing power" provisions:

Notwithstanding this endeavor to give pre-eminence to the dominion parliament in cases of a conflict of powers, it is obvious that in some cases where this apparent conflict exists, the legislature could not have intended that the powers exclusively assigned to the provincial legislature should be absorbed in those given to the dominion parliament. . . . So "the raising of money by any mode or system of taxation" is enumerated among the classes of subjects in sect. 91; but, though the description is sufficiently large and general to include "direct taxation within the province, in order to the raising of a revenue for provincial purposes," assigned to the provincial legislatures by sect. 92, it obviously could not have been intended that, in this instance also, the general power should override the particular one.

[35]*Citizens Insurance Co.* v. *Parsons* (1882), 7 A.C. 96, at 108.

In *Bank of Toronto* v. *Lambe*,[36] 1887, Lord Hobhouse applied the above formula to a conflict between section 91(3) and section 92(2):

It is impossible to give exclusively to the Dominion the whole subject of raising money by any mode of taxation, and at the same time to give to the provincial legislatures, exclusively or at all, the power of direct taxation for provincial or any other purposes. This very conflict between the two sections was noticed by way of illustration in the case of *Parsons*. Their Lordships there said: "So 'the raising of money by any mode or system of taxation' is enumerated among the classes of subjects in sect. 91; but, though the description is sufficiently large and general to include 'direct taxation within the province, in order to the raising of a revenue for provincial purposes,' assigned to the provincial legislatures by sect. 92, it obviously could not have been intended that, in this instance also, the general power should override the particular one." Their Lordships adhere to that view, and hold that, as regards direct taxation within the province to raise revenue for provincial purposes, that subject falls wholly within the jurisdiction of the provincial legislatures.

However, in *Caron* v. *The King*,[37] 1924, Lord Phillimore proposed an alternative principle: "Both sections of the Act of Parliament [i.e., section 91(3) and section 92(2)] must be construed together; and it matters not whether the principle to be applied is that the particular provision in head 2 of s. 92 effects a deduction from the general provision in head 3 of s. 91, or whether the general principle be that head 3 of s. 91 is confined to Dominion taxes for Dominion purposes." This new principle has the advantage of covering indirect as well as direct taxation; for except in so far as section 92(2) applies, the federal parliament may now impose both types. This power might derive from the fact that section 91(3) covers all taxes other than those assigned to the provincial legislatures by section 92(2). Alternatively, on the assumption that it covers taxation for federal purposes only, head 3 of section 91 might reflect the residuary authority of the federal parliament. But in either case, only the federal parliament may impose indirect taxes.[38]

---

[36]12 A.C. 575, at 585.

[37][1924] A.C. 999, at 1004.

[38]Hence the federal parliament's Agricultural Products Marketing Act, R.S.C. 1952, c. 6 (amended and enacted by R.S.C. 1957, c. 15, consequent on the decision of the Supreme Court of Canada in *Reference re Farm Products Marketing Act, R.S.O. 1950, c. 131, as Amended*, [1957] S.C.R. 198): see Laskin, *Constitutional Law*, 712–16. The prohibition against provincially imposed indirect taxes was confirmed in *Lower Mainland Dairy Products Sales Adjustment Committee* v. *Crystal Dairy*, [1933] A.C. 168. Attempts to invoke s. 92(16) have also failed: see Kennedy and Wells, *Taxing Power*, 152. On the other hand, provincial licence fees, imposed on the authority of s. 92(9), need not conform to the test of direct taxation: see *Shannon* v. *Lower Mainland Dairy Products Board*, [1938] A.C. 708.

On the other hand, since there is no constitutional bar to the imposition of double taxation, and since income tax has been defined as a form of "Direct Taxation," this type of tax may be imposed by the provincial legislatures as well as the federal parliament. Thus in *Forbes* v. *Attorney-General for Manitoba*,[39] 1937, Lord Macmillan decided that "both income taxes may co-exist and be enforced without clashing." In practice, however, this situation has usually been avoided by means of the "Tax Agreements":[40] until very recently the provinces were generally willing to relinquish the taxation of income in return for certain payments from the federal authorities.

But the major taxation questions are concerned not so much with the relationship between section 91(3) and section 92(2), as with the relationship between both these heads and the other heads of sections 91 and 92. To what extent may either the federal parliament or a provincial legislature use its taxing powers for a regulatory purpose? May the federal parliament employ section 91(3) to enable the passage of legislation that would otherwise concern section 92(13)? When is a taxing law "regulatory legislation" coming within section 92(13)? And when is it simply an extension of the provincial taxing power under section 92(2)?

In so far as they apply to the federal taxing power, these questions were first considered by Lord Dunedin during *In re the Insurance Act of Canada*,[41] 1932:

Now as to the power of the Dominion Parliament to impose taxation there is no doubt. But if the tax imposed is linked up with an object which is illegal the tax for that purpose must fall. Sect. 16 [of the *Special War Revenue Act*, R.S.C., 1927, c. 179] clearly assumes that a Dominion license to prosecute insurance business is a valid license all over Canada and carries with it the right to transact insurance business. But it has been already decided that this is not so; that a Dominion license, so far as authorizing transactions of insurance business in a Province is concerned, is an idle piece of paper conferring no rights which the party transacting in accordance with Provincial legislation has not already got, if he has complied with Provincial requirements. It is really the same old attempt in another way.

Their Lordships cannot do better than quote and then paraphrase a portion of the words of Duff J. in the *Reciprocal Insurers'* case. He says: In accordance with the principle inherent in these decisions their Lordships think it is no longer open to dispute that the Parliament of Canada cannot, by purporting to create penal sanctions under s. 91, head 27, appropriate to itself

---

[39][1937] A.C. 260, at 274.

[40]Especially, the Dominion-Provincial Taxation Agreement Act, R.S.C. 1942, c. 13; the Dominion-Provincial Tax Rental Agreements Act, R.S.C. 1947, c. 58, am. 149 (2nd sess.), c. 19; and the Tax Rental Agreements Act, R.S.C. 1952, c. 49.

[41][1932] A.C. 41, at 52–53.

exclusively a field of jurisdiction in which, apart from such a procedure, it could exert no legal authority, and that if, when examined as a whole, legislation in form criminal is found, in aspects and for purposes exclusively within the Provincial sphere, to deal with matters committed to the Provinces, it cannot be upheld as valid." If instead of the words "create penal sanctions under s. 91, head 27" you substitute the words "exercise taxation powers under s. 91, head 3," and for the word "criminal" substitute "taxing," the sentence expresses precisely their Lordships' views.

In the *Unemployment Insurance* judgment[42] of 1937, Lord Atkin developed a similar argument:

That the Dominion may impose taxation for the purpose of creating a fund for special purposes, and may apply that fund for making contributions in the public interest to individuals, corporations or public authorities, could not as a general proposition be denied. Whether in such an Act as the present compulsion applied to an employed person to make a contribution to an insurance fund out of which he will receive benefit for a period proportionate to the number of his contributions is in fact taxation it is not necessary finally to decide. It might seem difficult to discern how it differs from a form of compulsory insurance, or what the difference is between a statutory obligation to pay insurance premiums to the State or to an insurance company. But assuming that the Dominion has collected by means of taxation a fund, it by no means follows that any legislation which disposes of it is necessarily within Dominion competence.

It may still be legislation affecting the classes of subjects enumerated in s. 92, and, if so, would be ultra vires. In other words, Dominion legislation, even though it deals with Dominion property, may yet be so framed as to invade civil rights within the Province, or encroach upon the classes of subjects which are reserved to Provincial competence. It is not necessary that it should be a colourable device, or a pretence. If on the true view of the legislation it is found that in reality in pith and substance the legislation invades civil rights within the Province, or in respect of other classes of subjects otherwise encroaches upon the provincial field, the legislation will be invalid. To hold otherwise would afford the Dominion an easy passage into the Provincial domain. In the present case, their Lordships agree with the majority of the Supreme Court in holding that in pith and substance this Act is an insurance Act affecting the civil rights of employers and employed in each Province, and as such is invalid.

And Mr. Justice Laskin adds the following observation:

This statement has not had any noticeable effect upon Dominion spending. Indeed, the rejection of an attack on the constitutionality of the *Family Allowances Act* lends emphasis to the view that the Courts have no concern with the disbursement of public funds which have been validly raised: see *Angers* v. *Minister of National Revenue*, [1957] Ex. C.R. 83. It ought to be said that in contrasting taxation and regulation, the courts have not been

---

[42]*A.-G. Can.* v. *A.-G. Ont.*, [1937] A.C. 355, at 366.

influenced so much by a belief in "pure taxation" (*i.e.* taxation which produces revenue but has no economic effects—an imaginary situation in the modern world) as by a legal view of the distribution of legislative power and of the "pith and substance" doctrine.[43]

As for the provincial taxing power, Part I of the British Columbia Workmen's Compensation Act[44] was designed "to confer on workmen, out of an accident fund which it established, compensation for personal injury by accident arising out of and in course of their employment." In *Workmen's Compensation Board* v. *Canadian Pacific Railway*,[45] 1920, Lord Haldane decided that this Part could be considered a matter of "Direct Taxation," and so was not a matter of "Property and Civil Rights." The same legislature then passed the Dairy Products Sales Adjustment Act,[46] which was intended "to transfer compulsorily a portion of the returns obtained by the traders in the fluid milk market to the traders in the manufactured products market," and to "afford the machinery by which this is enabled to be done." In *Lower Mainland Dairy Products Sales Adjustment Committee* v. *Crystal Dairy*,[47] 1933, Lord Thankerton decided that the resulting tax was "indirect taxation," and so was *ultra vires* the provincial legislature. And in *Attorney-General for British Columbia* v. *Esquimalt and Nanaimo Railway*,[48] 1950, Lord Greene decided that section 124 of the British Columbia Forest Act[49]— which imposed on the owners of timber land an annual levy as a contribution to the development of a "forest protection fund"—was also an indirect tax (rather than a service charge), and so, once again, was *ultra vires* the provincial legislature.[50]

These interpretations have served not only to curtail the regulatory power of the provincial legislatures, but practically to force the federal parliament into constitutional improprieties. In the case of marketing regulation, since the *Crystal Dairy* judgment[51] of 1933 had shown equalization levies to be indirect taxes, the provincial legislatures were effectively prevented from developing a system of price fixing. The

[43]Laskin, *Constitutional Law*, 655.
[44]R.S.B.C. 1916, c. 77. [45][1920] A.C. 184, at 188 and 190.
[46]R.S.B.C. 1929, c. 20. [47][1933] A.C. 168, at 174–77.
[48][1950] A.C. 87, at 121. [49]R.S.B.C. 1936, c. 102.
[50]This decision was reached despite the acknowledged circumstances "first, that the levy is on a defined class of interested individuals and, secondly, that the fund raised does not fall into the general mass of the proceeds of taxation but is applicable for a special and limited purpose" (at 121).
[51]*Lower Mainland Dairy Products Sales Adjustment Committee* v. *Crystal Dairy*, [1933] A.C. 168. See the discussion of this judgment—and of *Shannon* v. *Lower Mainland Dairy Products Board*, [1938] A.C. 708, and *Crawford, Hillside Farm Dairy* v. *A.-G. B.C.* (1960), 22 D.L.R. (2d) 321—in Laskin, *Constitutional Law*, 656, 658, 701–4, and 712–13.

present system was therefore probably achieved in an unconstitutional manner; for the federal parliament got round the difficulty by authorizing the provincial marketing boards to impose the necessary levies.

But even on the assumption that executive authority may be delegated at all, it is doubtful whether such delegation may be made in respect of intra-provincial, as distinct from inter-provincial and export trade.[52] It is also questionable whether sections 54 and 90 of the British North America Act permit the federal government to assume the responsibility of raising revenue for provincial purposes in the first place. Certainly, it is not surprising that in the *Shannon* judgment[53] of 1938, the Judicial Committee preferred to uphold the British Columbia Natural Products Marketing Act[54] on the basis of heads 9, 13, and 16 of section 92, rather than that of section 92(2): as Lord Atkin remarked, "without deciding the matter either way, they can see difficulties in holding this to be direct taxation within the province."[55]

3. The Ambit of Section 132

Section 132 might also appear expansible. This section reads as follows:

132. The Parliament and Government of Canada shall have all Powers necessary or proper for performing the Obligations of Canada or any Province thereof, as Part of the British Empire, towards Foreign Countries, arising under Treaties between the Empire and such Foreign Countries.

The section is thus concerned with treaty legislation only—with the power of "performing the Obligations . . . arising under Treaties"—and so is not concerned with the executive action of making treaties. However, this distinction entails a possibility of extending federal legislative authority; for it might be argued that an increase in the power of the federal government to make treaties should produce a corresponding increase in the power of the federal parliament to pass enabling legislation.

[52]Cf. the limits fixed by the Judicial Committee's construction of s. 91(2): see above, chap. 7, sec. 2.
[53]*Shannon* v. *Lower Mainland Dairy Products Board*, [1938] A.C. 708, at 721.
[54]R.S.B.C. 1936, c. 165.
[55]The 19 major references to s. 91(3), as well as the 42 to s. 92(2), are marked in col. D of the Analytical Table. The references to ss. 91(1A), 91(8), 92(4), 92(9), 100, 118, 121, 122 and 125 can be traced through col. C. For a fuller discussion of the "taxing powers," see Laskin, *Constitutional Law*, 653–760.

This possibility was first considered by Lord Sankey, in the *Aeronautics* judgment[56] of 1932. Since the Canadian government had subscribed to the Aerial Navigation Convention of October 13, 1919, and since the terms of this convention "include almost every conceivable matter relative to aerial navigation," it seemed to follow—chiefly on the basis of section 132[57]—"that substantially the whole field of legislation in regard to aerial navigation belongs to the Dominion":[58]

As far as s. 132 is concerned, their Lordships are not aware of any decided case which is of assistance on the present occasion. It will be observed, however, from the very definite words of the section, that it is the Parliament and Government of Canada who are to have all powers necessary or proper for performing the obligations of Canada, or any Province thereof. It would therefore appear to follow that any convention of the character under discussion necessitates Dominion legislation in order that it may be carried out. It is only necessary to look at the Convention itself to see what wide powers are necessary for performing the obligations arising thereunder. . . .

To sum up, having regard (*a*) to the terms of s. 132; (*b*) to the terms of the Convention which covers almost every conceivable matter relating to aerial navigation; and (*c*) to the fact that further legislative powers in relation to aerial navigation reside in the Parliament of Canada by virtue of s. 91, items 2, 5 and 7, it would appear that substantially the whole field of legislation in regard to aerial navigation belongs to the Dominion. There may be a small portion of the field which is not by virtue of specific words in the British North America Act vested in the Dominion; but neither is it vested by specific words in the Provinces. As to that small portion it appears to the Board that it must necessarily belong to the Dominion under its power to make laws for the peace, order and good government of Canada. Further, their Lordships are influenced by the facts that the subject of aerial navigation and the fulfilment of Canadian obligations under s. 132 are matters of national interest and importance; and that aerial navigation is a class of subject which has attained such dimensions as to affect the body politic of the Dominion.

As far as the possibility of increasing federal legislative authority is concerned, the critical factor in the *Aeronautics* judgment was the form of the 1919 Convention. This convention had been "ratified by His Majesty on behalf of the British Empire," and the subsequent legislation was passed by the parliament of Canada "with a view to performing her obligations as part of the British Empire."[59] Such a convention definitely comes within section 132, which covers obligations incurred

[56]*In re the Regulation and Control of Aeronautics in Canada*, [1932] A.C. 54, at 74 and 77.
[57]For the other possible reasons, see *ibid.*, at 69–73 and 77.
[58]*Ibid.*, at 63.
[59]*Ibid.* The legislation referred to was the Aeronautics Act, R.S.C. 1927, c. 3.

"as part of the British Empire," and arising under treaties between foreign states and "the Empire."

Suppose, however, that a treaty involved not "the Empire," but Canada alone. Should section 132 be expanded, so as to cover "Canadian," as opposed to "imperial" treaties? Or should it be confined, so as to cover only "imperial," and not strictly Canadian treaties? Should it, in other words, be liberally interpreted—and so adapted to the evolution of Canada's imperial and international status? Or should it be literally construed—and so divorced from that evolution?

The dilemma was posed by Lord Dunedin, in the *Radio* judgment[60] of 1932:

This idea of Canada as a Dominion being bound by a convention equivalent to a treaty with foreign powers was quite unthought of in 1867. It is the outcome of the gradual development of the position of Canada vis-à-vis to the mother country, Great Britain, which is found in these later days expressed in the Statute of Westminster. It is not, therefore, to be expected that such a matter should be dealt with in explicit words in either s. 91 or s. 92. The only class of treaty which would bind Canada was thought of as a treaty by Great Britain, and that was provided for by s. 132.

For this reason, Lord Dunedin favoured a liberal construction:

Being, therefore, not mentioned explicitly in either s. 91 or s. 92, such legislation falls within the general words at the opening of s. 91 which assign to the Government of the Dominion the power to make laws "for the peace, order, and good government of Canada in relation to all matters not coming within the classes of subjects by this Act assigned exclusively to the legislatures of the Provinces." In fine, though agreeing that the Convention was not such a treaty as is defined in s. 132, their Lordships think that it comes to the same thing. On August 11, 1927, the Privy Council of Canada with the approval of the Governor-General chose a body to attend the meeting of all the powers to settle international agreements as to wireless. The Canadian body attended and took part in deliberations. The deliberations ended in the convention with general regulations appended being signed at Washington on November 25, 1927, by the representatives of all the powers who had taken part in the conference, and this convention was ratified by the Canadian Government on July 12, 1928.

The result is in their Lordships' opinion clear. It is Canada as a whole which is amenable to the other powers for the proper carrying out of the convention; and to prevent individuals in Canada infringing the stipulations of the convention it is necessary that the Dominion should pass legislation which should apply to all the dwellers in Canada. . . .

But the question does not end with the consideration of the convention. Their Lordships draw attention to the provisions of head 10 of s. 92. These

[60]*In re the Regulation and Control of Radio Communication in Canada*, [1932] A.C. 304, at 312–14.

115

provisions, as has been explained in several judgments of the Board, have the effect of reading the excepted matters into the preferential place enjoyed by the enumerated subjects of s. 91, and the exceptions run that the works or undertakings are to be other than such as are of the following classes:—

(a) Lines of steam or other ships, railways, canals, telegraphs, and other works and undertakings connecting the Province with any other or others of the Provinces, or extending beyond the limits of the Province; (b) Lines of steamships between the Province and any British or foreign country; (c) Such works as, although wholly situate within the Province, are before or after their execution declared by the Parliament of Canada to be for the general advantage of Canada or for the advantage of two or more of the Provinces. Now, does broadcasting fall within the excepted matters? Their Lordships are of opinion that it does, falling in (a) within both the word "telegraphs" and the general words "undertakings connecting the Province with any other or others of the Provinces or extending beyond the limits of the Province."

From Lord Dunedin's words alone, it might be argued that the *ratio* of the *Radio* judgment consists in this reasoning: that the legislation in question[61] was *intra vires* the federal parliament because it was enabling legislation for a convention which, though not a treaty as defined in section 132, "comes to the same thing." It might then be concluded that as a result of the new treaty-making authority of the Canadian government, the Canadian parliament must have acquired additional legislative authority. For it must have been enabled to control those "subjects" that would formerly have belonged to the exclusive legislative authority of the provincial legislatures, but which could now be affected by such federal legislation as was necessary for performing obligations arising out of Canadian treaties. Alternatively, it might be argued that the *ratio* of the *Radio* judgment consists in this reasoning: that the disputed law was *intra vires* the federal parliament either because it was covered by the Peace, Order, and good Government clause (since the "subject" is "not mentioned explicitly in either s. 91 or s. 92"), or because it came within the heads of section 91 (since the "subject" falls within the exceptions specifically mentioned in head 10 of section 92). It might then be concluded that the possibility of using section 132 as a justification for extending the legislative authority of the federal parliament was still open to question.

This doubt was finally settled in the *Labour Conventions* judgment[62] of 1937. Confirming Lord Dunedin's opinion that the *Aeronautics* judgment was based on the imperial form of the 1919 Convention, Lord Atkin ruled that the *ratio* of the *Radio* judgment consists in the argument

[61]Viz., the Supreme Court Act, R.S.C. 1927, c. 35.
[62]*A.-G. Can.* v. *A.-G. Ont.*, [1937] A.C. 326, at 349–50, 351–52, and 353–54.

involving sections 91 and 92, rather than that involving section 132. He accordingly decided that the evolution in Canada's imperial and international status entailed mainly executive effects; that the legislative authority of the federal parliament was essentially defined by sections 91 and 92; and that section 132 was not so expansible as had been hoped, or feared.

The first ground upon which counsel for the Dominion sought to base the validity of the legislation was s. 132. So far as it is sought to apply this section to the conventions when ratified the answer is plain. The obligations are not obligations of Canada as part of the British Empire, but of Canada, by virtue of her new status as an international person, and do not arise under a treaty between the British Empire and foreign countries. This was clearly established by the decision in the *Radio* case, and their Lordships do not think that the proposition admits of any doubt. It is unnecessary, therefore, to dwell upon the distinction between legislative powers given to the Dominion to perform obligations imposed upon Canada as part of the Empire by an Imperial executive responsible to and controlled by the Imperial Parliament, and the legislative power of the Dominion to perform obligations created by the Dominion executive responsible to and controlled by the Dominion Parliament. While it is true, as was pointed out in the *Radio* case, that it was not contemplated in 1867 that the Dominion would possess treaty-making powers, it is impossible to strain the section so as to cover the uncontemplated event. . . .

For the purposes of ss. 91 and 92, i.e., the distribution of legislative powers between the Dominion and the Provinces, there is no such thing as treaty legislation as such. The distribution is based on classes of subjects; and as a treaty deals with a particular class of subjects so will the legislative power of performing it be ascertained. No one can doubt that this distribution is one of the most essential conditions, probably the most essential condition, in the inter-provincial compact to which the British North America Act gives effect. . . . It would be remarkable that while the Dominion could not initiate legislation, however desirable, which affected civil rights in the Provinces, yet its Government not responsible to the Provinces nor controlled by Provincial Parliaments need only agree with a foreign country to enact such legislation, and its Parliament would be forthwith clothed with authority to affect Provincial rights to the full extent of such agreement. Such a result would appear to undermine the constitutional safeguards of Provincial constitutional autonomy.

It follows from what has been said that no further legislative competence is obtained by the Dominion from its accession to international status, and the consequent increase in the scope of its executive functions. It is true, as pointed out in the judgment of the Chief Justice, that as the executive is now clothed with the powers of making treaties so the Parliament of Canada, to which the executive is responsible, has imposed upon it responsibilities in connection with such treaties, for if it were to disapprove of them they would either not be made or the Ministers would meet their constitutional fate. But this is true of all executive functions in their relation

117

to Parliament. There is no existing constitutional ground for stretching the competence of the Dominion Parliament so that it becomes enlarged to keep pace with enlarged functions of the Dominion executive. If the new functions affect the classes of subjects enumerated in s. 92 legislation to support the new functions is in the competence of the Provincial Legislatures only. If they do not, the competence of the Dominion Legislature is declared by s. 91 and existed ab origine. In other words, the Dominion cannot, merely by making promises to foreign countries, clothe itself with legislative authority inconsistent with the constitution which gave it birth. . . .

It must not be thought that the result of this decision is that Canada is incompetent to legislate in performance of treaty obligations. In totality of legislative powers, Dominion and Provincial together, she is fully equipped. But the legislative powers remain distributed, and if in the exercise of her new functions derived from her new international status Canada incurs obligations they must, so far as legislation be concerned, when they deal with Provincial classes of subjects, be dealt with by the totality of powers, in other words by co-operation between the Dominion and the Provinces. While the ship of state now sails on larger ventures and into foreign waters she still retains the water-tight compartments which are an essential part of her original structure.[63]

---

[63]Though only the above three cases were concerned with the implementation of treaty obligations, s. 132 also figured in *A.-G. B.C.* v. *A.-G. Can.*, [1924] A.C. 203, and *A.-G. N.B.* v. *Canadian Pacific Railway*, [1925] 2 D.L.R. 732. All 5 references are marked in col. D of the Analytical Table. As usual, the foregoing account is merely an outline, which should be supplemented by other analyses (several useful articles are listed in the Select Bibliography).

Chapter Nine

THE CONSIGNMENT PROBLEM: I

1. Consignment Difficulties in the B.N.A. Act

The Compartment and Ambit Problems are concerned with the construction of the British North America Act, whereas the Consignment Problem is concerned with the disposition of impugned laws. Because that disposition affected the framework of the Act, however, an analysis of the Judicial Committee's interpretative scheme must take into account the solutions devised for the problem of consigning impugned legislation.

This problem could not be solved either by settling the number of compartments or by delimiting their ambits. Since "subjects" are not disjunctive,[1] a law could involve a "subject" assigned to the federal parliament, and at the same time, a "subject" assigned to the provincial legislatures. Temperance legislation, for example, could involve such "subjects" as "The Regulation of Trade and Commerce," in section 91(2); "Municipal Institutions in the Province," in section 92(8); "Shop, Saloon, Auctioneer, and other Licences . . .," in section 92(9); "Property and Civil Rights in the Province," in section 92(13); "Generally all Matters of a merely local or private Nature in the Province," in section 92(16); and even "the Peace, Order, and good Government of Canada." As Sir Barnes Peacock observed in *Hodge* v. *The Queen*,[2] 1883, "subjects which in one aspect and for one purpose fall within sect. 92, may in another aspect and for another purpose fall within sect. 91." A decision must therefore be made as to which aspects of a disputed law are "principal," and which "incidental." In other words, to use the language of the Judicial Committee,[3] it is necessary

[1] See above, 75–76.
[2] 9 A.C. 117, at 130. See Jackett, in Corry *et al.*, eds., *Legal Essays*, 170.
[3] See *Russell* v. *The Queen* (1882), 7 A.C. 829, at 839–40; *Union Colliery Co.* v. *Bryden*, [1899] A.C. 580, at 587; *A.-G. Ont.* v. *Reciprocal Insurers*, [1924] A.C. 328, at 337–38; *In re the Insurance Act of Canada*, [1932] A.C. 41, at 49 *et. seq.*; *A.-G. Alta.* v. *A.-G. Can.*, [1939] A.C. 117, at 130–31; *Lethbridge Northern Irrigation Board of Trustees* v. *I.O.F.*, [1940] A.C. 513, at 529.

to determine the "leading feature" of the law, its "true nature and character," its "pith and substance"; or in the terms of the Act itself, the "matter" a law is "in relation to" must be distinguished from the "matters" it merely affects.[4]

But before this distinguishing can be done, the term "matter" must be defined; and here the solution to the Consignment Problem was influenced by the solution to the Problem of Compartments. If the two-compartment view were adopted, "matter" would signify primarily "scope," and secondarily "subject." A law would then be consigned to a provincial legislature if it concerned any of the "subjects" enumerated in section 92, and also were of provincial "scope." Alternatively, if it were of national "scope," it would be consigned to the federal parliament regardless of what its "subject" might be.[5]

If the three-compartment view were adopted, however, a reverse emphasis would follow: "matter" would signify primarily "subject," and only under exceptional circumstances, "scope." And a law would be consigned chiefly according to its "subject"—that is, on the basis of whether it concerned "government property and finance," "public services," "specific classes of persons," "physical objects," "rights and obligations as between individuals," or "divisions of jurisprudence." Alternatively, under exceptional circumstances, a law would be consigned according to its "scope"—that is, on the basis of whether it were of such national import as to bring it within the Peace, Order, and good Government clause, despite its concern with the "subjects" enumerated in section 92.

The priority considerations implicit in the Compartment Problem are also influential in the consignment of legislation. If the two-compartment view were adopted, a law that was of national "scope" would be consigned to section 91, and so upheld because this section is "prior" to section 92. The only check on the parliament of Canada would be the stipulation that federal legislation must not be employed as a "colour-

[4]This general distinction was made in *Proprietary Articles Trade Association* v. *A.-G. Can.*, [1931] A.C. 310, at 326–27. For particular applications—and some indication as to the type of law that might enable the federal parliament to "affect" provincial "subjects" (or vice versa)—see *Cushing* v. *Dupuy* (1880), 5 A.C. 409, at 415–16; *Russell* v. *The Queen* (1882), 7 A.C. 829, at 837–39; *A.-G. Man.* v. *Manitoba Licence Holders' Association*, [1902] A.C. 73, at 79–80; *Grand Trunk Railway* v. *A.-G. Can.*, [1907] A.C. 65, at 68; *Toronto Railway* v. *Toronto*, [1920] A.C. 426, at 439–40; *Great West Saddlery Co.* v. *The King*, [1921] 2 A.C. 91, at 117–18; *A.-G. B.C.* v. *Kingcome Navigation Co.*, [1934] A.C. 45, at 59–60; *Ladore* v. *Bennett*, [1939] A.C. 468, at 480–82.

[5]These and the following arguments were developed in chaps. 3, 6 and 7; see above, especially at 38, 40–41, 73–77, 86–87, 96–98.

able" device for controlling the provinces; and even then, the onus would be on the provinces to prove that it was. The legislative activities of the federal parliament would thus be practically unconfined—and the courts might tend to presume in favour of federal statutes.

If the three-compartment view were adopted, however, a law would be consigned to the compartment that contained the "subject" embracing the "matter" the law was "in relation to." The emphasis would now be placed not only on the two lists of enumerated heads, as opposed to the Peace, Order, and good Government clause, but also (because the most expansible part of the act is head 13 of section 92) on section 92, as opposed to the heads of section 91. Indeed, the relative priority of these three compartments would affect the consignment of a law at an even earlier stage, when the "matter" of that law was being determined. For if the law concerned a "subject" that overlapped the heads enumerated in sections 91 and 92, the aspect of the "subject" that fell within the former heads would probably (because those heads are prior to section 92) enjoy an advantage. Similarly, in the case of a "subject" that overlapped section 92 and the Peace, Order, and good Government clause, the aspect of the "subject" that fell within section 92 would probably (because that section is prior to the Peace, Order, and good Government clause) be considered paramount.[6] The application of the three-compartment view would consequently serve to confine the legislative authority of the federal parliament—if not to encourage a presumption in favour of provincial, rather than federal statutes.

The connection between the Compartment and Consignment problems is further complicated by the relation of these problems to the question of jurisprudential assumptions. If the two-compartment view were adopted, a federal law could not be judged invalid unless it were proved not to have a national import. Faced with the difficulty of providing such proof, the courts would probably tend to endorse most federal statutes. But even if they were willing to declare federal legislation invalid, they would still be placed in an awkward situation; for they would be forced to emphasize the particular facts of a situation, and at the same time, to consider the "national interest." Both the responsibility of establishing precedents and the need to exercise judicial restraint would become correspondingly difficult.

If the three-compartment view were adopted, however, a law would normally be judged invalid if it were proved to be "in relation to" a "matter" coming within the list of enumerated "subjects" that are

[6]Unless, of course, exceptional circumstances warranted the invocation of "scope" considerations.

121

assigned to the non-legislating authority. The only departure from this procedure would occur when "scope" was taken into account. Accordingly, the courts could apply a pair of "tests" that would not be available under the two-compartment procedure: they could first list all the "subjects" concerned, and then "weigh" those "subjects" in three-compartment terms. These "tests" would in turn lend themselves to the formulation of generalizations, and so to the establishing of precedents. And the courts would be able not only to concentrate on what the law "is," rather than what it should be, but also to make some show of exercising judicial restraint.

It is now possible to review the various solutions to the Consignment Problem. Section 91 and 92 assign legislative authority by means of a "two remove" formula: laws are described as "in relation to matters," which are in turn described as "coming within classes of subjects" (or in the case of the Peace, Order, and good Government clause, as not coming within the classes of subjects) assigned exclusively to the provincial legislatures. The Consignment solutions can thus be divided into two groups: those concerned with determining the "matter" of a law; and those concerned with classifying a law, once its "matter" has been determined.

2. The "Matter" Solutions, in General

Since a law cannot concern a "subject" without involving a design for affecting this "subject," the efforts of the Judicial Committee to determine the "matter" of an impugned law were largely directed towards identifying the "object" of that law. However, since the "expressed intention" of a legislature is not an infallible guide to the "true purpose" of its legislation, the "declared" object of a law is not always the same as its "legal" object.[7] The Judicial Committee therefore considered impugned laws, at least in part, from the standpoint of their "probable effect."[8]

At the same time, the Board preferred to confine itself to "immediate"[9]

[7]These are Mr. Jackett's terms: see Corry *et al.*, eds., *Legal Essays*, 162–65. The others in the following account have been employed by him, by other writers, and by the Judicial Committee itself—though not always with the same meaning: see Laskin, *Constitutional Law*, 76–83. The resulting confusion is not helped by the uncertainty as to what the Judicial Committee did, let alone meant; and this account might well suggest a greater consistency than was actually the case.

[8]See *A.-G. Alta.* v. *A.-G. Can.*, [1939] A.C. 117, at 130–31.

[9]See *A.-G. B.C.* v. *A.-G. Can.*, [1937] A.C. 391, at 397–98 and 403–4.

outcomes, and so to avoid speculating over "consequential effects,"[10] let alone "ultimate economic results."[11] In the *Farm Security Act* judgment[12] of 1949, Lord Simon—rejecting the contention that "the impeached paragraph is intra vires of the Province . . . [because] its 'pith and substance' is 'agriculture in the Province' "—illustrated this preference in the following statement:

There was abundant evidence that agriculture is the main industry of Saskatchewan and that it is the principal source of revenue of its inhabitants. It is moreover clear that the result of the impeached legislation, if it is validly enacted, would be to relieve in some degree a certain class of farmers from financial difficulties due to the uncertainties of their farming operations. But, as Rand J. points out, there is a distinction between legislation "in relation to" agriculture and legislation which may produce a favourable effect on the strength and stability of that industry. Consequential effects are not the same thing as legislative subject-matter. It is "the true nature and character of the legislation"—not its ultimate economic results— that matters (*Russell* v. *The Queen*). Here, what is sought to be statutorily modified is a contract between two parties one of which is an agriculturist but the other of which is a lender of money. However broadly the phrase "agriculture in the Province" may be construed, and whatever advantages to farmers the re-shaping of their mortgages or agreements for sale might confer, their Lordships are unable to take the view that this legislation can be regarded as valid on the ground that it is enacted in relation to agriculture.

Nevertheless, the first source of information as to the "legal object" of a statute is the "declared object" of the legislature that passed it.[13] The importance of this "declared object" (or "expressed intention") was recognized by Lord Atkin, in *Abitibi Power and Paper Company* v. *Montreal Trust Company*,[14] 1943:

It was pressed on their Lordships that the real substance of the legislation was an attempt to coerce the bondholders into accepting a plan of reconstruction, and that arrangements such as were contemplated by the report of the Royal Commission were within the exclusive field of dominion legislation. So they are, but this Board must have cogent grounds before it

---

[10]*A.-G. Sask.* v. *A.-G. Can.*, [1949] A.C. 110, at 123.
[11]*Ibid.*
[12]*Ibid.*, at 122–23. See Laskin, *Constitutional Law*, 81–82.
[13]See *Russell* v. *The Queen* (1882), 7 A.C. 829, at 841.
[14][1943] A.C. 536, at 548. See also *Russell* v. *The Queen* (1882), 7 A.C. 829, at 841; *Madden* v. *Nelson and Fort Sheppard Railway*, [1899] A.C. 626, at 628; *Fort Frances Pulp and Power Co.* v. *Manitoba Free Press Co.*, [1923] A.C. 695, at 705–6; *A.-G. B.C.* v. *A.-G. Can.*, [1937] A.C. 368, at 375; *A.-G. Alta.* v. *A.-G. Can.*, [1939] A.C. 117, at 130–31; *Co-operative Committee on Japanese Canadians* v. *A.-G. Can.*, [1947] A.C. 87, at 101.

arising from the nature of the impugned legislation before it can impute to a provincial legislation [*sic*] some object other than what is to be seen on the face of the enactment itself. In the present case their Lordships see no reason to reject the statement of the Ontario legislature, contained in the preamble to the Act, that the power to stay the action is given so that an opportunity may be given to all the parties concerned to consider the plan submitted in the report of the Royal Commission. That the Act was renewed in March, 1942, by another temporary Act expiring in June, 1943, affords no reason for modifying this view, nor does the fact that the plan suggested by the Royal Commission involves recourse to dominion legislation. The pith and substance of this Act is to regulate property and civil rights within the province.

Moreover, a court may not disregard the "declared object" of a statute either because the statute would be inadequate to the fulfilment of that object, or because the object itself seemed "indiscreet" or "unwise."[15] As Lord Loreburn warned, in the *Companies* judgment[16] of 1912, "it cannot be too strongly put that with the wisdom or expediency or policy of an Act, no Court has a word to say"; and the Judicial Committee was accordingly much more sensitive in its treatment of "declared objects" than is sometimes implied. In fact, it actually decided that the construction of particularly ambiguous statutes should be weighted by the desirability of placing them within the jurisdiction of the enacting legislature.[17]

On the other hand, since a "declared object" could be partial, mistaken, or misleading, it cannot be relied on exclusively. In the *Grain Futures Taxation* judgment[18] of 1925—despite a declaration in the impugned statute that "the tax imposed by this Act shall be a direct tax upon the person actually entering into the contract of sale"—Lord Haldane decided that the legislation really sought to impose indirect taxation. And in the *Sale of Company Shares* judgment[19] of 1929, Lord Sumner ruled that "the matter depends upon the effect of the legislation not upon its purpose." The Judicial Committee has consequently insisted that the "declared object" of a statute must rep-

[15]*Union Colliery Co.* v. *Bryden*, [1899] A.C. 580, at 585. See also *Cunningham* v. *Tomey Homma*, [1903] A.C. 151, at 155–56; *Grand Trunk Railway* v. *A.-G. Can.*, [1907] A.C. 65. at 68–69; *A.-G. Ont.* v. *A.-G. Can.*, [1912] A.C. 571, at 583–84; *Lymburn* v. *Mayland*, [1932] A.C. 318, at 326.

[16]*A.-G. Ont.* v. *A.-G. Can.*, [1912] A.C. 571, at 583.

[17]See *A.-G. Can.* v. *Cain*, [1906] A.C. 542, at 545; *Smith* v. *Vermillion Hills Rural Council*, [1916] 2 A.C. 569, at 574; *A.-G. Ont.* v. *Reciprocal Insurers*, [1924] A.C. 328, at 345.

[18]*A.-G. Man.* v. *A.-G. Can.*, [1925] A.C. 561, at 565. See also *A.-G. Can.* v. *A.-G. Ont.*, [1937] A.C. 326.

[19]*A.-G. Man.* v. *A.-G. Can.*, [1929] A.C. 260, at 268.

resent a "genuine determination."[20] For a legislature, whether federal or provincial, must not be enabled to do indirectly that which it is prohibited from doing directly[21]—or to regulate "colourably," under the form of a valid law, a "subject" which it is prohibited from regulating at all.[22]

In the *Proprietary Articles Trade Association* judgment[23] of 1931, Lord Atkin suggested that this "declared object" might be tested by considering the legislative history of a statute (though "time alone will not validate an Act which when challenged is found to be ultra vires; nor will a history of a gradual series of advances till this boundary is finally crossed avail to protect the ultimate encroachment"[24]). In the *Criminal Code* judgment[25] of 1937 and *Ladore* v. *Bennett*,[26] 1939, he also considered "the materials which the Government of the Province had before them before promoting in the Legislature the statute now impugned" (though such materials may not be cited as "evidence of the facts there found," and need not "necessarily be treated as conclusive"). And in the *Alberta Bank Taxation* judgment[27] of 1939, Lord Maugham went further: "the Court must take into account any public general knowledge of which the Court would take judicial notice, and may in a proper case require to be informed by evidence as to what the effect of the legislation will be."

Even so, all these sources of information are relatively subsidiary. For the statute itself has the principal "evidential value"; and it is through reading this, as a whole, that the "declared object" can be most convincingly tested, and the "true purpose" of the impugned legislation most readily discerned. Basically, the Judicial Committee tried to determine the "matter" a law was "in relation to," and so to characterize it in terms of the "subjects" enumerated in sections 91 and 92, by correlating this "true purpose" with the "subject" concerned.

[20]Paraphrasing Lord Atkin, in *Proprietary Articles Trade Association* v. *A.-G. Can.*, [1931] A.C. 310, at 323–24.

[21]See *Madden* v. *Nelson and Fort Sheppard Railway*, [1899] A.C. 626, at 627–28, and *A.-G. Sask.* v. *A.-G. Can.*, [1949] A.C. 110, at 124.

[22]See *A.-G. Ont.* v. *Reciprocal Insurers*, [1924] A.C. 328, at 342; *A.-G. Alta.* v. *A.-G. Can.*, [1928] A.C. 475, at 487; *A.-G. Alta.* v. *A.-G. Can.*, [1939] A.C. 117, at 130; *Ladore* v. *Bennett*, [1939] A.C. 468, at 482; *A.-G. B.C.* v. *Esquimalt and Nanaimo Railway*, [1950] A.C. 87, at 117.

[23]*Proprietary Articles Trade Association* v. *A.-G. Can.*, [1931] A.C. 310, at 317.
[24]*Ibid.*
[25]*A.-G. B.C.* v. *A.-G. Can.*, [1937] A.C. 368, at 376.
[26][1939] A.C. 468, at 477.
[27]*A.-G. Alta.* v. *A.-G. Can.*, [1939] A.C. 117, at 130.

3. The "Classification" Solutions, in General

One way of consigning laws that concern "subjects" in both section 91 and section 92 would be to sever the projecting parts. As Lord Atkin showed in *Lymburn* v. *Mayland*,[28] 1932, and *Toronto* v. *York*,[29] 1938, a statute could be declared partly valid, and partly invalid. As he also showed in the *Natural Products Marketing Act* judgment[30] of 1937, however, the part declared valid must represent the "pith and substance" of the Act, and the severed part only "incidental" provisions. Expressed negatively, this means that the incidental provisions of an Act may not be upheld if the Act itself, in "pith and substance," is invalid.

But the provisions of most Acts are usually inextricable;[31] to transpose Sir Barnes Peacock's remark in *Hodge* v. *The Queen*,[32] 1883, most impugned laws are valid in some aspects, but invalid in others. The Judicial Committee accordingly had to devise some other method of classifying legislation, and the Aspect (or as it is sometimes called, Double Aspect, or Pith and Substance) Doctrine was the general result: a law should be judged valid if, "in pith and substance," it concerns a "subject" assigned exclusively to the enacting legislature— even though it "incidentally affects" a "subject" assigned exclusively to the other legislature.[33]

In order to stress the legitimacy of such "incidental affecting," the term "trenching" is sometimes applied.[34] However, this term implies an "encroachment" by one legislature on the authority of another, and so a violation of the federal principle of exclusive legislative spheres.[35] In contrast, since it merely concerns the consignment of legislation, and not the extension of legislative authority, the Aspect Doctrine is

[28][1932] A.C. 318, at 327.
[29][1938] A.C. 415, at 427–28.
[30]*A.-G. B.C.* v. *A.-G. Can.*, [1937] A.C. 377, at 389.
[31]See *In re the Initiative and Referendum Act*, [1919] A.C. 935, at 944.
[32]9 A.C. 117, at 130.
[33]See *Hodge* v. *The Queen* (1883), 9 A.C. 117, at 130; *John Deere Plow Co.* v. *Wharton*, [1915] A.C. 330, at 339; *A.-G. Can.* v. *A.-G. Alta.*, [1916] 1 A.C. 588, at 596; *Paquet* v. *Quebec Pilots' Corporation*, [1920] A.C. 1029, at 1031; *A.-G. Ont.* v. *Reciprocal Insurers*, [1924] A.C. 328, at 343; *A.-G. Ont.* v. *Canada Temperance Federation*, [1946] A.C. 193, at 205–6; *A.-G. B.C.* v. *Esquimalt and Nanaimo Railway*, [1950] A.C. 87, at 120.
[34]See *Tennant* v. *Union Bank*, [1894] A.C. 31, at 45, and *A.-G. Can* v. *A.-G. B.C.*, [1930] A.C. 111, at 118.
[35]See above, 51–52, with regard to Lord Tomlin's "second proposition" in *A.G. Can.* v. *A.-G. B.C.*, [1930] A.C. 111, at 118.

quite compatible with the federal principle. As Mr. Justice Laskin suggests, then, the term "trenching" might well be allowed to disappear.[36]

But Mr. Justice Laskin does not object simply to the theoretical incongruity of the term "trenching"; he is even more disturbed by the restriction of "legitimate trenching," on the part of the federal parliament, to laws that concern the heads of section 91 only.[37] Yet without such a restriction, the third-compartment status of the Peace, Order, and good Government clause could not have been ensured, and the Aspect Doctrine thereby confined within the framework of the three-compartment view. It is the failure to appreciate this connection between the Compartment and Consignment Problems that explains the confusion over the Judicial Committee's resolution of the latter. The Board might not have employed the most precise or consistent language; it might even have changed old solutions, and developed new ones, as it went along. Nonetheless, the various Consignment Doctrines that eventually emerged are not merely congruous, but, given the three-compartment view, necessary.

For the Aspect Doctrine, given that view, is only a general principle,[38] which must be applied to particular conflicts between the heads of section 91 and section 92, and between section 92 and the Peace, Order, and good Government clause. It is submitted that the Doctrines of Ancillary Powers, Occupied Field, and Co-operation represent attempts to apply it to the former; and that the Dimensions and Emergency Doctrines represent attempts to apply it to the latter. It is also submitted that this "general" character both explains and justifies Lord Haldane's warning, in the *Insurance Act* judgment[39] of 1916, that the Aspect Principle "ought to be applied only with great caution."

Mr. Justice Laskin suspects that "the caution was sounded not because of any desire to find a more functional principle of assessing legislative competence but because of a desire to limit legislative competence according to subject matter rather than purpose or effect."[40]

---

[36]See Laskin, *Constitutional Law*, 88–89. See also O'Connor, *Report*, Annex 1, 92; Plaxton, *Canadian Constitutional Decisions*, xiv–xv; Varcoe, *Legislative Power*, 73–76; Rand J., in *A.-G. Can.* v. *C.P.R. and C.N.R.*, [1958] S.C.R. 285, at 290.

[37]See Lord Tomlin in *A.-G. Can.* v. *A.-G. B.C.* [1930] A.C. 111, at 118.

[38]This term was used by Lord Haldane in *A.-G. Can.* v. *A.-G. Alta.*, [1916] 1 A.C. 588, at 596.

[39]*Ibid.* See also *A.-G. B.C.* v. *Esquimalt and Nanaimo Railway*, [1950] A.C. 87, at 120.

[40]Laskin, *Constitutional Law*, 80.

He neglects to note, however, that this desire was related to the other parts of the Judicial Committee's interpretative scheme, and above all, to the fundamental three-compartment view. Unless the Aspect Principle were applied "with great caution" (which is to say, within the framework of that view), it could become not just an incongruity, but an escape mechanism. For it could make "scope," rather than "subject," the guiding consideration in the consignment of impugned legislation, and thus be used to evade the three-compartment view.[41]

Still, Mr. Justice Laskin is correct in one respect: unless the Aspect Principle is related to that view, the Ancillary (or Necessarily Incidental) Doctrine would become a "verbal rationalization."[42] According to this doctrine, the federal parliament may enact provisions that are ancillary (or necessarily incidental) to legislation concerning the "subjects" enumerated in section 91—even though these provisions concern "subjects" mentioned in section 92.[43] But this is not simply "a tortuous method of explaining the 'aspect doctrine' ";[44] on the contrary, it is a particular, and necessary, application of that principle to conflicts between the heads of section 91 and section 92. And the fact that this Ancillary Doctrine has the effect "not only of bisecting Dominion legislation but of enlarging the area of exercise of provincial legislative power,"[45] seems to be a result, rather than an object.

Suppose, however, that the federal parliament makes a law requiring "ancillary" provisions. May the provincial legislatures make laws concerning the "subjects" that are now covered by this law? To put the question another way, suppose the federal parliament makes a law covering a "field" in which federal and provincial legislative authority appears to overlap (a "field" that might be considered "common," in the sense of being liable to "legitimate trenching," by the federal parliament, in aid of legislation which is in relation to a matter coming within the classes of "subjects" enumerated in section 91). May the provincial legislatures also make laws covering that field?

The two, or perhaps three answers to this question established the Doctrine of the Occupied (or Unoccupied, or Overlapping) Field. If

[41]See the *O'Connor Report*, especially at 12–13, and Annex 1, 39–40.

[42]Laskin, *Constitutional Law*, 94.

[43]See *A.-G. Ont.* v. *A.-G. Can.*, [1894] A.C. 189, at 198–99 and 200–1. The same notion can be discerned in *L'Union St. Jacques de Montréal* v. *Bélisle* (1874), 6 A.C. 31, at 36–37; *Cushing* v. *Dupuy* (1880), 5 A.C. 409, at 415–16; *Tennant* v. *Union Bank*, [1894] A.C. 31, at 45. A more advanced explanation was made in *A.-G. Ont.* v. *A.-G. Can.*, [1896] A.C. 348, at 359–60.

[44]Laskin, *CBR*, XXV (1947), 1061, and *Constitutional Law*, 94. See also MacDonald, *UTLJ*, I (1936), 274.

[45]Laskin, *ibid.*

the "common" field is occupied by a federal law, the provinces may not legislate in any way that would interfere with this law.[46] If the field is unoccupied, the provinces may legislate so as to cover it (though such laws must give way to federal laws should the parliament of Canada enter the field).[47] But in no case may the provinces legislate in relation to a matter that would constitute the "pith and substance" of a federal law overlapping a common field.[48]

The Occupied Field Doctrine, like the Doctrine of Ancillary Powers, was applied to the heads of section 91 only. That is probably why Mr. Justice Laskin wants to discard it as well: "regarded from another standpoint,"[49] he argues, the Doctrine of the Occupied Field is merely a particular application of the Paramountcy Doctrine.[50] Moreover, since the latter doctrine makes no distinction between the heads of section 91 and the Peace, Order, and good Government clause,[51] it is more suited to Mr. Justice Laskin's two-compartment preference—though incompatible with the Judicial Committee's three-compartment view.

However, it is doubtful whether the Paramountcy Doctrine should be described as a "doctrine" at all. Like the Aspect "Doctrine," it would seem to be only a "principle"; and in any case, it is of a different order from the Doctrine of Ancillary Powers or Occupied Field. For it cannot be used to consign legislation until it is made consistent with the basic three-compartment view; and when that is done, the general Paramountcy Principle, being now applicable to the heads of section 91 only, becomes the particular Doctrine of the Occupied Field.

The last of these particular doctrines, so far as conflicts between the heads of section 91 and section 92 are concerned, is the Co-operation Doctrine. Although relatively recent, and rather nebulous,[52] this doctrine implies an approach that seems especially noteworthy today, when the "shared" aspects of federal government are beginning to receive attention.[53] While control over the "subjects" enumerated in section 92

---

[46]See *A.-G. Ont.* v. *A.-G. Can.*, [1894] A.C. 189, at 200–1, and *Grand Trunk Railway* v. *A.-G. Can.*, [1907] A.C. 65, at 68.

[47]See *ibid.*

[48]See *A.-G. Can.* v. *A.'s-G. Ont., Que., N.S.*, [1898] A.C. 700, at 715.

[49]Laskin, *Constitutional Law*, 95.

[50]According to which, if "valid provincial and valid Dominion legislation cannot stand together, the latter must prevail" (*ibid.*).

[51]According to Mr. Justice Laskin; cf. his arguments in *Constitutional Law*, 95–96, and the analysis made above, in chaps. 3 and 4.

[52]And thus often neglected—as by Mr. Justice Laskin and Mr. Jackett; cf. Cameron.

[53]See Corry, in Fox, ed., *Politics*, 26–40; Elazer, *American Partnership*; Vile, *American Federalism*.

might be essential to effective legislation by the federal parliament in relation to matters coming within the classes of subjects enumerated in section 91, legislation that attempted to secure this control might not be judged "necessarily incidental." But if it were not, then the only way the "field" could be covered would be through the "co-operation" of the federal parliament and the provincial legislatures.[54] Admittedly, "the legislation will have to be carefully framed, and will not be achieved by either party leaving its own sphere and encroaching upon that of the other."[55] Nevertheless, "it cannot be assumed that either body will decline to co-operate with the other in a reasonable way."[56]

Finally, the Dimensions and Emergency Doctrines reflect an application of the Aspect Principle to the other three-compartment conflict, between section 92 and the Peace, Order, and good Government clause. According to the Dimensions Doctrine,[57] the federal parliament may make laws concerning "subjects" enumerated in section 92, even though these "subjects are not included in the heads of section 91, providing the laws are of national "scope." According to the Emergency Doctrine,[58] however, the federal parliament may so legislate only when an "emergency" occurs. It is probably more illuminating to consider the latter doctrine as a modified version of the former, rather than a separate doctrine embodying a contrasting principle. But the main point, for present purposes, is that both doctrines reflect the influence of the Aspect Principle. And in this connection, the Judicial Committee's interpretative scheme involves not only the application of a "scope," rather than "subject" test, but also the control of this test within the framework of the three-compartment view.

[54]See *A.-G. Can.* v. *A.-G. Ont.*, [1937] A.C. 326, at 353–54; *A.-G. Can.* v. *A.-G. Ont.*, [1937] A.C. 355, at 356–57; *A.-G. B.C.* v. *A.-G. Can.*, [1937] A.C. 377, at 389.
[55]*Montreal* v. *Montreal Street Railway*, [1912] A.C. 333, at 346.
[56]*Ibid.*
[57]See *A.-G. Ont.* v. *A.-G. Can.*, [1896] A.C. 348, at 361–62.
[58]See *A.-G. Can.* v. *A.-G. Alta.*, [1916] 1 A.C. 588, at 597, and *Fort Frances Pulp and Power Co.* v. *Manitoba Free Press Co.*, [1923] A.C. 695, at 703–5.

Chapter Ten

THE CONSIGNMENT PROBLEM: II

1. The Severability Doctrine

When the notion of severability was first raised, during *In re The Initiative and Referendum Act*,[1] 1919, Lord Haldane dismissed it briefly: it was not possible to save the "residue" of the act in question by severing the invalid parts because "the offending provisions are in their Lordships' view so interwoven with the scheme that they are not severable." In *Great West Saddlery Company* v. *The King*,[2] 1921, Lord Haldane was more sympathetic: while he did not consider the mortmain provisions of the Manitoba and Saskatchewan acts inseverable, he did sever the valid Ontario Mortmain Act from the invalid Ontario Corporations Act. But it was not until *Lymburn* v. *Mayland*,[3] 1932, that part of an act was severed from the whole; according to Lord Atkin, even though the section of the impugned statute that attempted to impose penalties for fraudulent actions probably "encroaches on the exclusive legislative power of the Dominion as to criminal law," since "so far as the section is invalid it appears to be clearly severable," the statute could be upheld. Similarly, in *Toronto* v. *York*,[4] 1938, Lord Atkin decided that because the invalid provisions in the impugned Act were severable, the Act itself was *intra vires*.

However, those are the only instances of a statute being severed. Lord Atkin's qualification, in the *Natural Products Marketing Act* judgment[5] of 1937, probably accounts for this reluctance to employ the severability solution: "as the main legislation is invalid as being in pith and substance an encroachment upon the Provincial rights the sections must fall with them as being in part merely ancillary to it." In the

[1][1919] A.C. 935, at 944.
[2][1921] 2 A.C. 91, at 119–24.
[3][1932] A.C. 318, at 327.
[4][1938] A.C. 415, at 427–28.
[5]*A.-G. B.C.* v. *A.-G. Can.*, [1937] A.C. 377, at 389.

Alberta Bill of Rights Act judgment[6] of 1947, Lord Simon, though reasoning somewhat differently, reached the same conclusion:[7]

There remains the second question, whether when Part II has been struck out from the Act as invalid what is left should be regarded as surviving, or whether, on the contrary, the operation of cutting out Part II involves the consequence that the whole Act is a dead letter. This sort of question arises not infrequently and is often raised (as in the present instance) by asking whether the legislation is intra vires "either in whole or in part," but this does not mean that when Part II is declared invalid what remains of the Act is to be examined bit by bit in order to determine whether the legislature would be acting within its powers if it passed what remains. The real question is whether what remains is so inextricably bound up with the part declared invalid that what remains cannot independently survive, or, as it has sometimes been put, whether on a fair review of the whole matter it can be assumed that the legislature would have enacted what survives without enacting the part that is ultra vires at all.

2. The Aspect "Principle"

The Aspect Principle is so general as to make it sometimes indiscernible. In *Hodge* v. *The Queen*,[8] 1883, Sir Barnes Peacock not only suggested that "subjects which in one aspect and for one purpose fall within sect. 92, may in another aspect and for another purpose fall within sect. 91," but argued that this principle had already been implied by the *Parsons* judgment[9] of 1881. In contrast, while he does not mention the latter judgment, Mr. Jackett cites both *L'Union St. Jacques de Montréal* v. *Bélisle*,[10] 1874, and *Dobie* v. *Temporalities Board*,[11] 1881. And O'Connor, not surprisingly, would include *Russell* v. *The Queen*,[12] 1882.

Among the subsequent references to the Aspect Principle, two judgments are notable for the caution they advise. In the *Insurance Act* judgment[13] of 1916, Lord Haldane made this comment on *Russell* v. *The Queen*, 1882:

No doubt the Canada Temperance Act contemplated in certain events the use of different licensing boards and regulations in different districts and

---

[6]*A.-G. Alta.* v. *A.-G. Can.*, [1947] A.C. 503, at 518.

[7]The 11 major references to the Severability Doctrine are marked in col. D of the Analytical Table.

[8]9 A.C. 117, at 130.

[9]*Citizens Insurance Co.* v. *Parsons* (1881), 7 A.C. 96.

[10]6 A.C. 31.

[11]7 A.C. 136.   [12]7 A.C. 829.

[13]*A.-G. Can.* v. *A.-G. Alta.*, [1916] 1 A.C. 588, at 596.

to this extent legislated in relation to local institutions. But the Judicial Committee appear to have thought that this purpose was subordinate to a still wider and legitimate purpose of establishing a uniform system of legislation for prohibiting the liquor traffic throughout Canada excepting under restrictive conditions. The case must therefore be regarded as illustrating the principle which is now well established, but none the less ought to be applied only with great caution, that subjects which in one aspect and for one purpose fall within the jurisdiction of the provincial Legislatures may in another aspect and for another purpose fall within Dominion legislative jurisdiction.

In the same manner, during the *Esquimalt and Nanaimo Railway* judgment[14] of 1950, Lord Greene (describing the Aspect Principle as the "pith and substance principle") made this comment on *Atlantic Smoke Shops* v. *Conlon*,[15] 1943:

In the latter case a somewhat complicated method of taxing the consumption of tobacco was adopted. It was held to be a direct tax because it was imposed on the actual consumer on the occasion of a purchase by him. A similar result from the revenue point of view could no doubt have been secured by imposing the tax on the manufacturer or on the vendor. But such a tax would have been an indirect tax since the operation of passing the burden of the tax to the consumer in the shape of an increase of price would have been in practice almost automatic. This case, in their Lordships' view, affords a good example of the caution with which the "pith and substance" principle ought to be applied. The object of that principle is to discover what the tax really is; it must not be used for the purpose of holding that what is really a direct tax is an indirect tax on the ground that an equivalent result could have been obtained by using the technique of indirect taxation. The use of the word "camouflage" in the argument of the respondents appears to their Lordships to be due to a misapplication of the principle.

The constant attempts to employ the Aspect Principle regardless of its congruity with the Judicial Committee's interpretative scheme—and above all, outside the framework of the three-compartment view—would seem to justify both these statements.[16]

3. The Ancillary Doctrine

In the *Local Prohibition* judgment[17] of 1896, Lord Watson remarked that the federal parliament may "deal with matters local or private in

---

[14]*A.-G. B.C.* v. *Esquimalt and Nanaimo Railway*, [1950] A.C. 87, at 119–20.
[15][1943] A.C. 550.
[16]The 7 fairly clear, as well as the 37 more debatable references to the Aspect Principle are all marked in col. D of the Analytical Table.
[17]*A.-G. Ont.* v. *A.-G. Can.*, [1896] A.C. 348, at 359–60.

133

those cases where such legislation is necessarily incidental to the exercise of the powers conferred upon it by the enumerative heads of clause 91." He thereby confined the Doctrine of Ancillary Powers to conflicts between the heads of section 91 and section 92. This fact probably explains both Mr. Justice Laskin's wish to discard the doctrine altogether,[18] and O'Connor's attempt to deny that it had a three-compartment implication before 1896.[19] But at least the latter attempt appears to be unfounded; in the *Voluntary Assignments* judgment[20] of 1894, Lord Herschell referred specifically to head 21 of section 91, as distinct from the Peace, Order, and good Government clause:

In their Lordships' opinion these considerations must be borne in mind when interpreting the words "bankruptcy" and "insolvency" in the British North America Act. It appears to their Lordships that such provisions as are found in the enactment in question, relating as they do to assignments purely voluntary, do not infringe on the exclusive legislative power conferred upon the Dominion Parliament. They would observe that a system of bankruptcy legislation may frequently require various ancillary provisions for the purpose of preventing the scheme of the Act from being defeated. It may be necessary for this purpose to deal with the effect of executions and other matters which would otherwise be within the legislative competence of the provincial legislature. Their Lordships do not doubt that it would be open to the Dominion Parliament to deal with such matters as part of a bankruptcy law, and the provincial legislature would doubtless be then precluded from interfering with this legislation inasmuch as such interference would affect the bankruptcy law of the Dominion Parliament. But it does not follow that such subjects, as might properly be treated as ancillary to such a law and therefore within the powers of the Dominion Parliament are excluded from the legislative authority of the provincial legislature when there is no bankruptcy or insolvency legislation of the Dominion Parliament in existence.

Actually, the notion of "ancillary" powers had been recognized well before the *Voluntary Assignments* judgment of 1894.[21] In *L'Union St. Jacques de Montréal* v. *Bélisle*,[22] 1874, Lord Selborne went this far:

The hypothesis was suggested in argument by Mr. *Benjamin*, who certainly argued this case with his usual ingenuity and force, of a law having been previously passed by the Dominion Legislature, to the effect that any association of this particular kind throughout the Dominion, on certain specified conditions assumed to be exactly those which appear upon the face of this statute, should thereupon, *ipso facto*, fall under the legal administration in

[18]See Laskin, *Constitutional Law*, 84 and 92–95.
[19]See the *O'Connor Report*, Annex 1, 46.
[20]*A.-G. Ont.* v. *A.-G. Can.*, [1894] A.C. 189, at 200–1.
[21]See Cameron, *Canadian Constitution*, I, 78–79.
[22]6 A.C. 31, at 36–37.

bankruptcy or insolvency. Their Lordships are by no means prepared to say that if any such law as that had been passed by the Dominion Legislature, it would have been beyond their competency: nor that, if it had been so passed, it would have been within the competency of the provincial legislature afterwards to take a particular association out of the scope of a general law of that kind, so competently passed by the authority which had power to deal with bankruptcy and insolvency. But no such law ever has been passed; and to suggest the possibility of such a law as a reason why the power of the provincial legislature over this local and private association should be in abeyance or altogether taken away, is to make a suggestion which, if followed up to its consequences, would go very far to destroy that power in all cases.

In *Cushing* v. *Dupuy*,[23] 1880, Sir Montague Smith added the following:

It was contended for the Appellant that the provisions of the *Insolvency Act* interfered with property and civil rights, and was therefore *ultra vires*. This objection was very faintly urged, but it was strongly contended that the Parliament of *Canada* could not take away the right of appeal to the Queen from final judgments of the Court of Queen's Bench, which, it was said, was part of the procedure in civil matters exclusively assigned to the Legislature of the Province.

The answer to these objections is obvious. It would be impossible to advance a step in the construction of a scheme for the administration of insolvent estates without interfering with and modifying some of the ordinary rights of property, and other civil rights, nor without providing some mode of special procedure for the vesting, realisation, and distribution of the estate, and the settlement of the liabilities of the insolvent. Procedure must necessarily form an essential part of any law dealing with insolvency. It is therefore to be presumed, indeed it is a necessary implication, that the Imperial statute, in assigning to the Dominion Parliament the subjects of bankruptcy and insolvency, intended to confer on it legislative power to interfere with property, civil rights, and procedure within the Provinces, so far as a general law relating to those subjects might affect them.

And in *Tennant* v. *Union Bank*,[24] 1894, Lord Watson not only expanded these "ancillary" gestures, but confined them to the case of conflicts between the heads of section 91 and section 92:

Statutory regulations with respect to the form and legal effect, in Ontario, of warehouse receipts and other negotiable documents, which pass the property of goods without delivery, unquestionably relate to property and civil rights in that province; and the objection taken by the appellant to the provisions of the Bank Act would be unanswerable if it could be shewn that, by the Act of 1867, the Parliament of Canada is absolutely debarred from trenching to any extent upon the matters assigned to the provincial legislature by sect. 92. But sect. 91 expressly declares that, "notwithstanding anything

---

[23]5 A.C. 409, at 415–16.
[24][1894] A.C. 31, at 45.

in this Act," the exclusive legislative authority of the Parliament of Canada shall extend to all matters coming within the enumerated classes; which plainly indicates that the legislation of that Parliament, so long as it strictly relates to these matters, is to be of paramount authority. To refuse effect to the declaration would render nugatory some of the legislative powers specially assigned to the Canadian Parliament. For example, among the enumerated classes of subjects in·sect. 91, are "Patents of Invention and Discovery," and "Copyrights." It would be practically impossible for the Dominion Parliament to legislate upon either of these subjects without affecting the property and civil rights of individuals in the provinces.

As for the judgments after 1896, the Ancillary Doctrine was not applied to a provincial law until *Ladore* v. *Bennett*,[25] 1939. Although he agreed that it "incidentally" affected the "subject" of "interest," Lord Atkin decided that the impugned statute did not come within section 91(2):

For the reasons given the attack upon the Acts and scheme on the ground either that they infringe the Dominion's exclusive power relating to bankruptcy and insolvency, or that they deal with civil rights outside the Province, breaks down. The statutes are not directed to insolvency legislation; they pick out insolvency as one reason for dealing in a particular way with unsuccessful institutions; and though they affect rights outside the Province they only so affect them collaterally, as a necessary incident to their lawful powers of good government within the Province.

This decision was then followed by Lord Caldecote, in *Lethbridge Northern Irrigation District Board of Trustees* v. *Independent Order of Foresters*,[26] 1940:

Their Lordships were pressed with the decision of the Board in *Ladore* v. *Bennett*. In that case a Provincial Legislature passed Acts amalgamating and incorporating in one city four municipalities which were in financial difficulties. As part of the consignment adjustment of the finances of the municipalities, debentures of the new city of equal nominal amount to those of the old municipalities were issued to the creditors, but with the rate of interest reduced. It was held by the Judicial Committee that a Provincial Legislature, which could dissolve a Municipal Corporation and create a new one to take its place, could legislate concerning the financial powers of the new corporation, and incidentally might define the amount of interest which the obligations incurred by the new city should bear. On this ground it was decided that legislation directed bona fide to the creation and control of municipal institutions is in no way an encroachment upon the general exclusive power of the Dominion Legislation [*sic*] over interest. Having come to the conclusion that the pith and substance of the legislation in question related to one or more of the classes of subjects under s. 92, the Board had no difficulty in holding that the regulation of the interest payable on the

[25][1939] A.C. 468, at 482–83.
[26][1940] A.C. 513, at 532.

136

debentures of the new city was not an invasion of Dominion powers under head 19 of s. 91.

Two other post-1896 judgments—*Toronto* v. *Canadian Pacific Railway*,[27] 1908, and *Toronto Railway* v. *Toronto*,[28] 1920—might reflect a different use of the "ancillary" notion.[29] But although Lord Collins and Lord Finlay applied this notion to legislation that was probably *ultra vires* the provincial legislatures, it is questionable whether they recognized that probability. In any case, a more significant difference is apparent in *Montreal* v. *Montreal Street Railway*,[30] 1912, and the *Fish Canneries* decision[31] of 1930; for in these judgments Lord Atkinson and Lord Tomlin suggested that legislation should not be classified as ancillary to a federal statute unless it was clear that the provincial legislatures would refuse to pass such legislation. This suggestion might have laid the basis for the Co-operation Doctrine.[32]

4. The Occupied Field Doctrine

In the *Voluntary Assignments* judgment[33] of 1894, Lord Herschell considered "common fields" that were occupied by federal laws, as well as those that were unoccupied:

Their Lordships do not doubt that it would be open to the Dominion Parliament to deal with such matters [viz., "executions and other matters which would otherwise be within the legislative competence of the provincial legislature"] as part of a bankruptcy law, and the provincial legislature would doubtless be then precluded from interfering with this legislation inasmuch as such interference would affect the bankruptcy law of the Dominion Parliament. But it does not follow that such subjects, as might properly be treated as ancillary to such a law and therefore within the powers of the Dominion Parliament, are excluded from the legislative authority of the provincial legislature when there is no bankruptcy or insolvency legislation of the Dominion Parliament in existence.

The resulting "propositions" were then summarized by Lord Dunedin in *Grand Trunk Railway* v. *Attorney-General of Canada*,[34] 1907: "First, that there can be a domain in which provincial and Dominion legislation

---

[27][1908] A.C. 54. [28][1920] A.C. 446.
[29]See Varcoe, *Legislative Power*, 57. [30][1912] A.C. 333.
[31]*A.-G. Can.* v. *A.-G. B.C.*, [1930] A.C. 111.
[32]The 22 major references to the Ancillary Doctrine are marked in col. D of the Analytical Table.
[33]*A.-G. Ont.* v. *A.-G. Can.*, [1894] A.C. 189, at 200–1.
[34][1907] A.C. 65, at 68.

may overlap, in which case neither legislation will be ultra vires, if the field is clear; and, secondly, that if the field is not clear, and in such a domain the two legislations meet, then the Dominion legislation must prevail."

However, there is a third requirement in the Doctrine of the Occupied Field: the provincial legislatures may not make laws concerning "subjects" that would constitute the "pith and substance" of federal laws which necessarily affected "subjects" mentioned in section 92. In other words, the provincial legislatures may not make laws that are substantially concerned with "subjects" mentioned in the heads of section 91 —even though the making of such laws by the federal parliament would necessarily affect "subjects" mentioned in section 92. Otherwise, as Lord Herschell pointed out in the *Fisheries* judgment[35] of 1898, the principle of "exclusivity" would be violated:

It has been suggested, and this view has been adopted by some of the judges of the Supreme Court, that although any Dominion legislation dealing with the subject [viz., "Sea-Coast and Inland Fisheries," in section 91(12)] would override provincial legislation, the latter is nevertheless valid, unless and until the Dominion Parliament so legislates. Their Lordships think that such a view does not give their due effect to the terms of s. 91, and in particular to the word "exclusively." It would authorize, for example, the enactment of a bankruptcy law or a copyright law in any of the provinces unless and until the Dominion Parliament passed enactments dealing with those subjects. Their Lordships do not think this is consistent with the language and manifest intention of the British North America Act.

Lord Herschell consequently distinguished his *Voluntary Assignments* judgment as follows:

It is true that this Board held in the case of *Attorney-General of Canada v. Attorney-General of Ontario* [*sic*; i.e., *A.-G. Ont.* v. *A.-G. Can.* (1894) A.C. 189] that a law passed by a Provincial Legislature which affected the assignments and property of insolvent persons was valid as falling within the heading "Property and Civil Rights," although it was of such a nature that it would be a suitable ancillary provision to a bankruptcy law. But the ground of this decision was that the law in question did not fall within the class "Bankruptcy and Insolvency" in the sense in which those words were used in s. 91.

And in *Union Colliery Company* v. *Bryden*,[36] 1899, Lord Watson not only repeated Lord Herschell's argument, but emphasized the connection between the Occupied Field Doctrine and the Aspect Principle:

The provisions of which the validity has been thus affirmed by the Courts below are capable of being viewed in two different aspects, according to one

---

[35]*A.-G. Can.* v. *A.'s-G. Ont., Que., N.S.,* [1898] A.C. 700, at 715.
[36][1899] A.C. 580, at 587–88.

of which they appear to fall within the subjects assigned to the provincial parliament by s. 92 of the British North America Act, 1867, whilst, according to the other, they clearly belong to the class of subjects exclusively assigned to the legislature of the Dominion by s. 91, sub-s. 25. They may be regarded as merely establishing a regulation applicable to the working of underground coal mines; and, if that were an exhaustive description of the substance of the enactments, it would be difficult to dispute that they were within the competency of the provincial legislature, by virtue either of s. 92, sub-s. 10, or s. 92, sub-s. 13. But the leading feature of the enactments consists in this—that they have, and can have, no application except to Chinamen who are aliens or naturalized subjects, and that they establish no rule or regulation except that these aliens or naturalized subjects shall not work, or be allowed to work, in underground coal mines within the Province of British Columbia.

Their Lordships see no reason to doubt that, by virtue of s. 91, sub-s. 25, the legislature of the Dominion is invested with exclusive authority in all matters which directly concern the rights, privileges, and disabilities of the class of Chinamen who are resident in the provinces of Canada. They are also of opinion that the whole pith and substance of the enactments of s. 4 of the Coal Mines Regulation Act, in so far as objected to by the appellant company, consists in establishing a statutory prohibition which affects aliens or naturalized subjects, and therefore trench upon the exclusive authority of the Parliament of Canada. The learned judges who delivered opinions in the Full Court noticed the fact that the Dominion legislature had passed a "Naturalization Act, No. 113 of the Revised Statutes of Canada, 1886," by which a partial control was exercised over the rights of aliens. Walkem J. appears to regard that fact as favourable to the right of the provincial parliament to legislate for the exclusion of aliens being Chinamen from underground coal mines. The abstinence of the Dominion Parliament from legislating to the full limit of its powers, could not have the effect of transferring to any provincial legislature the legislative power which had been assigned to the Dominion by s. 91 of the Act of 1867.

The Occupied Field Doctrine was raised most frequently in cases involving section 91(15), "Banking . . ."; section 91(21), "Bankruptcy and Insolvency"; section 92(10), "Local Works and Undertakings . . ."; section 92(11), "The Incorporation of Companies with Provincial Objects"; and section 92(2), "Direct Taxation within the Province. . . ." But the last two sections required special solutions. Since they are excepted from section 92(11), and yet not mentioned in the heads of section 91, federal companies are incorporated under the authority of the Peace, Order, and good Government clause. On the other hand, the third-compartment character of that clause has made these companies peculiarly subject to provincial laws;[37] for they are not only registered, licensed, and taxed by the provincial legislatures, but also required to

[37]See Varcoe, *Legislative Power*, 51.

obey provincial regulations as to mortmain and the form of contracts. In fact, the only real check on the provincial legislatures—as was shown in *John Deere Plow Company* v. *Wharton*,[38] 1915, *Great West Saddlery Company* v. *King*,[39] 1921, and the *Sale of Company Shares* judgment[40] of 1929—is that they may not deprive a federal company of its status or powers.

As for section 92(2), the judgments in *Forbes* v. *Attorney-General for Manitoba*,[41] 1937, and *Judges* v. *Attorney-General for Saskatchewan*,[42] 1937, showed that situations could occur in which the Occupied Field Doctrine would not apply: that is, when no conflict was involved. In addition, they showed that the taxation of incomes is a common field, in which federal and provincial legislation may co-exist, and be enforced simultaneously. These disclosures might also be connected with the Co-operation Doctrine.[43]

5. The Co-operation Doctrine

This doctrine is usually dated from *Montreal* v. *Montreal Street Railway*,[44] 1912. After denying that a federal law concerning federal railways may necessarily affect "subjects" mentioned in section 92, Lord Atkinson recommended that the conduct of through traffic should be secured by means of legislative "co-operation." It must be noted, however, that this recommendation was based on certain assumptions:

> . . . the Act and Order if justified at all must be justified on the ground that they are necessarily incidental to the exercise by the Dominion Parliament of the powers conferred upon it by the enumerated heads of s. 91. Well, the only one of the heads enumerated in s. 91 dealing expressly or impliedly with railways is that which is interpolated by the transfer into it of sub-heads (*a*), (*b*), and (*c*) of sub-s. 10 of s. 92. Lines such as the Street Railway are not amongst these.

Yet even if it were confined to federal legislation that was not in relation to the heads of section 91, Lord Atkinson's recommendation would be provocative; and his further suggestion is still more so:

> One of the arguments urged on behalf of the appellants was this: The through traffic must, it is said, be controlled by some legislative body. It

[38][1915] A.C. 330.   [39][1921] 2 A.C. 91.
[40]*A.-G. Man.* v. *A.-G. Can.*, [1929] A.C. 260.
[41][1937] A.C. 260.   [42]53 T.L.R. 464.
[43]The 39 major references to the Occupied Field Doctrine are marked in col. D of the Analytical Table.
[44][1912] A.C. 333, at 344 and 346.

cannot be controlled by the provincial Legislature because that Legislature has no jurisdiction over a federal line, therefore it must be controlled by the Legislature of Canada. The answer to that contention is this, that so far as the "through" traffic is carried on over the federal line, it can be controlled by the Parliament of Canada. And that so far as it is carried over a non-federal provincial line it can be controlled by the provincial Legislature, and the two companies who own these lines can thus be respectively compelled by these two Legislatures to enter into such agreement with each other as will secure that this "through" traffic shall be properly conducted; and further that it cannot be assumed that either body will decline to co-operate with the other in a reasonable way to effect an object so much in the interest of both the Dominion and the province as the regulation of "through" traffic.

In the *Fish Canneries* judgment[45] of 1930, Lord Tomlin shared this reluctance to invoke the Ancillary Doctrine.[46] While admitting that some power of enforcing prescribed regulations "may be" necessary to effective fishery control, he decided that federal legislation requiring fish canneries to be licensed was not "necessarily incidental" to federal legislation respecting a sea-coast fishery. But this decision would seem to have raised more questions than it settled. Could such legislation be enforced by any method other than licensing? If not, could the provincial legislatures be forced to license on behalf of the federal parliament? Or if the connection between regulating and licensing a sea-coast fishery were shown to be "necessary," could the Ancillary Doctrine be invoked, after all? Did the federal contention really fail because of insufficient factual evidence? Was it really impossible to establish the "necessary connection between the two subject matters"? Does "necessary" mean "logically," or only "practically" necessary?

Whatever Lord Tomlin's views might have been, Lord Atkin definitely favoured the principle of co-operative action. Thus in the *Labour Conventions* judgment[47] of 1937—after denying that the new ability of the federal government to make treaties must have enabled the federal parliament to pass any law necessary for the implementation of such treaties—he made the following comment:

It must not be thought that the result of this decision is that Canada is incompetent to legislate in performance of treaty obligations. In totality of legislative powers, Dominion and Provincial together, she is fully equipped. But the legislative powers remain distributed, and if in the exercise of her new functions derived from her new international status Canada incurs obligations they must, so far as legislation be concerned, when they deal with

---

45*A.-G. Can.* v. *A.-G. B.C.*, [1930] A.C. 111, at 121–22.
46See Varcoe, *Legislative Power*, 59.
47*A.-G. Can.* v. *A.-G. Ont.*, [1937] A.C. 326, at 353–54.

Provincial classes of subjects, be dealt with by the totality of powers, in other words by co-operation between the Dominion and the Provinces.

Similarly, in the *Unemployment Insurance* case[48] of 1937, Lord Atkin implied that the only way to establish an effective unemployment insurance scheme would be through the passage of co-operative legislation by the federal parliament and the provincial legislatures;[49] for he argued that although "the Dominion may impose taxation for the purpose of creating a fund for special purposes . . . it by no means follows that any legislation which disposes of it is necessarily within Dominion competence." And in the *Natural Products Marketing Act* judgment[50] of 1937, he added this statement:

The Board were given to understand that some of the Provinces attach much importance to the existence of marketing schemes such as might be set up under this legislation [e.g., the federal parliament's Natural Products Marketing Act of 1934]: and their attention was called to the existence of Provincial legislation setting up Provincial schemes for various Provincial products. It was said that as the Provinces and the Dominion between them possess a totality of complete legislative authority, it must be possible to combine Dominion and Provincial legislation so that each within its own sphere could in co-operation with the other achieve the complete power of regulation which is desired. Their Lordships appreciate the importance of the desired aim. Unless and until a change is made in the respective legislative functions of Dominion and Province it may well be that satisfactory results for both can only be obtained by co-operation. But the legislation will have to be carefully framed, and will not be achieved by either party leaving its own sphere and encroaching upon that of the other.

In so far as they revealed the existence of a "common field" of income taxation, Lord Macmillan's judgment in *Forbes* v. *Attorney-General for Manitoba*,[51] 1937, as well as Lord Rowlatt's judgment in *Judges* v. *Attorney-General for Saskatchewan*,[52] 1937, would also appear to reflect a co-operative presumption.[53]

[48]*A.-G. Can.* v. *A.-G. Ont.*, [1937] A.C. 355, at 366.
[49]See the arguments of counsel for the Dominion, at 356–57. "Unemployment insurance" was later added to s. 91 (as head 2A) by the British North America Act, 1940, 3–4 Geo. VI, c. 36.
[50]*A.-G. B.C.* v. *A.-G. Can.*, [1937] A.C. 377, at 389.
[51][1937] A.C. 260.
[52]53 T.L.R. 464.
[53]The 7 possible references to the Co-operation Doctrine are marked in col. D of the Analytical Table.

Chapter Eleven

THE CONSIGNMENT PROBLEM: III

1. The Dimensions Doctrine

Even in the judgment characterized by O'Connor as the first three-compartment decision, the Judicial Committee ascribed more than a residuary quality to the Peace, Order, and good Government clause. In fact, the *Local Prohibition* judgment[1] of 1896 might be considered the genesis of the "Dimensions Doctrine"; for Lord Watson accompanied his approval of the three-compartment view with a novel admission:

Their Lordships do not doubt that some matters, in their origin local and provincial, might attain such dimensions as to affect the body politic of the Dominion, and to justify the Canadian Parliament in passing laws for their regulation or abolition in the interest of the Dominion. But great caution must be observed in distinguishing between that which is local and provincial, and therefore within the jurisdiction of the provincial legislatures, and that which has ceased to be merely local or provincial, in such sense as to bring it within the jurisdiction of the Parliament of Canada. An Act restricting the right to carry weapons of offence, or their sale to young persons, within the province would be within the authority of the provincial legislature. But traffic in arms, or the possession of them under such circumstances as to raise a suspicion that they were to be used for seditious purposes, or against a foreign State, are matters which, their Lordships conceive, might be competently dealt with by the Parliament of the Dominion.

This admission would have enabled the federal parliament to make laws concerning "subjects" that are listed in section 92, but not enumerated in section 91. In Ambit terms, it would have thereby provided an excuse for extending the federal sphere of legislative authority at the expense of the provincial legislatures.

According to some critics, however, that excuse had already been exploited, in *Russell* v. *The Queen*,[2] 1882. For Sir Montague Smith not only upheld the Canada Temperance Act of 1878 because it "does not

[1] *A.-G. Ont.* v. *A.-G. Can.*, [1896] A.C. 348, at 361–62.
[2] 7 A.C. 829.

fall within any of the classes of subjects assigned exclusively to the Provincial Legislatures,"[3] but explicitly denied the relevance of heads 9, 13, and 16 of section 92.[4] Head 9 ("Shop, Saloon, Tavern, Auctioneer, and other Licences in order to the raising of a Revenue for Provincial, Local, or Municipal Purposes") was held not to apply for these reasons:

If the argument of the appellant that the power given to the Provincial Legislatures to raise a revenue by licenses prevents the Dominion Parliament from legislating with regard to any article or commodity which was or might be covered by such licenses were to prevail, the consequence would be that laws which might be necessary for the public good or the public safety could not be enacted at all. Suppose it were deemed to be necessary or expedient for the national safety, or for political reasons, to prohibit the sale of arms, or the carrying of arms, it could not be contended that a Provincial Legislature would have authority, by virtue of sub-sect. 9 (which alone is now under discussion), to pass any such law, nor, if the appellant's argument were to prevail, would the Dominion Parliament be competent to pass it, since such a law would interfere prejudicially with the revenue derived from licenses granted under the authority of the Provincial Legislature for the sale or the carrying of arms. Their Lordships think that the right construction of the enactment does not lead to any such inconvenient consequence. It appears to them that legislation of the kind referred to, though it might interfere with the sale or use of an article included in a license granted under sub-sect. 9, is not in itself legislation upon or within the subject of that sub-section, and consequently is not by reason of it taken out of the general power of the Parliament of the Dominion.

Head 13 was dismissed like this:

What Parliament is dealing with in legislation of this kind is not a matter in relation to property and its rights, but one relating to public order and safety. That is the primary matter dealt with, and though incidentally the free use of things in which men may have property is interfered with, that incidental interference does not alter the character of the law. Upon the same considerations, the Act in question cannot be regarded as legislation in relation to civil rights. In however large a sense these words are used, it could not have been intended to prevent the Parliament of Canada from declaring and enacting certain uses of property, and certain acts in relation to property, to be criminal and wrongful. Laws which make it a criminal offence for a man wilfully to set fire to his own house on the ground that such an act endangers the public safety, or to overwork his horse on the ground of cruelty to the animal, though affecting in some sense property and the right of a man to do as he pleases with his own, cannot properly be regarded as legislation in relation to property or to civil rights. Nor could a law which prohibited or restricted the sale or exposure of cattle having a contagious disease be so regarded. Laws of this nature designed for the promotion of public order, safety, or morals, and which subject those who contravene them

[3]*Ibid.*, at 842.
[4]*Ibid.*, at 837–41.

to criminal procedure and punishment, belong to the subject of public wrongs rather than to that of civil rights. They are of a nature which fall within the general authority of Parliament to make laws for the order and good government of Canada, and have direct relation to criminal law which is one of the enumerated classes of subjects assigned exclusively to the Parliament of Canada. It was said in the course of the judgment of this Board in the case of the *Citizens Insurance Company of Canada* v. *Parsons*, that the two sections (91 and 92) must be read together, and the language of one interpreted, and, where necessary, modified by that of the other. Few, if any, laws could be made by Parliament for the peace, order, and good government of Canada which did not in some incidental way affect property and civil rights; and it could not have been intended, when assuring to the provinces exclusive legislative authority on the subjects of property and civil rights, to exclude the Parliament from the exercise of this general power whenever any such incidental interference would result from it. The true nature and character of the legislation in the particular instance under discussion must always be determined, in order to ascertain the class of subject to which it really belongs. In the present case it appears to their Lordships, for the reasons already given, that the matter of the Act in question does not properly belong to the class of subjects "Property and Civil Rights" within the meaning of sub-sect. 13.

And the claims of head 16 were rejected as follows:

It was not, of course, contended for the appellant that the Legislature of New Brunswick could have passed the Act in question, which embraces in its enactments all the provinces; nor was it denied, with respect to this last contention that the Parliament of Canada might have passed an Act of the nature of that under discussion to take effect at the same time throughout the whole Dominion. Their Lordships understand the contention to be that, at least in the absence of a general law of the Parliament of Canada, the provinces might have passed a local law of a like kind, each for its own province, and that, as the prohibitory and penal parts of the Act in question were to come into force in those counties and cities only in which it was adopted in the manner prescribed, or, as it was said, "by local option," the legislation was in effect, and on its face, upon a matter of a merely local nature. . . .

Their Lordships cannot concur in this view. The declared object of Parliament in passing the Act is that there should be uniform legislation in all the provinces respecting the traffic in intoxicating liquors, with a view to promote temperance in the Dominion. Parliament does not treat the promotion of temperance as desirable in one province more than in another, but as desirable everywhere throughout the Dominion. The Act as soon as it was passed became a law for the whole Dominion, and the enactments of the first part, relating to the machinery for bringing the second part into force, took effect and might be put in motion at once and everywhere within it. It is true that the prohibitory and penal parts of the Act are only to come into force in any county or city upon the adoption of a petition to that effect by a majority of electors, but this conditional application of these parts of the Act does not convert the Act itself into legislation in relation to a merely local matter. The objects and scope of the legislation are still general, viz., to promote temperance by means of a uniform law throughout the Dominion.

2. The Emergency Doctrine

If the Canada Temperance Act had been upheld on the basis of the Peace, Order, and good Government clause alone, *Russell v. The Queen* might have established a precedent for the Dimensions Doctrine. This precedent, in turn, might have entailed not only an enlargement of the federal legislative sphere, but a departure from the three-compartment view. Accordingly, Lord Haldane felt it necessary to emphasize the exceptional circumstances in the *Russell* case, and thus the extraordinary requirements of the Dimensions Doctrine.[5] As a result of his efforts, it is now almost impossible to justify federal legislation affecting a "subject" enumerated in section 92 by invoking the Peace, Order, and good Government clause alone.

The Doctrine of Emergency Powers is consequently best explained, not as a separate theory, but as a modified version of the Dimensions Doctrine. This modification was begun in the *Insurance Act* judgment[6] of 1916. While recognizing that "the business of insurance is a very important one, which has attained to great dimensions in Canada," Lord Haldane insisted that the federal parliament may not pass legislation which "trenched upon" the exclusive authority conferred on the provincial legislatures by head 13 of section 92. He then elaborated this opinion in the *Board of Commerce* judgment[7] of 1922:

No doubt the initial words of s. 91 of the British North America Act confer on the Parliament of Canada power to deal with subjects which concern the Dominion generally, provided that they are not withheld from the powers of that Parliament to legislate, by any of the express heads in s. 92, untrammelled by the enumeration of special heads in s. 91. It may well be that the subjects of undue combination and hoarding are matters in which the Dominion has a great practical interest. In special circumstances, such as those of a great war, such an interest might conceivably become of such paramount and overriding importance as to amount to what lies outside the

5See *A.-G. Can. v. A.-G. Alta.*, [1916] 1 A.C. 588; *In re the Board of Commerce Act, 1919, and the Combines and Fair Prices Act, 1919*, [1922] 1 A.C. 191; *Fort Frances Pulp and Power Co. v. Manitoba Free Press Co.*, [1922] A.C. 695; *Toronto Electric Commissioners v. Snider*, [1925] A.C. 396.
6*A.-G. Can. v. A.-G. Alta.*, [1916] 1 A.C. 588, at 597.
7*In re the Board of Commerce Act, 1919, and the Combines and Fair Prices Act, 1919*, [1922] 1 A.C. 191, at 197–98.

heads in s. 92, and is not covered by them. The decision in *Russell* v. *The Queen* appears to recognize this as constitutionally possible, even in time of peace; but it is quite another matter to say that under normal circumstances general Canadian policy can justify interference, on such a scale as the statutes in controversy involve, with the property and civil rights of the inhabitants of the Provinces. It is to the Legislatures of the Provinces that the regulation and restriction of their civil rights have in general been exclusively confided, and as to these the Provincial Legislatures possess quasi-sovereign authority. It can, therefore, be only under necessity in highly exceptional circumstances, such as cannot be assumed to exist in the present case, that the liberty of the inhabitants of the Provinces may be restricted by the Parliament of Canada, and that the Dominion can intervene in the interests of Canada as a whole in questions such as the present one. For, normally, the subject-matter to be dealt with in the present case would be one falling within s. 92.

However, it was not until the *Fort Frances* judgment[8] of 1923, that the modification of Lord Watson's original admission—from the vague description of "such dimensions as to affect the body politic of the Dominion,"[9] through the more precise (and restrictive) definitions of "special circumstances," "highly exceptional circumstances," and "altogether exceptional situation"[10]—was carried to its most extreme state, and the test of "emergency" introduced. Having already recommended the consideration of "temporary purpose," as well as the practicability of attaining the end sought "without the co-operation of the Provincial Legislatures," Lord Haldane formulated this "new" doctrine as follows:[11]

It is clear that in normal circumstances the Dominion Parliament could not have so legislated as to set up the machinery of control over the paper manufacturers which is now in question. The recent decision of the Judicial Committee in the *Board of Commerce Case*, as well as earlier decisions, show that as the Dominion Parliament cannot ordinarily legislate so as to interfere with property and civil rights in the Provinces, it could not have done what the two statutes under consideration purport to do had the situation been normal. But it does not follow that in a very different case, such as that of sudden danger to social order arising from the outbreak of a great war, the Parliament of the Dominion cannot act under other powers which may well be implied in the constitution. The reasons given in the *Board of Commerce Case* recognize exceptional cases where such a power may be implied.

In the event of war, when the national life may require for its preservation the employment of very exceptional means, the provision of peace, order

[8]*Fort Frances Pulp and Power Co.* v. *Manitoba Free Press Co.*, [1923] A.C. 695.
[9]*A.-G. Ont.* v. *A.-G. Can.*, [1896] A.C. 348, at 361.
[10]*In re the Board of Commerce Act, 1919, and the Combines and Fair Prices Act, 1919*, [1922] 1 A.C. 191, at 197 and 198.
[11]*Fort Frances Pulp and Power Co.* v. *Manitoba Free Press Co.*, [1923] A.C. 695, at 703–5.

and good government for the country as a whole may involve effort on behalf of the whole nation, in which the interests of individuals may have to be subordinated to that of the community in a fashion which requires s. 91 to be interpreted as providing for such an emergency. The general control of property and civil rights for normal purposes remains with the Provincial Legislatures. But questions may arise by reason of the special circumstances of the national emergency which concern nothing short of the peace, order and good government of Canada as a whole.

The overriding powers enumerated in s. 91, as well as the general words at the commencement of the section, may then become applicable to new and special aspects which they cover of subjects assigned otherwise exclusively to the Provinces. It may be, for example, impossible to deal adequately with the new questions which arise without the imposition of special regulations on trade and commerce of a kind that only the situation created by the emergency places within the competency of the Dominion Parliament. It is proprietary [sic] and civil rights in new relations, which they do not present in normal times, that have to be dealt with; and these relations, which affect Canada as an entirety, fall within s. 91, because in their fullness they extend beyond what s. 92 can really cover. The kind of power adequate for dealing with them is only to be found in that part of the constitution which establishes power in the State as a whole. For it is not one that can be reliably provided for by depending on collective action of the Legislatures of the individual Provinces agreeing for the purpose. That the basic instrument on which the character of the entire constitution depends should be construed as providing for such centralised power in an emergency situation follows from the manifestation in the language of the Act of the principle that the instrument has among its purposes to provide for the State regarded as a whole, and for the expression and influence of its public opinion as such. This principle of a power so implied has received effect also in countries with a written and apparently rigid constitution such as the United States, where the strictly federal character of the national basic agreement has retained the residuary powers not expressly conferred on the Federal Government for the component States. The operation is all the more to be looked for in a constitution such as that established by the British North America Act, where the residuary powers are given to the Dominion Central Government; and the preamble of the statute declares the intention to be that the Dominion should have a constitution similar in principle to that of the United Kingdom.

Their Lordships, therefore, entertain no doubt that however the wording of ss. 91 and 92 may have laid down a framework under which, as a general principle, the Dominion Parliament is to be excluded from trenching on property and civil rights in the Provinces of Canada, yet in a sufficiently great emergency such as that arising out of war, there is implied a power to deal adequately with that emergency for the safety of the Dominion as a whole. The enumeration in s. 92 is not in any way repealed in the event of such an occurrence, but a new aspect of the business of Government is recognized as emerging, an aspect which is not covered or precluded by the general words in which powers are assigned to the Legislatures of the Provinces as individual units. Where such an exact line of demarcation will lie in such cases it may not be easy to lay down a priori, nor is it necessary.

148

For in the solution of the problem regard must be had to the broadened field covered, in case of exceptional necessity, by the language of s. 91, in which the interests of the Dominion generally are protected. As to those interests the Dominion Government, which in its Parliament represents the people as a whole, must be deemed to be left with considerable freedom to judge.

The difference between this argument and that developed in the *Board of Commerce* judgment consists in the extremity of the circumstances that are now required. Before the Peace, Order, and good Government clause can be held to validate federal legislation concerning "subjects" enumerated in section 92, the federal authorities must establish not merely "a sufficiently great emergency" and "exceptional necessity," but "sudden danger to the social order," the "preservation of national life," and "nothing short of the peace, order and good government of Canada as a whole." Indeed, the requisite circumstances are so extreme as to be practically confined to those produced by "a great war";[12] for as Lord Atkin showed in the "New Deal" judgments[13] of 1937, not even the Great Depression met the required standard. At the same time, Lord Haldane suggested that in estimating the extremity of a situation, the federal government should be "left with considerable freedom to judge"; and this suggestion was repeated by Lord Wright, in the *Japanese Canadians* judgment[14] of 1947.

The precision with which Lord Haldane described the consignment situation—in notable contrast to Lord Tomlin's ambiguous remarks, in the *Fish Canneries* judgment[15] of 1930—is also remarkable. "The enumeration in s. 92 is not in any way repealed in the event of such an occurrence"; nor does the federal parliament "trench on" (in the sense of "encroach on") the exclusive sphere of the provincial legislatures. Instead, the "field is broadened"—so that "matter" becomes of such "scope" as to place it outside section 92, and therefore inside the Peace, Order, and good Government clause. For "a new aspect of the business of Government is recognized as emerging, an aspect which is not covered or precluded by the general words in which powers are assigned to the Legislatures of the Provinces as individual units." In other words, the

---

[12]In the only two cases where the Emergency Doctrine was successfully invoked —*Fort Frances Pulp and Power Co.* v. *Manitoba Free Press Co.*, [1923] A.C. 695, and *Co-operative Committee on Japanese Canadians* v. *A.-G. Can.*, [1947] A.C. 87—the legislation passed by the federal parliament was said to have been impelled by wartime conditions.

[13]Especially, *A.-G. Can.* v. *A.-G. Ont.*, [1937] A.C. 326; *A.-G. Can.* v. *A.-G. Ont.*, [1937] A.C. 355; *A.-G. B.C.* v. *A.-G. Can.*, [1937] A.C. 377.

[14]*Co-operative Committee on Japanese Canadians* v. *A.-G. Can.*, [1947] A.C. 87, at 101–2.

[15]*A.-G. Can.* v. *A.-G. B.C.*, [1930] A.C. 111. See above, 51–52.

Aspect Principle is applied to the particular case of conflicts between the second and third compartments of the three-compartment view.

Finally, in the *Snider* judgment[16] of 1925, Lord Haldane put the finishing gloss on both *Russell* v. *The Queen* and the Dimensions Doctrine:

> It appears to their Lordships that it is not now open to them to treat *Russell* v. *The Queen* as having established the general principle that the mere fact that Dominion legislation is for the general advantage of Canada, or is such that it will meet a mere want which is felt throughout the Dominion, renders it competent if it cannot be brought within the heads enumerated specifically in s. 91. Unless that is so, if the subject matter falls within any of the enumerated heads in s. 92, such legislation belongs exclusively to Provincial competency. No doubt there may be cases arising out of some extraordinary peril to the national life of Canada, as a whole, such as the cases arising out of a war, where such legislation is required of an order that passes beyond the heads of exclusive Provincial competency. Such cases may be dealt with under the words at the commencement of s. 91, conferring general powers in relation to peace, order and good government, simply because such cases are not otherwise provided for. But instances of this, as was pointed out in the judgment in *Fort Frances Pulp and Power Co.* v. *Manitoba Free Press* are highly exceptional. Their Lordships think that the decision in *Russell* v. *The Queen* can only be supported to-day, not on the footing of having laid down an interpretation, such as has sometimes been invoked of the general words at the beginning of s. 91, but on the assumption of the Board, apparently made at the time of deciding the case of *Russell* v. *The Queen*, that the evil of intemperance at that time amounted in Canada to one so great and so general that at least for the period it was a menace to the national life of Canada so serious and pressing that the National Parliament was called on to intervene to protect the nation from disaster. An epidemic of pestilence might conceivably have been regarded as analogous. It is plain from the decision in the *Board of Commerce* case that the evil of profiteering could not have been so invoked, for Provincial powers, if exercised, were adequate to it. Their Lordships find it difficult to explain the decision in *Russell* v. *The Queen* as more than a decision of this order upon facts, considered to have been established at its date rather than upon general law.

3. Reversions to the Dimensions Doctrine

Lord Haldane's interpretation[17] of *Russell* v. *The Queen* was subsequently affirmed, and the Emergency Doctrine established, in a series of

[16]*Toronto Electric Commissioners* v. *Snider*, [1925] A.C. 396, at 412–13.
[17]For Lord Haldane's earlier attempts to distinguish *Russell* v. *The Queen*, see *A.-G. Can.* v. *A.-G. Alta.*, [1916] 1 A.C. 588, at 595–97, and *In re the Board of*

six judgments.[18] Meanwhile, however, the Judicial Committee occasionally reverted to a "dimensions" outlook. Lord Tomlin's second proposition, in the *Fish Canneries* judgment[19] of 1930, is an example:

(2) The general power of legislation conferred upon the Parliament of the Dominion by s. 91 of the Act in supplement of the power to legislate upon the subjects expressly enumerated must be strictly confined to such matters as are unquestionably of national interest and importance, and must not trench on any of the subjects enumerated in s. 92 as within the scope of the provincial legislation, unless these matters have attained such dimensions as to affect the body politic of the Dominion: see *Attorney-General for Ontario* v. *Attorney-General for the Dominion* [the *Local Prohibition* judgment of 1896].

Lord Tomlin thus suggested that a federal law which is made under the sole authority of the Peace, Order, and good Government clause may still be upheld on the basis of its "dimensions."[20] On the other hand, he ruled that in so far as the matters covered by the impugned Act were concerned, "it is not suggested that they are of national importance and have attained such dimensions as to affect the body politic of the Dominion."[21]

In the *Aeronautics* judgment[22] of 1932, Lord Sankey made a similar reference to the Dimensions Doctrine:

But while the Courts should be jealous in upholding the charter of the Provinces as enacted in s. 92 it must no less be borne in mind that the real object of the Act was to give the central Government those high functions and almost sovereign powers by which uniformity of legislation might be secured on all questions which were of common concern to all the Provinces as members of a constituent whole. . . .

To sum up, having regard (*a*) to the terms of s. 132; (*b*) to the terms of the Convention which covers almost every conceivable matter relating to aerial navigation; and (*c*) to the fact that further legislative powers in relation to aerial navigation reside in the Parliament of Canada by virtue of

---

Commerce Act, 1919, and the Combines and Fair Prices Act, 1919, [1922] 1 A.C. 191, at 197–98. He did not mention the *Russell* decision in *Fort Frances Pulp and Power Co.* v. *Manitoba Free Press Co.*, [1923] A.C. 695—though counsel for the Dominion did (at 697).

[18]Viz., *A.-G. Can.* v. *A.-G. Ont.*, [1937] A.C. 326; *A.-G. Can.* v. *A.-G. Ont.*, [1937] A.C. 355; *A.-G. B.C.* v. *A.-G. Can.*, [1937] A.C. 377; *Co-operative Committee on Japanese Canadians* v. *A.-G. Can.*, [1947] A.C. 87; *Canadian Pacific Railway* v. *A.-G. B.C.*, [1950] A.C. 122; *Canadian Federation of Agriculture* v. *A.-G. Que.*, [1951] A.C. 179.

[19]*A.-G. Can* v. *A.-G. B.C.*, [1930] A.C. 111, at 118.

[20]The looseness of his wording has already been criticized: see above, 51–52.

[21][1930] A.C. 111, at 122.

[22]*In re the Regulation and Control of Aeronautics in Canada*, [1932] A.C. 54, at 70–71 and 77.

s. 91, items 2, 5 and 7, it would appear that substantially the whole field of legislation in regard to aerial navigation belongs to the Dominion. There may be a small portion of the field which is not by virtue of specific words in the British North America Act vested in the Dominion; but neither is it vested by specific words in the Provinces. As to that small portion it appears to the Board that it must necessarily belong to the Dominion under its power to make laws for the peace, order and good government of Canada. Further, their Lordships are influenced by the facts that the subject of aerial navigation and the fulfilment of Canadian obligations under s. 132 are matters of national interest and importance; and that aerial navigation is a class of subject which has attained such dimensions as to affect the body politic of the Dominion.

But again the context must be noted: in the *Labour Conventions* judgment[23] of 1937, Lord Atkin not only identified the *ratio* in the *Aeronautics* judgment as consisting of an application of section 132, but declared that "the additional remark at the end of the judgment" [viz., Lord Sankey's "dimensions" comment] was "clearly *obiter*." It is therefore uncertain whether Lord Sankey's remarks in 1932 represent a reflection on the possibilities disclosed by Sir Montague Smith in 1882, and Lord Watson in 1896.

The *Radio* judgment[24] of 1932 appears to have been more definite. Lord Dunedin held that the International Radiotelegraph Convention "comes to the same thing" as "a treaty as is defined in s. 132"; for "the persons who might infringe some of the stipulations in the convention... must so to speak be kept in order by legislation and the only legislation that can deal with them all at once is Dominion legislation." He accordingly developed a "dimensions" argument:

In other words the argument of the Province comes to this: Go through all the stipulations of the convention and each one you can pick out which fairly falls within one of the enumerated heads of s. 91, that can be held to be appropriate for Dominion legislation; but the residue belongs to the Province under the head either of head 13 of s. 92—property and civil rights, or head 16—matters of a merely local or private nature in the Province.

Their Lordships cannot agree that the matter should be so dealt with. Canada as a Dominion is one of the signatories to the convention. In a question with foreign powers the persons who might infringe some of the stipulations in the convention would not be the Dominion of Canada as a whole but would be individual persons residing in Canada. These persons must so to speak be kept in order by legislation and the only legislation that can deal with them all at once is Dominion legislation. This idea of Canada as a Dominion being bound by a convention equivalent to a treaty with foreign

[23]*A.-G. Can.* v. *A.-G. Ont.*, [1937] A.C. 326, at 351.
[24]*In re the Regulation and Control of Radio Communication in Canada*, [1932] A.C. 304, at 311–12.

powers was quite unthought of in 1867. It is the outcome of the gradual development of the position of Canada vis-à-vis to the mother country, Great Britain, which is found in these later days expressed in the Statute of Westminster. It is not, therefore, to be expected that such a matter should be dealt with in explicit words in either s. 91 or s. 92. The only class of treaty which would bind Canada was thought of as a treaty by Great Britain, and that was provided for by s. 132. Being, therefore, not mentioned explicitly in either s. 91 or s. 92, such legislation falls within the general words at the opening of s. 91 which assign to the Government of the Dominion the power to make laws "for the peace order and good government of Canada in relation to all matters not coming within the classes of subjects by this Act assigned exclusively to the legislatures of the Provinces."

When he considered this decision in the *Labour Conventions* judgment[25] of 1937, Lord Atkin was concerned with denying its application to section 132. He thus decided, simply, that "the true ground of the decision was that the convention in that case dealt with classes of subjects which did not fall within the enumerated classes of subjects in s. 92, or even within the enumerated classes in s. 91." If the latter classes did not apply, however, the federal legislation must have been upheld because of the Peace, Order, and good Government clause; and if so, then (on the basis of Lord Dunedin's reasoning) the *Radio* judgment must represent an application of the Dimensions Doctrine. But whether or not this conclusion follows, Lord Atkin could not have intended such a construction himself. On the contrary, it would be difficult to find a firmer advocate of the Doctrine of Emergency Powers, or a stronger affirmation of that doctrine than his *Labour Conventions* judgment of 1937:

But the validity of the legislation under the general words of s. 91 was sought to be established not in relation to the treaty-making power alone, but also as being concerned with matters of such general importance as to have attained "such dimensions as to affect the body politic," and to have "ceased to be merely local or provincial," and to have "become matter of national concern." It is interesting to notice how often the words used by Lord Watson in *Attorney-General for Ontario* v. *Attorney-General for the Dominion* [the *Local Prohibition* judgment of 1896] have unsuccessfully been used in attempts to support encroachments on the Provincial legislative powers given by s. 92. They laid down no principle of constitutional law, and were cautious words intended to safeguard possible eventualities which no one at the time had any interest or desire to define. The law of Canada on this branch of constitutional law has been stated with such force and clarity by the Chief Justice in his judgment in the reference concerning the Natural Products Marketing Act dealing with the six Acts there referred to, that their Lordships abstain from stating it afresh. The Chief Justice,

---

[25]*A.-G. Can.* v. *A.-G. Ont.*, [1937] A.C. 326, at 352–53.

153

naturally from his point of view, excepted legislation to fulfil treaties. On this their Lordships have expressed their opinion. But subject to this, they agree with and adopt what was there said. They consider that the law is finally settled by the current of cases cited by the Chief Justice on the principles declared by him. It is only necessary to call attention to the phrases in the various cases, "abnormal circumstances," "exceptional conditions," "standard of necessity" (*Board of Commerce* case), "some extraordinary peril to the national life of Canada," "highly exceptional," "epidemic of pestilence" (*Snider's* case), to show how far the present case is from the conditions which may override the normal distribution of powers in ss. 91 and 92. The few pages of the Chief Justice's judgment will, it is to be hoped, form the locus classicus of the law on this point, and preclude further disputes.

Actually, the only unequivocal protest against Lord Haldane's views was made in the *Canada Temperance Act* judgment[26] of 1946. Expressly repudiating Lord Haldane's interpretation of *Russell* v. *The Queen*, Lord Simon not only disputed the validity of the Emergency Doctrine, but re-invoked Lord Watson's original Doctrine of Dimensions:

> But in 1925 *Russell's* case was commented on in a judgment of the Judicial Committee delivered by Lord Haldane in *Toronto Electric Commissioners* v. *Snider*, and it is on this comment that the present appellants largely rely in support of their contention that it was wrongly decided. . . .
>
> The first observation which their Lordships would make on this explanation of *Russell's* case is that the British North America Act nowhere gives power to the Dominion Parliament to legislate in matters which are properly to be regarded as exclusively within the competence of the provincial legislatures merely because of the existence of an emergency. Secondly, they can find nothing in the judgment of the Board in 1882 which suggests that it proceeded on the ground of emergency; there was certainly no evidence before that Board that one existed. The Act of 1878 was a permanent, not a temporary, Act, and no objection was raised to it on that account. In their Lordships' opinion the true test must be found in the real subject matter of the legislation: if it is such that it goes beyond local or provincial concern or interests and must from its inherent nature be the concern of the Dominion as a whole (as, for example, in the *Aeronautics* case and the *Radio* case), then it will fall within the competence of the Dominion Parliament as a matter affecting the peace, order and good government of Canada, though it may in another aspect touch on matters specially reserved to the provincial legislatures. War and pestilence, no doubt, are instances; so, too, may be the drink or drug traffic, or the carrying of arms. In *Russell* v. *The Queen*, Sir Montague Smith gave as an instance of valid Dominion legislation a law which prohibited or restricted the sale or exposure of cattle having a contagious disease. Nor is the validity of the legislation, when due to its inherent nature, affected because there may still be room for enactments by a provincial legislature dealing with an aspect of the same subject in so far as it specially affects that province.

---

[26]*A.-G. Ont.* v. *Canada Temperance Federation*, [1946] A.C. 193, at 205–6.

It is to be noticed that the Board in *Snider's* case nowhere said that *Russell* v. *The Queen* was wrongly decided. What it did was to put forward an explanation of what it considered was the ground of the decision, but in their Lordships' opinion the explanation is too narrowly expressed. True it is that an emergency may be the occasion which calls for the legislation, but it is the nature of the legislation itself, and not the existence of emergency, that must determine whether it is valid or not.

Here, at last, was a clear invitation to exploit the Aspect Doctrine; to adopt a flexible view of the Peace, Order, and good Government clause; and, perhaps, to expand the sphere of legislative authority available to the federal parliament.

4. Reaffirmations of the Emergency Doctrine

In the *Japanese Canadians* judgment[27] of 1947, however, Lord Wright reaffirmed "certain general matters of principle," on which "there is not, since the decision in *Fort Frances Pulp and Power Co.* v. *Manitoba Free Press Co.*, any room for dispute." These matters were admittedly re-shaped, if not relaxed; and in particular, Lord Haldane's suggestion,[28] concerning the need to leave the federal government "considerable freedom to judge," was not only reiterated, but extended. For the onus was now effectively placed on the courts, to show that an emergency did not exist, rather than on the federal authorities, to show that it did:

But very clear evidence that an emergency has not arisen, or that the emergency no longer exists, is required to justify the judiciary, even though the question is one of ultra vires, in overruling the decision of the Parliament of the Dominion that exceptional measures were required or were still required. To this may be added as a corollary that it is not pertinent to the judiciary to consider the wisdom or the propriety of the particular policy which is embodied in the emergency legislation. Determination of the policy to be followed is exclusively a matter for the Parliament of the Dominion and those to whom it has delegated its powers. Lastly, it should be observed that the judiciary are not concerned when considering a question of ultra vires with the question whether the executive will in fact be able to carry into effective operation the emergency provisions which the Parliament of the Dominion either directly or indirectly has made. It is unnecessary, therefore, for their Lordships to take into review or even to recount the particular circumstances obtaining within the Dominion that

---

[27]*Co-operative Committee on Japanese Canadians* v. *A.-G. Can.*, [1947] A.C. 87, at 101–2.
[28]See *Fort Frances Pulp and Power Co.* v. *Manitoba Free Press Co.*, [1923] A.C. 695, at 705.

led to the Orders in question or the arrangements made with a view to their execution.

Nevertheless, whatever re-shaping or relaxing Lord Wright might have accomplished, the fact remains that in the *Japanese Canadians* judgment of 1947, he definitely reaffirmed the Doctrine of Emergency Powers: "Again, if it be clear that an emergency has not arisen, or no longer exists, there can be no justification for the exercise of the exceptional powers. The rule of law as to the distribution of powers between the Parliament of the Dominion and the Parliaments of the Provinces comes into play."

This reaffirmation was repeated in the *Hours of Work Act*[29] and *Margarine*[30] judgments of 1950 and 1951. During the former, Lord Reid argued that the Dimensions Doctrine, as initiated by Lord Watson in the *Local Prohibition* judgment of 1896, must be interpreted in view of Lord Atkin's comments in the *Labour Conventions* judgment of 1937:

It is true that many matters which from one aspect are local and fall within the scope of s. 92 are nevertheless withdrawn from the competence of the provincial legislature, but that is by virtue of the terms of the last sentence of s. 91. That provision makes it clear that a matter which is truly one of civil rights in the province will be withdrawn from the provincial legislature and come within the competence of the Parliament of Canada if it comes within, or is necessarily incidental to, any of the subjects enumerated in s. 91 or expressly excepted from s. 92. But their Lordships can find neither principle nor authority to support the competence of the Parliament of Canada to legislate on a matter which clearly falls within the enumerated heads in s. 92 and cannot be brought within any of the enumerated heads in s. 91 merely because the activities of one of the parties concerned in the matter have created a unified system which is widespread and important in the Dominion. "It is interesting to notice how often the words used by Lord Watson in *Attorney-General for Ontario* v. *Attorney-General for the Dominion* have unsuccessfully been used in attempts to support encroachments on the provincial legislative powers given by s. 92. They laid down no principle of constitutional law, and were cautious words intended to safeguard possible eventualities which no one at the time had any interest or desire to define" (*Attorney-General for Canada* v. *Attorney-General for Ontario*). In their Lordships' judgment the present case is very different from any of those exceptional cases to which the words used by Lord Watson are applicable.

Similarly, in the *Margarine* judgment of 1951, Lord Morton of Henryton declared that the *Canada Temperance Act* decision of 1946 must "be considered with the words used by Lord Atkin when delivering the judgment of the Board in the *Labour Conventions* case": "Their Lord-

[29]*Canadian Pacific Railway* v. *A.-G. B.C.*, [1950] A.C. 122, at 140.
[30]*Canadian Federation of Agriculture* v. *A.-G. Que.*, [1951] A.C. 179, at 197–98.

ships think it sufficient to say, in answer to this third argument, that the prohibition now under consideration relates to civil rights within each of the provinces and that neither the facts set out in the Order of Reference, nor any other facts of which their Lordships could take judicial notice, lead to the conclusion that there exist in the present case the conditions which may override the normal distribution of powers in ss. 91 and 92."

The supremacy of the Emergency Doctrine was thus established. From the standpoint of the Consignment Problem, this meant that the Aspect Principle was not only confined within the framework of the three-compartment view, but practically restricted to very exceptional legislation: if a law even affects a matter coming within a subject enumerated in section 92, the argument that this law is also of "national dimensions" will probably not suffice to secure its consignment to the Peace, Order, and good Government clause. Furthermore, from the standpoint of the Ambit Problem, the Judicial Committee's "third compartment" became essentially residuary: the federal parliament may not extend its sphere of legislative authority through the Peace, Order, and good Government clause—any more than it may through heads 2, 3, and 27 of section 91, or section 132.[31]

[31]The 5 possible references to the Dimensions Doctrine, as well as the 12 to the Emergency Doctrine (the *Russell* case being considered as either), are marked in col. D of the Analytical Table.

Chapter Twelve

CONCLUSION

1. The Framework of the Scheme

Most accounts of the Judicial Committee's interpretative scheme tend not only to confuse evaluation and analysis, but to neglect interrelationships and implications. Yet the most remarkable feature of that scheme is the fundamental congruity of its major components. The Rule of Precedent, the Theory of Judicial Restraint, and the Federal Principle are all in harmony; the three-compartment view corresponds with them; the delimitation of the ambits of legislative authority is in accordance with both that view and those jurisprudential assumptions; and the Consignment Doctrines agree, essentially, with the rest. Such interrelationships might not always be logically necessary, or causally connected; but they do amount to at least a coincidental, and remarkable, congruity. This congruity might be remembered when any component of the Judicial Committee's interpretative scheme is either analysed or evaluated.

To retrace these interrelationships and implications: while the Emergency Doctrine has been generally criticized, much of this criticism is actually concerned with separable, if associated, questions. Thus Lord Haldane's attempt to distinguish *Russell* v. *The Queen*, and to base his new doctrine on an implied power, is not an integral part of the Doctrine of Emergency Powers. But even when it is disassociated from such questions, this doctrine still raises objections. Why was it necessary to constrain the general legislative authority of the federal parliament? What was the trouble with the Dimensions Doctrine?

The Judicial Committee has frequently been charged with harbouring a "provincial bias"; and there is no denying that some of the judges were preoccupied with the "principle of co-ordinate and independent authorities." Still, that is neither the most plausible, nor the most illuminating explanation of the Emergency Doctrine. For the urge to establish this doctrine can also be connected with the major components in the interpretative scheme—and above all, with the basic three-compartment

158

view and underlying jurisprudential assumptions. Unless some constraint were placed on the ability of the federal parliament to make laws under the sole authority of the Peace, Order, and good Government clause, the relative "priority" of section 92, the emphasis on "subject" rather than "scope," and the position of the courts with regard to the Rule of Precedent, as well as the Theory of Judicial Restraint, would all be threatened. The trouble with the Dimensions Doctrine was that it might have encouraged too great a reliance on "scope" considerations.

Both this alarm, and the consequent urge to confine the Dimensions Doctrine, make sense. The Doctrine of Emergency Powers might have led to such absurdities (if not "aspersions"[1]) as Lord Haldane's interpretation of the *Russell* judgment; and it was undeniably eccentric to apply this doctrine to legislation passed during a war, to deny its applicability to legislation needed for a depression, and then to vindicate its use as a means of promoting national temperance. Similarly, the Emergency Doctrine might have been enforced too rigorously; the estimations of the federal government (at least as to the existence of an emergency) might have received more attention; and the emergency notion might be difficult to justify in the first place. There might even be an argument in favour of reviving the Dimensions Doctrine—at least for cases like *Russell* v. *The Queen*, when a law is not "in relation to" (or concerned in its main aspect with) a "matter" coming within a "subject" enumerated in either section 91 or section 92. Nevertheless, whether these or any other criticisms are valid, is of secondary importance. It must first be realized that given the three-compartment view, as well as the Judicial Committee's jurisprudential assumptions, some confinement of the Dimensions Doctrine was necessary; and that the transformation of this doctrine into the Doctrine of Emergency Powers is correspondingly understandable. Both these doctrines must be looked at in context.

The same recommendation applies to the other set of Consignment Doctrines, involving conflicts between the heads of section 91 and section 92. Considered alone, the Doctrines of Ancillary Powers, Occupied Field, and Co-operation might well appear tortuous, if not "nonsensical." In the context of the three-compartment view, however, they seem not only reasonable, but unavoidable. It is rather the Aspect and Paramountcy "doctrines" that are difficult to appreciate. In fact, those "doctrines" do not appear practicable (especially from the standpoint of the Rule of Precedent and the Theory of Judicial Restraint) unless

---

[1]"On the fair fame of Canada": Anglin C.J.C., dissenting in *R.* v. *Eastern Terminal Elevator Co.*, [1925] S.C.R. 434, at 438.

159

they are viewed in three-compartment terms; and then they assume the form of general "principles," which must be translated into the particular "doctrines" of Ancillary Powers, Occupied Field, and Co-operation.

But it may not be concluded that the latter doctrines were developed because they serve to reinforce the framework of the Judicial Committee's interpretative scheme, The fact that they do would hardly have proved an obstacle to their development; but this is no proof that they must have been developed for such a purpose. On the contrary, the fact that they are meaningless out of context would seem to indicate that these three doctrines were developed because of, rather than for the sake of, the three-compartment view and the Judicial Committee's jurisprudential assumptions.

The first part of the Consignment Problem—that of determining the "matter" of a law, as opposed to classifying the law—appears to have been resolved within the same context. The critical consideration, when distinguishing between "in relation to" and "affecting," was the relative "weight" of the "subjects" concerned (that is, the position they occupied in sections 91 and 92). If a law were concerned with a "subject" enumerated in the heads of section 91, it was usually consigned to this first compartment. Alternatively, if the law were concerned with a "subject" enumerated in section 92, it was usually consigned to this second compartment. And if there were a conflict between the second compartment and the third, then (because of the contrast between the particular and general language of these two compartments, as well as the inclusive character of head 13) section 92 usually prevailed over the Peace, Order, and Good Government clause.[2]

However, the determining of "matter" was not accomplished solely by considering the relative weight of the "subjects" concerned; for the "object" of an impugned law also had to be taken into account. Accordingly, the Judicial Committee not only distinguished between "declared" and "legal" objects, but drew a line, consonant with its judicial sphere, between "immediate" and "consequential" effects. These distinctions, in turn, required decisions as to "evidential value"; and again it was "subject," and not "scope," that came to be the vital consideration.

The solution to the second part of the Consignment Problem—that of classifying laws (or characterizing legislation concerned with "subjects" that overlap sections 91 and 92)—is also based on the definition of "matter" in terms of "subject," rather than "scope." And the results of this definition are likewise consistent with the federal principle of

[2]That is, unless it were held that circumstances were sufficiently exceptional to warrant the invocation of "scope" considerations.

"co-ordinate and independent authorities." But again, it may not be concluded that either the establishment of an effective power to restrain federal legislation, or the presumption in favour of the validity of provincial statutes, was the cause of that definition. For such a conclusion not only reverses the probable course of events, but overlooks the consistency between those results and the urge to develop a system of precedents, while exercising judicial restraint. The solutions to the Consignment Problem must also be considered in the context of the three-compartment view and the Judicial Committee's jurisprudential assumptions.

As for the solutions to the Ambit Problem, the very emphasis on construing the various provisions—so as to restrict the ambits of those that overlap—was the outcome of a three-compartment presumption: that these provisions indicate "subjects" which are assigned exclusively to one legislative authority or the other. Moreover, the constrictive interpretation of the Peace, Order, and good Government clause, together with the expansive interpretation of section 92, connects the Ambit and Compartment Problems to the question of jurisprudential assumptions. If section 92 were "prior" to the Peace, Order, and good Government clause, there would be a tendency to fit as much legislation as possible into the former, before resorting to the latter. At the same time, this tendency would accord with a preference for classifying laws on the basis of "subject," rather than "scope"; and that classification, in turn, would facilitate the establishment of precedents, as well as the exercise of judicial restraint. Finally, a tendency to expand section 92 at the expense of the Peace, Order, and good Government clause would probably serve to strengthen the authority of the provincial legislatures—though once again, this does not prove that the tendency must have been an effect, rather than a cause.

The particular wording of section 92, as contrasted with the general wording of the Peace, Order, and good Government clause, would have the same result. According to the Rules of Statutory Interpretation (which were applied partly because the Theory of Judicial Restraint was accepted) particular language should be given precedence. The expansion of section 92 was no doubt also induced by the nature of the "subjects" it contains: thus section 92(13), "Property and Civil Rights in the Province," not only cross-sections practically all the other heads in sections 91 and 92, but would be concerned in almost any federal law passed under the sole authority of the Peace, Order, and good Government clause. Nonetheless, because it is "subject" that counts, and also because section 92 is "prior" to the Peace, Order, and good

161

Government clause, such federal legislation would normally be characterized as "in relation to" a matter coming within section 92, as opposed to the Peace, Order, and good Government clause.

Short of discarding the three-compartment view and relinquishing the Judicial Committee's jurisprudential assumptions (which is what current orthodoxy entails), there would seem to be three main ways of enlarging the sphere of federal legislative authority: by expanding the Peace, Order, and good Government clause; by expanding the heads of section 91; and by contracting section 92. Because of its third-compartment status, however, the Peace, Order, and good Government clause could be appreciably expanded only by characterizing legislation in terms of "scope," rather than "subject." And the Emergency Doctrine denies that such a characterization is compatible with either the three-compartment view or the Judicial Committee's jurisprudential assumptions. Furthermore, while that doctrine might have been enforced too rigorously—and while there might even be a case for reviving the Dimensions Doctrine in certain circumstances—it seems advisable, in view of all the implications involved, to keep the primary emphasis on "subject." Similarly, the most expansible heads of section 91 can be stretched only so far; and while heads 2, 3, and 27, in particular, might be given a more liberal construction, the collocation arguments show that this way of enlarging the sphere of federal legislative authority is also limited. The most hopeful remedy would therefore appear to be the third: not to expand the first or third compartments, but to contract the second—or in other words, to find some way of restricting the ambit of head 13 of section 92, "Property and Civil Rights in the Province."

Suppose this head referred to section 92(16), "Generally all Matters of a merely local or private Nature in the Province." On the authority of the *Local Prohibition* judgment[3] of 1896 (as interpreted in the *Manitoba Liquor Act* judgment[4] of 1902), section 92(16) might then be assumed to possess a fourth-compartment status. Because a fourth compartment should give way to a third, conflicts between this head and the Peace, Order, and good Government clause might accordingly be resolved in favour of the latter. As much legislation as possible might thus be consigned to section 92(16), rather than to section 92(13). And that is why certain "federalists" have tried to promote the claims of head 16 of section 92.[5]

---

[3]*A.-G. Ont.* v. *A.-G. Can.*, [1896] A.C. 348.
[4]*A.-G. Man.* v. *Manitoba Licence Holders' Association*, [1902] A.C. 73, at 78.
[5]Especially with regard to taxation: see Kennedy and Wells, *Taxing Power*, 152, and Clokie, *Canadian Government, passim*.

It is doubtful, however, whether a successful promotion of this head would make much difference. For the whole argument depends on the fourth-compartment assumption; and that is not easy to establish. Apart from the very questionable authority of Lord Macnaghten's interpretation, the only basis for this assumption is the general wording of section 92(16)—while in opposition, there is not only the "linguistic principle," but also the structural fact that head 16 is on exactly the same compartment footing as the other heads in section 92 (that is, on a prior footing with regard to the Peace, Order, and good Government clause). Is it so surprising that the latter argument prevailed?

Alternatively, the ambit of section 92(13) might be restricted by reference to section 94. According to that section, while the federal parliament "may make Provision for the Uniformity of all or any of the Laws relative to Property and Civil Rights in Ontario, Nova Scotia, and New Brunswick," it may not do so (by omission) in Quebec. This exclusion of French Canada, particularly when contrasted with the inclusion of Quebec in sections 93 and 95, suggests that the phrase "Property and Civil Rights," as used in section 92(13), has a cultural significance: in the words of the Rowell-Sirois Commission,[6] it "was not designed to express genuinely local as against national interests nor to fix the spheres of the different levels of government but rather to protect regional interests only in so far as they were specifically cultural in character." Such an interpretation in turn suggests the following implications:

Accordingly, the phrase in question would include matters of civil law concerning the relations of citizen and citizen, such as ownership, transfer and various dealings in property, inheritance and succession by will, rights arising from personal status, such as minority and capacity to make contracts, and from the intimate domestic relations of the family. It would include a variety of other matters of private law but it would not include a number of matters inextricably bound up with the public law such as nation-wide regulation of industry and trade. Still less could it include social insurance which had formed no part of either French or English law and the idea of which was unknown to those who framed the British North America Act.

Even if the cultural assumption were granted, however, why should "Property and Civil Rights" cover only select parts of French civil law? And how, and by whom, would the relevant parts be selected? In any case, that is not the only way in which sections 92(13) and 94 can

---

[6]Canada, Royal Commission on Dominion-Provincial Relations, *Report*, Book I, 34–35. See also Laskin, *Constitutional Law*, 432; the *O'Connor Report*, Annex 1, 121–23; Scott, *CBR*, XX (1942), 525.

be related. On the contrary, if there is no reason (either because of the language itself, or because of any other part of the British North America Act) to restrict the meaning of the phrase "Property and Civil Rights," as used in section 94, then the omission of Quebec from this section would seem to imply that the phrase should be interpreted as widely there as it is in Ontario, Nova Scotia, and New Brunswick. And that is what the Judicial Committee decided: "in this statute [viz., the Quebec Act of 1774] the words 'property' and 'civil rights' are plainly used in their largest sense; and there is no reason for holding that in the statute under discussion they are used in a different and narrower one."[7]

But what of the phrase "in the Province"? Could this mean "in a provincial aspect"? If so, then any law that affected property and civil rights in a national aspect might be consigned to the federal parliament for the same reason that the Canada Temperance Act was probably consigned in the *Russell* judgment of 1882—because it did not come within any of the "subjects" enumerated in section 91 or section 92. Now this might be a way of enlarging the sphere of federal authority; and at least it seems more practicable than the distorted references to section 92(16) or section 94, let alone to O'Connor's two-compartment view or the "constituent statute argument." For those references violate not only the Judicial Committee's interpretative scheme, but also, as will now be shown, the most plausible reading of the British North America Act itself. The term "Property and Civil Rights" might thus be given the wide meaning that both the collocation argument and historical usage imply, and at the same time be restricted by reason of its modifying phrase, "in the Province."

Anyway, it would seem that the Judicial Committee's solutions to the Consignment and Ambit Problems were fundamentally determined by its resolution of the Compartment Problem, and in terms of its jurisprudential assumptions. For those solutions were based on the three-compartment view, the Rule of Precedent, and the Theory of Judicial Restraint. It follows that none of these basic components can be understood, or evaluated, without some appreciation of the interrelationships and implications of them all. This is the general answer to the critics of the Judicial Committee's interpretative scheme: the components of that scheme should be related to one another, and so examined in context.

---

[7] *Citizens Insurance Co.* v. *Parsons* (1881), 7 A.C. 96, at 111. See also Mignault, *La Revue du Droit*, XVI (1938), 577–79.

2. Some Evaluative Considerations

To comment on this context: if neither the expansion of the Peace, Order, and good Government clause, nor the expansion of the heads of section 91, nor even the contraction of section 92 can produce a sufficient enlargement of the federal legislative sphere, then the only way left would be to discard the three-compartment view. While O'Connor recognized this consequence, however, neither his analysis nor his evaluation seems adequate. This study has been mainly concerned with the first half of the question; but an evaluative comment might now be added, if only as a summing up.[8]

O'Connor makes a strong case for concluding that the deeming paragraph of section 91 refers to head 16 of section 92 only. The wording of the former ("Class of Matters of a local or private Nature") is almost identical with that of the latter ("Generally all Matters of a merely local or private Nature in the Province"). The use of the singular number, "class," seems an inappropriate way of referring to more than one class. And if that were the reference, it would be the sole instance of such use: the introductory words of section 91, for instance, refer to the "*Classes* of Subjects by this Act assigned exclusively to the Legislatures of the Provinces"; section 91(29) refers to "Such *Classes* of Subjects as are expressly excepted in the Enumeration of the *Classes* of Subjects by this Act assigned exclusively to the Legislatures of the Provinces"; and in the deeming paragraph, the ambiguous "Class of Matters" is said to be "comprised in the Enumeration of the *Classes* of Subjects by this Act assigned exclusively to the Legislatures of the Provinces."[9]

It could be replied that if "comprised in" meant "consisting of" (rather than "included within"), the reference in the deeming paragraph would be to all the heads of section 92. Alternatively, if the subject of the verb "comprised" (with either meaning) were "Matters," rather than "Class," the same effect would be achieved. But in either case, the above instances are all concerned with "Classes of *Subjects*," whereas the expression in question is "Class of *Matters*." Thus the word "Classes," as used in those instances, might have a distinguishing denotation;

---

[8]These considerations should be read in conjunction with the previous analyses of the Rules of Statutory Interpretation and the Compartment Problem: see above, chap. 1, sec. 2 and chap. 3, secs. 2 and 3.

[9]In addition, and possibly by way of analogy, the heads of both ss. 91 and 92 are referred to as the "*Classes* of Subjects next herein-after enumerated."

the word "Class," as used in relation to "Matters," might merely connote "group"; and the subject of the verb "comprised" might well be "Matters." Even so, on re-reading the deeming paragraph, it seems difficult to avoid the conclusion reached by Sir Montague Smith (and O'Connor): that "this paragraph applies in its grammatical construction only to No. 16 of sect. 92."[10]

O'Connor's other contentions are not so serious. It is hardly an argument to suggest that if the draftsman had intended to refer the deeming paragraph to all the heads of section 92, "he would have struck out of the paragraph the words 'the class of matters of a local or private nature comprised in the enumeration' and substituted the one simple word 'any'."[11] Moreover, to claim that unless it refers to head 16 only, this paragraph would duplicate a purpose already served by the *non obstante* clause, is not merely to assume that the framers considered the latter clause sufficiently clear, but to ignore all the dispute that has been provoked by its ambiguity. But that, of course, is exactly what O'Connor wants: if he could force the argument on to the ground of the introductory words of section 91, he could exploit this ambiguous use of the *non obstante* clause.

The crucial difference between the wording of the deeming paragraph and the second part of these introductory words (the part starting after the first semi-colon, with the phrase "and for greater Certainty") is that the former employs "enacting" terms ("shall not be deemed"), whereas the latter is in declaratory form ("it is hereby declared," and "extends"). O'Connor's effort to restrict the deeming paragraph to section 92(16) is based on this difference. If that paragraph refers to section 92 as a whole, the priority of the heads of section 91 over section 92 would be enacted—and this enactment would be confined to those heads. On the other hand, if the deeming paragraph refers to section 92(16) only, then the only enacting words in section 91 would be the very first ("It shall be lawful")—which cover the Peace, Order, and good Government clause in addition to the heads. The division of section 91 into two parts of unequal weight would consequently depend on a declaratory, instead of an enacted, provision.

This declaratory provision might in turn be re-interpreted on the basis of the other two-compartment arguments. Since the Rules of Statutory Interpretation state that "punctuation forms no part of the Act," the first semi-colon may be disregarded. The *non obstante* clause could therefore refer back to the Peace, Order, and good Government

[10]*Citizens Insurance Co.* v. *Parsons* (1881), 7 A.C. 96, at 108.
[11]*O'Connor Report*, Annex 1, 44.

clause; and in fact, the enacted equality of the latter clause and the heads of section 91 makes such a reference mandatory. The Peace, Order, and good Government clause is also expressly protected against any subtraction: the heads are listed merely "for greater Certainty, but not so as to restrict the Generality of the foregoing Terms of this Section." Above all, the exclusivity ascribed to the "Legislative Authority of the Parliament of Canada" (at the end of the introductory words) must refer to the Peace, Order, and good Government clause as well as to the heads. For "it *necessarily* follows that the powers of sections 91 and 92 are *naturally exclusive*, because, if not, section 92 does not *as between sections 91 and 92* contain all the provincial powers, for some of them are still in the only place where they *can be*, in section 91, which is, however, a place where they *cannot be*—which is nonsense."[12]

But what of the stipulation "not coming within the Classes of Subjects by this Act assigned exclusively to the Legislatures of the Provinces"? This seems the weakest point in O'Connor's two-compartment view. If the *non obstante* clause refers to the Peace, Order, and good Government clause, the federal parliament is enabled to make laws concerning any "subject"—including those enumerated in section 92. Yet the federal legislative power is expressly confined to "Matters" outside that section. Admittedly, this incompatibility could be avoided by interpreting the confining stipulation as a general prohibition (against federal legislation that is not of national import). However, such a reconciliation is dependent on the definition of "Matters" in terms of "scope," rather than "subject"; and even then the confining stipulation might appear strained.

Actually, the entire two-compartment view seems a contorted interpretation of sections 91 and 92. To begin with the "declaratory" argument, the division of section 91 into two parts of unequal weight would be more demonstrable if the priority of the heads of section 91 were enacted; and that is probably why the Judicial Committee tried to support the three-compartment view on the basis of the deeming paragraph. But what is "enacted" in the introductory words of section 91? If it is everything in those words, then the declaratory provision must be enacted too—so that that priority of the heads would be enacted, though indirectly, after all. On the other hand, if the "enacting" covers only the grant of legislative authority, then nothing is "enacted" concerning priority considerations—which may therefore be taken as "declared".

In any event, the fact that this priority is at least declared cannot be

---

[12]*Ibid.*, 84–85.

simply disregarded. A semi-colon is employed, with grammatical significance, if nothing more, to separate the two "parts" of section 91. The *non obstante* clause follows the semi-colon, and is affixed to the declaratory part. The only use of the term "exclusive," with regard to the federal legislative authority, is found in that declaratory part. The companionable use of "exclusively," in relation to provincial legislative authority, gives point to the position 'of the *non obstante* clause (which serves to ensure federal control over certain "subjects"). The exclusiveness of the provincial legislative authority is affirmed in no less than four separate places. And the classes of subjects enumerated in section 91 are so precise, so determinate, and so extensive as to make a merely illustrative purpose difficult to comprehend.

As for the other pair of two-compartment arguments, the exclusivity one is unintelligible. How can an open class be defined except by the definition of the closed? It would be meaningless to assert the exclusiveness of the federal parliament's total grant of legislative authority; the only sensible question is whether the heads of section 91 are a closed class. Nor is that the only, or even the most likely meaning of the word "restrict." For while this could mean a restriction in "quality" (signifying that the heads of section 91 are of no greater "weight" than the Peace, Order, and good Government clause), it could also mean a restriction in "quantity" (signifying that the heads of section 91 do not comprise all the powers of the federal parliament). And the latter seems the likelier meaning; for the word "restrict" would then mean that the Peace, Order, and good Government clause contains the residuary powers that are left over after the "exclusive" powers, defined by the two lists of enumerated "subjects," are subtracted from the total grant of legislative authority.

In short, O'Connor's two-compartment view fails to account for all the features of sections 91 and 92, and especially for the confinement of the federal power to "Matters not coming within the Classes of Subjects by this Act assigned exclusively to the Legislatures of the Provinces." In contrast, the Judicial Committee's three-compartment view not only manages to account for every one of those features, but is much more straightforward. In section 91 it is enacted that the federal parliament shall have all legislative authority not given exclusively to the provincial legislatures. It is then declared that legislative authority over the following list of "subjects" belongs exclusively to the federal parliament (notwithstanding any apparent overlapping of the "subjects" assigned to the provincial legislatures in section 92). However, this enumeration does not exhaust the federal legislative authority; for that

168

authority also includes the residuary power contained in the Peace, Order, and good Government clause. This is surely the first, and most natural reading of section 91.

It is also the more inclusive. The enacting words of section 91 might be interpreted as either covering everything that follows, or granting the federal parliament all authority not assigned to the provincial legislatures. The confining stipulation is given full effect. The exclusiveness of the provincial legislative authority, affirmed in four separate places, is assured. The use of the semi-colon becomes at least grammatically meaningful. The provision "and for greater Certainty" assumes its normal distinguishing implication. The caution "but not so as to restrict the Generality of the foregoing Terms" can be easily fitted to the other stipulations (by presuming a "quantity" construction of the word "restrict"). The declaratory remark acquires significance. The position of the *non obstante* clause is understandable. The "exclusive" description of the heads of section 91 seems apt. And all these features can be so interpreted whether the deeming paragraph remains ambiguous, or whether it is applied to section 92(16) only. Despite O'Connor, the Judicial Committee's three-compartment view remains the most plausible interpretation of sections 91 and 92, as well as the most consistent framework for interpreting the distribution of legislative powers in the British North America Act.

This does not mean that it is an entirely satisfactory framework, or that no improvements could be made. In particular, the Dimensions Doctrine might be partially revived; heads 2, 3, and 27 of section 91 might be given a more liberal construction; and the ambit of section 92(13)—especially the significance of the phrase "in the Province" —might be reassessed. But those are very different remedies from the orthodox attempts to undercut the three-compartment view, or more drastically, to discard the Judicial Committee's jurisprudential assumptions. Before resorting to such operations, one might try less dangerous treatments; and before feasible gains are reckoned, it seems only sensible to calculate present advantages, and possible losses.

To comment on the Judicial Committee's jurisprudential assumptions would lead to a discussion that is beyond the scope of this study. It might be noted, however, that the constitutent statute argument, so widely accepted today, is by no means conclusive. On the contrary, when it is related to the Rule of Precedent and the Theory of Judicial Restraint, this argument appears seriously deficient. There is still something to be said for stability and certainty in the law. And it might also be asked, particularly in the case of a federation like Canada, whether

169

political problems—including those that result from an extension of governmental activities, and a consequent need to readjust the federal balance—are not best resolved by political means.

But regardless of how they are evaluated, the Rule of Precedent and the Theory of Judicial Restraint should be at least remembered. Moreover, this requirement seems especially necessary, and has been notably lacking, in accounts of the Judicial Committee's interpretative scheme. For the Judicial Committee acted as the final court of appeal in Canadian constitutional cases during a period when those jurisprudential assumptions were at the height of their influence. Even if it were deliberately decided, in full awareness of all the factors and possibilities involved, that some "liberalization" was (or is) necessary, no account of the Board's activities between 1873 and 1960 should disregard this situation. In any case, whatever its practical defects, the Judicial Committee's interpretative scheme for the British North America Act is both fairly certain and generally congruous. That does not seem either a minor consideration or a mean achievement.

APPENDIXES

Appendix A

THE BRITISH NORTH AMERICA ACT, 1867*

Consolidated with amendments as of January 1, 1957

AN ACT for the Union of Canada, Nova Scotia, and New Brunswick, and the Government thereof; and for Purposes connected therewith.

29th March, 1867

WHEREAS the Provinces of Canada, Nova Scotia, and New Brunswick have expressed their Desire to be federally united into One Dominion under the Crown of the United Kingdom of Great Britain and Ireland, with a Constitution similar in Principle to that of the United Kingdom:

And whereas such a Union would conduce to the Welfare of the Provinces and promote the Interests of the British Empire:

And whereas on the Establishment of the Union by Authority of Parliament it is expedient, not only that the Constitution of the Legislative Authority in the Dominion be provided for, but also that the Nature of the Executive Government therein be declared:

And whereas it is expedient that Provision be made for the eventual Admission into the Union of other Parts of British North America:[1]

I. *Preliminary*

1.   This Act may be cited as The British North America Act, 1867.   Short title

2.   Repealed.[2]

*30 & 31 Vict. c. 3. This consolidation was prepared by Elmer A. Driedger, Q.C., B.A., LL.B., Assistant Deputy Minister and Parliamentary Counsel, Department of Justice, Ottawa.

[1]The enacting clause was repealed by the *Statute Law Revision Act, 1893*, 56–57 Vict., c. 14 (U.K.). It read as follows:

Be it therefore enacted and declared by the Queen's Most Excellent Majesty, by and with the Advice and Consent of the Lords Spiritual and Temporal, and Commons, in this present Parliament assembled, and by the Authority of the same, as follows:

[2]Section 2, repealed by the *Statute Law Revision Act, 1893*, 56–57 Vict., c. 14 (U.K.), read as follows:

2. The Provisions of this Act referring to Her Majesty the Queen extend also to the Heirs and Successors of Her Majesty, Kings and Queens of the United Kingdom of Great Britain and Ireland.

II. *Union*

3. It shall be lawful for the Queen, by and with the Advice of Her Majesty's Most Honourable Privy Council, to declare by Proclamation that, on and after a Day therein appointed, not being more than Six Months after the passing of this Act, the Provinces of Canada, Nova Scotia, and New Brunswick shall form and be One Dominion under the Name of Canada; and on and after that Day those Three Provinces shall form and be One Dominion under that Name accordingly.³

    Declaration of Union

4. Unless it is otherwise expressed or implied, the Name Canada shall be taken to mean Canada as constituted under this Act.⁴

    Construction of subsequent Provisions of Act

5. Canada shall be divided into Four Provinces, named Ontario, Quebec, Nova Scotia, and New Brunswick.⁵

    Four Provinces

³The first day of July, 1867, was fixed by proclamation dated May 22, 1867.

⁴Partially repealed by the *Statute Law Revision Act, 1893*, 56–57 Vict., c. 14 (U.K.). As originally enacted the section read as follows:

4. The subsequent Provisions of this Act shall, unless it is otherwise expressed or implied, commence and have effect on and after the Union, that is to say, on and after the Day appointed for the Union taking effect in the Queen's Proclamation; and in the same Provisions, unless it is otherwise expressed or implied, the Name Canada shall be taken to mean Canada as constituted under this Act.

⁵Canada now consists of ten provinces (Ontario, Quebec, Nova Scotia, New Brunswick, Manitoba, British Columbia, Prince Edward Island, Alberta, Saskatchewan and Newfoundland) and two territories (the Yukon Territory and the Northwest Territories).

The first territories added to the Union were Rupert's Land and the North-Western Territory, (subsequently designated the Northwest Territories), which were admitted pursuant to section 146 of the *British North America Act, 1867* and the *Rupert's Land Act, 1868*, 31–32 Vict., c. 105 (U.K.), by Order in Council of June 23, 1870, effective July 15, 1870. Prior to the admission of these territories the Parliament of Canada enacted the *Act for the temporary Government of Rupert's Land and the North-Western Territory when united with Canada* (32–33 Vict., c. 3), and the *Manitoba Act* (33 Vict., c. 3), which provided for the formation of the Province of Manitoba.

British Columbia was admitted into the Union pursuant to section 146 of the *British North America Act, 1867*, by Order in Council of May 16, 1871, effective July 20, 1871.

Prince Edward Island was admitted pursuant to section 146 of the *British North America Act, 1867*, by Order in Council of June 26, 1873, effective July 1, 1873.

On June 29, 1871, the United Kingdom Parliament enacted the *British North America Act, 1871* (34–35 Vict., c. 28) authorizing the creation of additional provinces out of territories not included in any province. Pursuant to this statute, the Parliament of Canada enacted *The Alberta Act*, (July 20, 1905, 4–5 Edw. VII, c. 3) and *The Saskatchewan Act*, (July 20, 1905, 4–5 Edw. VII, c. 42), providing for the creation of the provinces of Alberta and Saskatchewan respectively. Both these Acts came into force on Sept. 1, 1905.

Meanwhile, all remaining British possessions and territories in North America and the islands adjacent thereto, except the colony of

6. The Parts of the Province of Canada (as it exists at the passing of this Act) which formerly constituted respectively the Provinces of Upper Canada and Lower Canada shall be deemed to be severed, and shall form Two separate Provinces. The Part which formerly constituted the Province of Upper Canada shall constitute the Province of Ontario; and the Part which formerly constituted the Province of Lower Canada shall constitute the Province of Quebec.

Provinces of Ontario and Quebec

7. The Provinces of Nova Scotia and New Brunswick shall have the same Limits as at the passing of this Act.

Provinces of Nova Scotia and New Brunswick

8. In the general Census of the Population of Canada which is hereby required to be taken in the Year One thousand eight hundred and seventy-one, and in every Tenth Year thereafter, the respective Populations of the Four Provinces shall be distinguished.

Decennial Census

III. *Executive Power*

9. The Executive Government and Authority of and over Canada is hereby declared to continue and be vested in the Queen.

Declaration of Executive Power in the Queen

10. The Provisions of this Act referring to the Governor General extend and apply to the Governor General for the Time being of Canada, or other the Chief Executive Officer or Administrator for the Time being carrying on the Government of Canada, on behalf and in the Name of the Queen, by whatever Title he is designated.

Application of Provisions referring to Governor General

11. There shall be a Council to aid and advise in the Government of Canada, to be styled the Queen's Privy Council for Canada; and the Persons who are to be Members of that Council shall be from Time to Time chosen and summoned by the Governor General and sworn in as Privy Councillors, and Members thereof may be from Time to Time removed by the Governor General.

Constitution of Privy Council for Canada

Newfoundland and its dependencies, were admitted into the Canadian Confederation by Order in Council dated July 31, 1880.

The Parliament of Canada added portions of the Northwest Territories to the adjoining provinces in 1912 by *The Ontario Boundaries Extension Act*, 2 Geo. V, c. 40, *The Quebec Boundaries Extension Act, 1912*, 2 Geo. V, c. 45 and *The Manitoba Boundaries Extension Act, 1912*, 2 Geo. V. c. 32, and further additions were made to Manitoba by *The Manitoba Boundaries Extension Act, 1930*, 20–21 Geo. V, c. 28.

The Yukon Territory was created out of the Northwest Territories in 1898 by *The Yukon Territory Act*, 61 Vict., c. 6, (Canada).

Newfoundland was added on March 31, 1949, by the *British North America Act, 1949*, (U.K.), 12–13 Geo. VI, c. 22, which ratified the Terms of Union between Canada and Newfoundland.

12. All Powers, Authorities, and Functions which under any Act of Parliament of the United Kingdom of Great Britain and Ireland, or of the Legislature of Upper Canada, Lower Canada, Canada, Nova Scotia, or New Brunswick, are at the Union vested in or exerciseable by the respective Governors or Lieutenant Governors of those Provinces, with the Advice, or with the Advice and Consent, of the respective Executive Councils thereof, or in conjunction with those Councils, or with any Number of Members thereof, or by those Governors or Lieutenant Governors individually, shall, as far as the same continue in existence and capable of being exercised after the Union in relation to. the Government of Canada, be vested in and exerciseable by the Governor General, with the Advice or with the Advice and Consent of or in conjunction with the Queen's Privy Council for Canada, or any Members thereof, or by the Governor General individually, as the Case requires, subject nevertheless (except with respect to such as exist under Acts of the Parliament of Great Britain or of the Parliament of the United Kingdom of Great Britain and Ireland) to be abolished or altered by the Parliament of Canada.[6]

All Powers under Acts to be exercised by Governor General with Advice of Privy Council, or alone

13. The Provisions of this Act referring to the Governor General in Council shall be construed as referring to the Governor General acting by and with the Advice of the Queen's Privy Council for Canada.

Application of Provisions referring to Governor General in Council

14. It shall be lawful for the Queen, if Her Majesty thinks fit, to authorize the Governor General from Time to Time to appoint any Person or any Persons jointly or severally to be his Deputy or Deputies within any Part or Parts of Canada, and in that Capacity to exercise during the Pleasure of the Governor General such of the Powers, Authorities, and Functions of the Governor General as the Governor General deems it necessary or expedient to assign to him or them, subject to any Limitations or Directions expressed or given by the Queen; but the Appointment of such a Deputy or Deputies shall not affect the Exercise by the Governor General himself of any Power, Authority, or Function.

Power to Her Majesty to authorize Governor General to appoint Deputies

15. The Command-in-Chief of the Land and Naval Militia, and of all Naval and Military Forces, of and in Canada, is hereby declared to continue and be vested in the Queen.

Command of armed Forces to continue to be vested in the Queen

16. Until the Queen otherwise directs, the Seat of Government of Canada shall be Ottawa.

Seat of Government of Canada

IV. *Legislative Power*

17. There shall be One Parliament for Canada, consisting of the Queen, an Upper House styled the Senate, and the House of Commons.

Constitution of Parliament of Canada

[6]See the notes to section 129, *infra*.

18. The privileges, immunities, and powers to be held, enjoyed, and exercised by the Senate and by the House of Commons, and by the Members thereof respectively, shall be such as are from time to time defined by Act of the Parliament of Canada, but so that any Act of the Parliament of Canada defining such privileges, immunities, and powers shall not confer any privileges, immunities, or powers exceeding those at the passing of such Act held, enjoyed, and exercised by the Commons House of Parliament of the United Kingdom of Great Britain and Ireland, and by the Members thereof.[7]

Privileges, etc. of Houses

19. The Parliament of Canada shall be called together not later than Six Months after the Union.[8]

First Session of the Parliament of Canada

20. There shall be a Session of the Parliament of Canada once at least in every Year, so that Twelve Months shall not intervene between the last Sitting of the Parliament in one Session and its first Sitting in the next Session.[9]

Yearly Session of the Parliament of Canada

THE SENATE

21. The Senate shall, subject to the Provisions of this Act, consist of One Hundred and Two Members, who shall be styled Senators.[10]

Number of Senators

22. In relation to the Constitution of the Senate Canada shall be deemed to consist of Four Divisions:—
   1. Ontario;
   2. Quebec;

Representation of Provinces in Senate

[7]Repealed and re-enacted by the *Parliament of Canada Act, 1875*, 38–39 Vict., c. 38 (U.K.). The original section read as follows:
   18. The Privileges, Immunities, and Powers to be held, enjoyed, and exercised by the Senate and by the House of Commons and by the Members thereof respectively shall be such as are from Time to Time defined by Act of the Parliament of Canada, but so that the same shall never exceed those at the passing of this Act held, enjoyed, and exercised by the Commons House of Parliament of the United Kingdom of Great Britain and Ireland and by the Members thereof.
   [8]Spent. The first session of the first Parliament began on November 6, 1867.
   [9]The term of the twelfth Parliament was extended by the *British North America Act, 1916*, 6–7 Geo. V, c. 19 (U.K.), which Act was repealed by the *Statute Law Revision Act, 1927*, 17–18 Geo. V, c. 42 (U.K.).
   [10]As amended by the *British North America Act, 1915*, 5–6 Geo. V, c. 45 (U.K.), and modified by the *British North America Act, 1949*, 12–13 Geo. VI, c. 22 (U.K.).
   The original section read as follows:
   21. The Senate shall, subject to the Provisions of this Act, consist of Seventy-two Members, who shall be styled Senators.
   The Manitoba Act added two for Manitoba; the Order in Council admitting British Columbia added three; upon admission of Prince Edward Island four more were provided by section 147 of the *British North America Act, 1867*; *The Alberta Act* and *The Saskatchewan Act* each added four. The Senate was reconstituted at 96 by the *British North America Act, 1915*, and six more Senators were added upon union with Newfoundland.

177

3. The Maritime Provinces, Nova Scotia and New Brunswick, and Prince Edward Island;

4. The Western Provinces of Manitoba, British Columbia, Saskatchewan, and Alberta;

which Four Divisions shall (subject to the Provisions of this Act) be equally represented in the Senate as follows: Ontario by twenty-four senators; Quebec by twenty-four senators; the Maritime Provinces and Prince Edward Island by twenty-four senators, ten thereof representing Nova Scotia, ten thereof representing New Brunswick, and four thereof representing Prince Edward Island; the Western Provinces by twenty-four senators, six thereof representing Manitoba, six thereof representing British Columbia, six thereof representing Saskatchewan, and six thereof representing Alberta; Newfoundland shall be entitled to be represented in the Senate by six members.

In the Case of Quebec each of the Twenty-four Senators representing that Province shall be appointed for One of the Twenty-four Electoral Divisions of Lower Canada specified in Schedule A. to Chapter One of the Consolidated Statutes of Canada.[11]

23. The Qualification of a Senator shall be as follows: Qualifications of Senator

1. He shall be of the full age of Thirty Years:

2. He shall be either a natural-born Subject of the Queen, or a Subject of the Queen naturalized by an Act of the Parliament of Great Britain, or of the Parliament of the United Kingdom of Great Britain and Ireland, or of the Legislature of One of the Provinces of Upper Canada, Lower Canada, Canada, Nova Scotia, or New Brunswick, before the Union, or of the Parliament of Canada, after the Union:

3. He shall be legally or equitably seised as of Freehold for his own Use and Benefit of Lands or Tenements held in Free and Common Socage, or seised or possessed for his own Use and Benefit of Lands or Tenements held in Franc-alleu or in Roture, within the Province for which he is appointed, of the Value of Four thousand Dollars, over and above all Rents, Dues, Debts, Charges, Mortgages, and Incumbrances due or payable out of or charged on or affecting the same:

[11]As amended by the *British North America Act, 1915*, and the *British North America Act, 1949*, 12–13 Geo. VI, c. 22 (U.K.). The original section read as follows:

22. In relation to the Constitution of the Senate, Canada shall be deemed to consist of Three Divisions:
1. Ontario;
2. Quebec;
3. The Maritime Provinces, Nova Scotia and New Brunswick; which Three Divisions shall (subject to the Provisions of this Act) be equally represented in the Senate as follows: Ontario by Twenty-four Senators; Quebec by Twenty-four Senators; and the Maritime Provinces by Twenty-four Senators, Twelve thereof representing Nova Scotia, and Twelve thereof representing New Brunswick.

In the Case of Quebec each of the Twenty-four Senators representing that Province shall be appointed for One of the Twenty-four Electoral Divisions of Lower Canada specified in Schedule A. to Chapter One of the Consolidated Statutes of Canada.

4. His Real and Personal Property shall be together worth Four
thousand Dollars over and above his Debts and Liabilities:
5. He shall be resident in the Province for which he is appointed:
6. In the Case of Quebec he shall have his Real Property Qualification in the Electoral Division for which he is appointed, or
shall be resident in that Division.

24. The Governor General shall from Time to Time, in the Queen's
Name, by Instrument under the Great Seal of Canada, summon
qualified Persons to the Senate; and, subject to the Provisions of
this Act, every Person so summoned shall become and be a
Member of the Senate and a Senator.
Summons of Senator

25. Repealed.[12]

26. If at any Time on the Recommendation of the Governor General
the Queen thinks fit to direct that Four or Eight Members be
added to the Senate, the Governor General may by Summons to
Four or Eight qualified Persons (as the Case may be), representing equally the Four Divisions of Canada, add to the Senate
accordingly.[13]
Addition of Senators in certain cases

27. In case of such Addition being at any Time made, the Governor
General shall not summon any Person to the Senate, except upon
a further like Direction by the Queen on the like Recommendation, to represent one of the Four Divisions until such Division is
represented by Twenty-four Senators and no more.[14]
Reduction of Senate to normal Number

28. The Number of Senators shall not at any Time exceed One
Hundred and ten.[15]
Maximum Number of Senators

29. A Senator shall, subject to the Provisions of this Act, hold his
Place in the Senate for Life.
Tenure of Place in Senate

30. A Senator may by Writing under his Hand addressed to the
Governor General resign his Place in the Senate, and thereupon
the same shall be vacant.
Resignation of Place in Senate

[12]Repealed by the *Statute Law Revision Act, 1893*, 56–57 Vict.,
c. 14 (U.K.). The section read as follows:
25. Such Persons shall be first summoned to the Senate as the Queen by Warrant
under Her Majesty's Royal Sign Manual thinks fit to approve, and their Names shall
be inserted in the Queen's Proclamation of Union.
[13]As amended by the *British North America Act, 1915*, 5–6 Geo. V,
c. 45 (U.K.). The original section read as follows:
26. If at any Time on the Recommendation of the Governor General the Queen
thinks fit to direct that Three or Six Members be added to the Senate, the Governor
General may by Summons to Three or Six qualified Persons (as the Case may be),
representing equally the Three Divisions of Canada, add to the Senate accordingly.
[14]As amended by the *British North America Act, 1915*, 5–6 Geo. V,
c. 45 (U.K.). The original section read as follows:
27. In case of such Addition being at any Time made the Governor General shall
not summon any Person to the Senate, except on a further like Direction by the
Queen on the like Recommendation, until each of the Three Divisions of Canada is
represented by Twenty-four Senators and no more.
[15]As amended by the *British North America Act, 1915*, 5–6 Geo. V,
c. 45 (U.K.). The original section read as follows:
28. The Number of Senators shall not at any Time exceed Seventy-eight.

31. The Place of a Senator shall become vacant in any of the following Cases: Disqualification of Senators

1. If for Two consecutive Sessions of the Parliament he fails to give his Attendance in the Senate:

2. If he takes an Oath or makes a Declaration or Acknowledgment of Allegiance, Obedience, or Adherence to a Foreign Power, or does an Act whereby he becomes a Subject or Citizen, or entitled to the Rights or Privileges of a Subject or Citizen, of a Foreign Power:

3. If he is adjudged Bankrupt or Insolvent, or applies for the Benefit of any Law relating to Insolvent Debtors, or becomes a public Defaulter:

4. If he is attainted of Treason or convicted of Felony or of any infamous Crime:

5. If he ceases to be qualified in respect of Property or of Residence; provided, that a Senator shall not be deemed to have ceased to be qualified in respect of Residence by reason only of his residing at the Seat of the Government of Canada while holding an Office under that Government requiring his Presence there.

32. When a Vacancy happens in the Senate by Resignation, Death, or otherwise, the Governor General shall by Summons to a fit and qualified Person fill the Vacancy. Summons on Vacancy in Senate

33. If any Question arises respecting the Qualification of a Senator or a Vacancy in the Senate the same shall be heard and determined by the Senate. Questions as to Qualifications and Vacancies in Senate

34. The Governor General may from Time to Time, by Instrument under the Great Seal of Canada, appoint a Senator to be Speaker of the Senate, and may remove him and appoint another in his Stead.[16] Appointment of Speaker of Senate

35. Until the Parliament of Canada otherwise provides, the Presence of at least Fifteen Senators, including the Speaker, shall be necessary to constitute a Meeting of the Senate for the Exercise of its Powers. Quorum of Senate

36. Questions arising in the Senate shall be decided by a Majority of Voices, and the Speaker shall in all Cases have a Vote, and when the Voices are equal the Decision shall be deemed to be in the Negative. Voting in Senate

THE HOUSE OF COMMONS

37. The House of Commons shall, subject to the Provisions of this Act, consist of Two Hundred and sixty-five Members of whom Constitution of House of Commons in Canada

[16]Provision for exercising the functions of Speaker during his absence is made by the *Speaker of the Senate Act*, R.S.C. 1952, c. 255. Doubts as to the power of Parliament to enact such an Act were removed by the *Canadian Speaker (Appointment of Deputy) Act, 1895*, 59 Vict., c. 3, (U.K.).

Eighty-five shall be elected for Ontario, Seventy-five for Quebec, Twelve for Nova Scotia, Ten for New Brunswick, Fourteen for Manitoba, Twenty-two for British Columbia, Four for Prince Edward Island, Seventeen for Alberta, Seventeen for Saskatchewan, Seven for Newfoundland, One for the Yukon Territory and One for the Mackenzie district of the Northwest Territories.[17]

38. The Governor General shall from Time to Time, in the Queen's Name, by Instrument under the Great Seal of Canada, summon and call together the House of Commons.

Summoning of House of Commons

39. A Senator shall not be capable of being elected or of sitting or voting as a Member of the House of Commons.

Senators not to sit in House of Commons

40. Until the Parliament of Canada otherwise provides, Ontario, Quebec, Nova Scotia, and New Brunswick shall, for the Purposes of the Election of Members to serve in the House of Commons, be divided into Electoral Districts as follows:

Electoral districts of the Four Provinces

1. *Ontario.* Ontario shall be divided into the Counties, Ridings of Counties, Cities, Parts of Cities, and Towns enumerated in the First Schedule to this Act, each whereof shall be an Electoral District, each such District as numbered in that Schedule being entitled to return One Member.

2. *Quebec.* Quebec shall be divided into Sixty-five Electoral Districts, composed of the Sixty-five Electoral Divisions into which Lower Canada is at the passing of this Act divided under Chapter Two of the Consolidated Statutes of Canada, Chapter Seventy-five of the Consolidated Statutes for Lower Canada, and the Act of the Province of Canada of the Twenty-third Year of the Queen, Chapter One. or any other Act amending the same in force at the Union, so that each such Electoral Division shall be for the Purposes of this Act an Electoral District entitled to return One Member.

3. *Nova Scotia.* Each of the Eighteen Counties of Nova Scotia shall be an Electoral District. The County of Halifax shall be entitled to return Two Members, and each of the other Counties One Member.

4. *New Brunswick.* Each of the Fourteen Counties into which New Brunswick is divided, including the City and County of St. John, shall be an Electoral District. The City of St. John shall also be a separate Electoral District. Each of those Fifteen Electoral Districts shall be entitled to return One Member.[18]

41. Until the Parliament of Canada otherwise provides, all Laws in force in the several Provinces at the Union relative to the

Continuance of existing Election Laws

[17]As altered by the *Representation Act*, R.S.C. 1952, c. 334. The original section read as follows:
   37. The House of Commons shall, subject to the Provisions of this Act, consist of One hundred and eighty-one Members, of whom Eighty-two shall be elected for Ontario, Sixty-five for Quebec, Nineteen for Nova Scotia, and Fifteen for New Brunswick.
   [18]Spent. The electoral districts are now set out in the *Representation Act*, R.S.C. 1952, c. 334.

following Matters or any of them, namely,—the Qualifications and Disqualifications of Persons to be elected or to sit or vote as Members of the House of Assembly or Legislative Assembly in the several Provinces, the Voters at Elections of such Members, the Oaths to be taken by Voters, the Returning Officers, their Powers and Duties, the Proceedings at Elections, the Periods during which Elections may be continued, the Trial of controverted Elections, and Proceedings incident thereto, the vacating of Seats of Members, and the Execution of new Writs in case of Seats vacated otherwise than by Dissolution,—shall respectively apply to Elections of Members to serve in the House of Commons for the same several Provinces. *until Parliament of Canada otherwise provides*

Provided that, until the Parliament of Canada otherwise provides, at any Election for a Member of the House of Commons for the District of Algoma, in addition to Persons qualified by the Law of the Province of Canada to vote, every Male British Subject, aged Twenty-one Years or upwards, being a Householder, shall have a Vote.[19]

42. Repealed.[20]

43. Repealed.[21]

44. The House of Commons on its first assembling after a General Election shall proceed with all practicable Speed to elect One of its Members to be Speaker. *As to Election of Speaker of House of Commons*

45. In case of a Vacancy happening in the Office of Speaker by Death, Resignation, or otherwise, the House of Commons shall with all practicable Speed proceed to elect another of its Members to be Speaker. *As to filling up Vacancy in Office of Speaker*

[19]Spent. Elections are now provided for by the *Canada Elections Act*, R.S.C. '1952, c. 23; controverted elections by the *Dominion Controverted Elections Act*, R.S.C. 1952, c. 87; qualifications and disqualifications of members by the *House of Commons Act*, R.S.C. 1952, c. 143 and the *Senate and House of Commons Act*, R.S.C. 1952, c. 249.

[20]Repealed by the *Statute Law Revision Act, 1893*, 56–57 Vict:, c. 14 (U.K.). The section read as follows:

42. For the First Election of Members to serve in the House of Commons the Governor General shall cause Writs to be issued by such Person, in such Form, and addressed to such Returning Officers as he thinks fit.

The Person issuing Writs under this Section shall have the like Powers as are possessed at the Union by the Officers charged with the issuing of Writs for the Election of Members to serve in the respective House of Assembly or Legislative Assembly of the Province of Canada, Nova Scotia, or New Brunswick; and the Returning Officers to whom Writs are directed under this Section shall have the like Powers as are possessed at the Union by the Officers charged with the returning of Writs for the Election of Members to serve in the same respective House of Assembly or Legislative Assembly.

[21]Repealed by the *Statute Law Revision Act, 1893*, 56–57 Vict., c. 14 (U.K.). The section read as follows:

43. In case a Vacancy in the Representation in the House of Commons of any Electoral District happens before the Meeting of the Parliament, or after the Meeting of the Parliament before Provision is made by the Parliament in this Behalf, the Provisions of the last foregoing Section of this Act shall extend and apply to the issuing and returning of a Writ in respect of such vacant District.

46. The Speaker shall preside at all Meetings of the House of Commons. *Speaker to preside*

47. Until the Parliament of Canada otherwise provides, in case of the Absence for any Reason of the Speaker from the Chair of the House of Commons for a Period of Forty-eight consecutive Hours, the House may elect another of its Members to act as Speaker, and the Member so elected shall during the Continuance of such Absence of the Speaker have and execute all the Powers, Privileges, and Duties of Speaker.[22] *Provision in case of Absence of Speaker*

48. The Presence of at least Twenty Members of the House of Commons shall be necessary to constitute a Meeting of the House for the Exercise of its Powers, and for that Purpose the Speaker shall be reckoned as a Member. *Quorum of House of Commons*

49. Questions arising in the House of Commons shall be decided by a Majority of Voices other than that of the Speaker, and when the Voices are equal, but not otherwise, the Speaker shall have a Vote. *Voting in House of Commons*

50. Every House of Commons shall continue for Five Years from the Day of the Return of the Writs for choosing the House (subject to be sooner dissolved by the Governor General), and no longer. *Duration of House of Commons*

51(1). Subject as hereinafter provided, the number of members of the House of Commons shall be two hundred and sixty-three and the representation of the provinces therein shall forthwith upon the coming into force of this section and thereafter on the completion of each decennial census be readjusted by such authority, in such manner, and from such time as the Parliament of Canada from time to time provides, subject and according to the following rules: *Readjustment of representation in Commons*

1. There shall be assigned to each of the provinces a number of members computed by dividing the total population of the provinces by two hundred and sixty-one and by dividing the population of each province by the quotient so obtained, disregarding, except as hereinafter in this section provided, the remainder, if any, after the said process of division. *Rules*

2. If the total number of members assigned to all the provinces persuant to rule one is less than two hundred and sixty-one, additional members shall be assigned to the provinces (one to a province) having remainders in the computation under rule one commencing with the province having the largest remainder and continuing with the other provinces in the order of the magnitude of their respective remainders until the total number of members assigned is two hundred and sixty-one.

[22]Provision for exercising the functions of Speaker during his absence is now made by the *Speaker of the House of Commons Act*, R.S.C. 1952, c. 254.

3. Notwithstanding anything in this section, if upon completion of a computation under rules one and two, the number of members to be assigned to a province is less than the number of senators representing the said province, rules one and two shall cease to apply in respect of the said province, and there shall be assigned to the said province a number of members equal to the said number of senators.

4. In the event that rules one and two cease to apply in respect of a province then, for the purposes of computing the number of members to be assigned to the provinces in respect of which rules one and two continue to apply, the total population of the provinces shall be reduced by the number of the population of the province in respect of which rules one and two have ceased to apply and the number two hundred and sixty-one shall be reduced by the number of members assigned to such province pursuant to rule three.

5. On any such readjustment the number of members for any province shall not be reduced by more than fifteen per cent below the representation to which such province was entitled under rules one to four of this subsection at the last preceding readjustment of the representation of that province, and there shall be no reduction in the representation of any province as a result of which that province would have a smaller number of members than any other province that according to the results of the then last decennial census did not have a larger population; but for the purposes of any subsequent readjustment of representation under this section any increase in the number of members of the House of Commons resulting from the application of this rule shall not be included in the divisor mentioned in rules one to four of this subsection.

6. Such readjustment shall not take effect until the termination of the then existing Parliament.

(2) The Yukon Territory as constituted by chapter forty-one of the statutes of Canada, 1901, shall be entitled to one member, and such other part of Canada not comprised within a province as may from time to time be defined by the Parliament of Canada shall be entitled to one member.[23]

Yukon Territory and other part not comprised within a province

[23]As enacted by the *British North America Act, 1952*, R.S.C. 1952, c. 304, which came into force on June 18, 1952. The section, as originally enacted, read as follows:

51. On the Completion of the Census in the Year One Thousand eight hundred and seventy-one, and of each subsequent decennial Census, the Representation of the Four Provinces shall be re-adjusted by such Authority, in such Manner, and from such Time, as the Parliament of Canada from Time to Time provides, subject and according to the following Rules:

1. Quebec shall have the fixed Number of Sixty-five Members:

2. There shall be assigned to each of the other Provinces such a Number of Members as will bear the same Proportion to the Number of its Population (ascertained at such Census) as the Number Sixty-five bears to the Number of the Population of Quebec (so ascertained):

3. In the Computation of the Number of Members for a Province a fractional Part not exceeding One Half of the whole Number requisite for entitling the Province to a Member shall be disregarded; but a fractional Part exceeding One Half of that Number shall be equivalent to the whole Number:

4. On any such Re-adjustment the Number of Members for a Province shall not be

51A. Notwithstanding anything in this Act a province shall always be entitled to a number of members in the House of Commons not less than the number of senators representing such province.[24]

Constitution of House of Commons

52. The Number of Members of the House of Commons may be from Time to Time increased by the Parliament of Canada, provided the proportionate Representation of the Provinces prescribed by this Act is not thereby disturbed.

Increase of Number of House of Commons

MONEY VOTES; ROYAL ASSENT

53. Bills for appropriating any Part of the Public Revenue, or for imposing any Tax or Impost, shall originate in the House of Commons.

Appropriation and Tax Bills

---

reduced unless the Proportion which the Number of the Population of the Province bore to the Number of the aggregate Population of Canada at the then last preceding Re-adjustment of the Number of Members for the Province is ascertained at the then latest Census to be diminished by One Twentieth Part or upwards:

5. Such Re-adjustment shall not take effect until the Termination of the then existing Parliament.

The section was amended by the *Statute Law Revision Act, 1893,* 56–57 Vict., c. 14 (U.K.) by repealing the words from "of the census" to "seventy-one and" and the word "subsequent".

By the *British North America Act, 1943,* 6–7 Geo. VI, c..30 (U.K.) redistribution of seats following the 1941 census was postponed until the first session of Parliament after the war. The section was re-enacted by the *British North America Act, 1946,* 9–10 Geo. VI, c. 63 (U.K.) to read as follows:

51. (1) The number of members of the House of Commons shall be two hundred and fifty-five and the representation of the provinces therein shall forthwith upon the coming into force of this section and thereafter on the completion of each decennial census be readjusted by such authority, in such manner, and from such time as the Parliament of Canada from time to time provides, subject and according to the following rules:—

1. Subject as hereinafter provided, there shall be assigned to each of the provinces a number of members computed by dividing the total population of the provinces by two hundred and fifty-four and by dividing the population of each province by the quotient so obtained, disregarding, except as hereinafter in this section provided, the remainder, if any, after the said process of division.

2. If the total number of members assigned to all the provinces pursuant to rule one is less than two hundred and fifty-four, additional members shall be assigned to the provinces (one to a province) having remainders in the computation under rule one commencing with the province having the largest remainder and continuing with the other provinces in the order of the magnitude of their respective remainders until the total number of members assigned is two hundred and fifty-four.

3. Notwithstanding anything in this section, if upon completion of a computation under rules one and two, the number of members to be assigned to a province is less than the number of senators representing the said province, rules one and two shall cease to apply in respect of the said province, and there shall be assigned to the said province a number of members equal to the said number of senators.

4. In the event that rules one and two cease to apply in respect of a province then, for the purpose of computing the number of members to be assigned to the provinces in respect of which rules one and two continue to apply, the total population of the provinces shall be reduced by the number of the population of the province in respect of which rules one and two have ceased to apply and the number two hundred and fifty-four shall be reduced by the number of members assigned to such province pursuant to rule three.

5. Such readjustment shall not take effect until the termination of the then existing Parliament.

(2) The Yukon Territory as constituted by Chapter forty-one of the Statutes of Canada, 1901, together with any Part of Canada not comprised within a province which may from time to time be included therein by the Parliament of Canada for the purposes of representation in Parliament, shall be entitled to one member.

[24] As enacted by the *British North America Act, 1915,* 5–6 Geo. V, c. 45 (U.K.)

54. It shall not be lawful for the House of Commons to adopt or pass any Vote, Resolution, Address, or Bill for the Appropriation of any Part of the Public Revenue, or of any Tax or Impost, to any Purpose that has not been first recommended to that House by Message of the Governor General in the Session in which such Vote, Resolution, Address, or Bill is proposed. *Recommendation of Money Votes*

55. Where a Bill passed by the Houses of the Parliament is presented to the Governor General for the Queen's Assent, he shall declare, according to his Discretion, but subject to the Provisions of this Act and to Her Majesty's Instruction, either that he assents thereto in the Queen's Name, or that he withholds the Queen's Assent, or that he reserves the Bill for the Signification of the Queen's Pleasure. *Royal Assent to Bills, etc.*

56. Where the Governor General assents to a Bill in the Queen's Name, he shall by the first convenient Opportunity send an authentic Copy of the Act to one of Her Majesty's Principal Secretaries of State, and if the Queen in Council within Two Years after Receipt thereof by the Secretary of State thinks fit to disallow the Act, such Disallowance (with a Certificate of the Secretary of State of the Day on which the Act was received by him) being signified by the Governor General, by Speech or Message to each of the Houses of the Parliament or by Proclamation, shall annul the Act from and after the Day of such Signification. *Disallowance by Order in Council of Act assented to by Governor General*

57. A Bill reserved for the Signification of the Queen's Pleasure shall not have any Force unless and until, within Two Years from the Day on which it was presented to the Governor General for the Queen's Assent, the Governor General signifies, by Speech or Message to each of the Houses of the Parliament or by Proclamation, that it has received the Assent of the Queen in Council. *Signification of Queen's Pleasure on Bill reserved*

   An Entry of every such Speech, Message, or Proclamation shall be made in the Journal of each House, and a Duplicate thereof duly attested shall be delivered to the proper Officer to be kept among the Records of Canada.

V. *Provincial Constitutions*

EXECUTIVE POWER

58. For each Province there shall be an Officer, styled the Lieutenant Governor, appointed by the Governor General in Council by Instrument under the Great Seal of Canada. *Appointment of Lieutenant Governors of Provinces*

59. A Lieutenant Governor shall hold Office during the Pleasure of the Governor General; but any Lieutenant Governor after the Commencement of the First Session of the Parliament of Canada *Tenure of Office of Lieutenant Governor*

shall not be removeable within Five Years from his Appointment, except for Cause assigned, which shall be communicated to him in Writing within One Month after the Order for his Removal is made, and shall be communicated by Message to the Senate and to the House of Commons within One Week thereafter if the Parliament is then sitting,. and if not then within One Week after the Commencement of the next Session of the Parliament.

60. The Salaries of the Lieutenant Governors shall be fixed and provided by the Parliament of Canada.[25]   Salaries of Lieutenant Governors

61. Every Lieutenant Governor shall, before assuming the Duties of his Office, make and subscribe before the Governor General or some Person authorized by him Oaths of Allegiance and Office similar to those taken by the Governor General.   Oaths,. etc., of Lieutenant Governor

62. The Provisions of this Act referring to the Lieutenant Governor extend and apply to the Lieutenant Governor for the Time being of each Province, or other the Chief Executive Officer or Administrator for the Time being carrying on the Government of the Province, by whatever Title he is designated.   Application of provisions referring to Lieutenant Governor

63. The Executive Council of Ontario and of Quebec shall be composed of such Persons as the Lieutenant Governor from Time to Time thinks fit, and in the first instance of the following Officers, namely,—the Attorney General, the Secretary and Registrar of the Province, the Treasurer of the Province, the Commissioner of Crown Lands, and the Commissioner of Agriculture and Public Works, with in Quebec the Speaker of the Legislative Council and the Solicitor General.[26]   Appointment of Executive Offices for Ontario and Quebec

64. The Constitution of the Executive Authority in each of the Provinces of Nova Scotia and New Brunswick shall, subject to the Provisions of this Act, continue as it exists at the Union until altered under the Authority of this Act.[26a]   Executive Government of Nova Scotia and New Brunswick

65. All Powers, Authorities, and Functions which under any Act of the Parliament of Great Britain, or of the Parliament of the United Kingdom of Great Britain and Ireland, or of the Legislature of Upper Canada, Lower Canada, or Canada, were or are before or at the Union vested in or exerciseable by the respective Governors or Lieutenant Governors of those Provinces, with the Advice or with the Advice and Consent of the respective Execu-   Powers to be exercised by Lieutenant Governor of Ontario or Quebec with Advice, or alone

[25]Provided for by the *Salaries Act*, R.S.C. 1952, c. 243.

[26]Now provided for in Ontario by the *Executive Council Act*, R.S.O. 1950, c. 121, and in Quebec by the *Executive Power Act*, R.S.Q. 1941, c. 7.

[26a]A similar provision was included in each of the instruments admitting British Columbia, Prince Edward Island, and Newfoundland. The Executive Authorities for Manitoba, Alberta and Saskatchewan were established by the statutes creating those provinces. See the footnotes to section 5, *supra*.

tive Councils thereof, or in conjunction with those Councils, or with any Number of Members thereof, or by those Governors or Lieutenant Governors individually, shall, as far as the same are capable of being exercised after the Union in relation to the Government of Ontario and Quebec respectively, be vested in and shall or may be exercised by the Lieutenant Governor of Ontario and Quebec respectively, with the Advice or with the Advice and Consent of or in conjunction with the respective Executive Councils, or any Members thereof, or by the Lieutenant Governor individually, as the Case requires, subject nevertheless (except with respect to such as exist under Acts of the Parliament of Great Britain, or of the Parliament of the United Kingdom of Great Britain and Ireland,) to be abolished or altered by the respective Legislatures of Ontario and Quebec.[27]

66. The Provisions of this Act referring to the Lieutenant Governor in Council shall be construed as referring to the Lieutenant Governor of the Province acting by and with the Advice of the Executive Council thereof.

Application of Provisions referring to Lieutenant Governor in Council

67. The Governor General in Council may from Time to Time appoint an Administrator to execute the Office and Functions of Lieutenant Governor during his Absence, Illness, or other Inability.

Administration in Absence, etc., of Lieutenant Governor

68. Unless and until the Executive Government of any Province otherwise directs with respect to that Province, the Seats of Government of the Provinces shall be as follows, namely,—of Ontario, the City of Toronto; of Quebec, the City of Quebec; of Nova Scotia, the City of Halifax; and of New Brunswick, the City of Fredericton.

Seats of Provincial Governments

LEGISLATIVE POWER

1. ONTARIO

69. There shall be a Legislature for Ontario consisting of the Lieutenant Governor and of One House, styled the Legislative Assembly of Ontario.

Legislature for Ontario

70. The Legislative Assembly of Ontario shall be composed of Eighty-two Members, to be elected to represent the Eighty-two Electoral Districts set forth in the First Schedule to this Act.[28]

Electoral districts

2. QUEBEC

71. There shall be a Legislature for Quebec consisting of the Lieutenant Governor and of Two Houses, styled the Legislative Council of Quebec and the Legislative Assembly of Quebec.

Legislature for Quebec

[27]See the notes to section 129, *infra*.
[28]Spent. Now covered by the *Representation Act*, S.O. 1954, c. 84, which provides that the Assembly shall consist of 98 members, representing the electoral districts set forth in the Schedule to that Act.

72. The Legislative Council of Quebec shall be composed of Twenty-four Members, to be appointed by the Lieutenant Governor, in the Queen's Name, by Instrument under the Great Seal of Quebec, One being appointed to represent each of the Twenty-four Electoral Divisions of Lower Canada in this Act referred to, and each holding Office for the Term of his Life, unless the Legislature of Quebec otherwise provides under the Provisions of this Act.[29]

Constitution of Legislative Council

73. The Qualifications of the Legislative Councillors of Quebec shall be the same as those of the Senators for Quebec.[30]

Qualification of Legislative Councillors

74. The Place of a Legislative Councillor of Quebec shall become vacant in the Cases, *mutatis mutandis*, in which the Place of Senator becomes vacant.

Resignation, Disqualification, etc.

75. When a Vacancy happens in the Legislative Council of Quebec by Resignation, Death, or otherwise, the Lieutenant Governor, in the Queen's Name, by Instrument under the Great Seal of Quebec, shall appoint a fit and qualified Person to fill the Vacancy.

Vacancies

76. If any Question arises respecting the Qualification of a Legislative Councillor of Quebec, or a Vacancy in the Legislative Council of Quebec, the same shall be heard and determined by the Legislative Council.

Questions as to Vacancies, etc.

77. The Lieutenant Governor may from Time to Time, by Instrument under the Great Seal of Quebec, appoint a Member of the Legislative Council of Quebec to be Speaker thereof, and may remove him and appoint another in his Stead.[31]

Speaker of Legislative Council

78. Until the Legislature of Quebec otherwise provides, the Presence of at least Ten Members of the Legislative Council, including the Speaker, shall be necessary to constitute a Meeting for the Exercise of its Powers.

Quorum of Legislative Council

79. Questions arising in the Legislative Council of Quebec shall be decided by a Majority of Voices, and the Speaker shall in all Cases have a Vote, and when the Voices are equal the Decision shall be deemed to be in the Negative.

Voting in Legislative Council

80. The Legislative Assembly of Quebec shall be composed of Sixty-five Members, to be elected to represent the Sixty-five Electoral Divisions or Districts of Lower Canada in this Act referred to,

Constitution of Legislative Assembly of Quebec

[29]Spent. Now covered by the *Legislature Act*, R.S.Q. 1941, c. 4; the membership remains at twenty-four, representing the divisions set forth in the *Territorial Division Act*, R.S.Q. 1941, c. 3.

[30]Altered by the *Legislature Act*, R.S.Q. 1941, c. 4, s. 7, which provides that it shall be sufficient for any member to be domiciled, and to possess his property qualifications, within the Province of Quebec.

[31]Spent. Now covered by the *Legislature Act*, R.S.Q. 1941, c. 4, s. 9.

subject to Alteration thereof by the Legislature of Quebec: Provided that it shall not be lawful to present to the Lieutenant Governor of Quebec for Assent any Bill for altering the Limits of any of the Electoral Divisions or Districts mentioned in the Second Schedule to this Act, unless the Second and Third Readings of such Bill have been passed in the Legislative Assembly with the Concurrence of the Majority of the Members representing all those Electoral Divisions or Districts, and the Assent shall not be given to such Bill unless an Address has been presented by the Legislative Assembly to the Lieutenant Governor stating that it has been so passed.[32]

3. ONTARIO AND QUEBEC

81. Repealed.[33]

82. The Lieutenant Governor of Ontario and of Quebec shall from Time to Time, in the Queen's Name, by Instrument under the Great Seal of the Province, summon and call together the Legislative Assembly of the Province.

Summoning of Legislative Assemblies

83. Until the Legislature of Ontario or of Quebec otherwise provides, a Person accepting or holding in Ontario or in Quebec any Office, Commission, or Employment, permanent or temporary, at the Nomination of the Lieutenant Governor, to which an annual Salary, or any Fee, Allowance, Emolument, or Profit of any Kind or Amount whatever from the Province is attached, shall not be eligible as a Member of the Legislative Assembly of the respective Province, nor shall he sit or vote as such; but nothing in this Section shall make ineligible any Person being a Member of the Executive Council of the respective Province, or holding any of the following Offices, that is to say, the Offices of Attorney General, Secretary and Registrar of the Province, Treasurer of the Province, Commissioner of Crown Lands, and Commissioner of Agriculture and Public Works, and in Quebec Solicitor General, or shall disqualify him to sit or vote in the House for which he is elected, provided he is elected while holding such Office.[34]

Restriction on election of Holders of offices

84. Until the Legislatures of Ontario and Quebec respectively otherwise provide, all Laws which at the Union are in force in those Provinces respectively, relative to the following Matters, or any

Continuance of existing Election Laws

[32]Altered by the *Legislature Act*, R.S.Q. 1941, c. 4 and the *Territorial Division Act*, R.S.Q. 1941, c. 3; there are now 93 members representing the districts set out in the *Territorial Division Act*.
[33]Repealed by the *Statute Law Revision Act, 1893*, 56–57 Vict., c. 14 (U.K.). The section read as follows:
81. The Legislatures of Ontario and Quebec respectively shall be called together not later than Six Months after the Union.
[34]Probably spent. The subject-matter of this section is now covered in Ontario by the *Legislative Assembly Act*, R.S.O. 1950, c. 202, and in Quebec by the *Legislature Act*, R.S.Q. 1941, c. 4.

of them, namely,—the Qualifications and Disqualifications of Persons to be elected or to sit or vote as Members of the Assembly of Canada, the Qualifications or Disqualifications of Voters, the Oaths to be taken by Voters, the Returning Officers, their Powers and Duties, the Proceedings at Elections, the Periods during which such Elections may be continued, and the Trial of controverted Elections and the Proceedings incident thereto, the vacating of the Seats of Members and the issuing and execution of new Writs in case of Seats vacated otherwise than by Dissolution,—shall respectively apply to Elections of Members to serve in the respective Legislative Assemblies of Ontario and Quebec.

Provided that, until the Legislature of Ontario otherwise provides, at any Election for a Member of the Legislative Assembly of Ontario for the District of Algoma, in addition to Persons qualified by the Law of the Province of Canada to vote, every male British Subject, aged Twenty-one Years or upwards, being a Householder, shall have a Vote.[35]

85. Every Legislative Assembly of Ontario and every Legislative Assembly of Quebec shall continue for Four Years from the Day of the Return of the Writs for choosing the same (subject nevertheless to either the Legislative Assembly of Ontario or the Legislative Assembly of Quebec being sooner dissolved by the Lieutenant Governor of the Province), and no longer.[36]

Duration of Legislative Assemblies

86. There shall be a Session of the Legislature of Ontario and of that of Quebec once at least in every Year, so that Twelve Months shall not intervene between the last Sitting of the Legislature in each Province in one Session and its first Sitting in the next Session.

Yearly Session of Legislature

87. The following Provisions of this Act respecting the House of Commons of Canada shall extend and apply to the Legislative Assemblies of Ontario and Quebec, that is to say,—the Provisions relating to the Election of a Speaker originally and on Vacancies, the Duties of the Speaker, the Absence of the Speaker, the Quorum, and the Mode of voting, as if those Provisions were here re-enacted and made applicable in Terms to each such Legislative Assembly.

Speaker, Quorum, etc.

[35]Probably spent. The subject-matter of this section is now covered in Ontario by the *Election Act*, 1951, c. 21, the *Controverted Elections Act*, R.S.O. 1950, c. 67 and the *Legislative Assembly Act*, R.S.O. 1950, c. 202, and in Quebec by the *Quebec Election Act*, 1945, c. 15, the *Quebec Controverted Elections Act*, R.S.Q. 1941, c. 6, and the *Legislature Act*, R.S.Q. 1941, c. 4.

[36]The maximum duration of the Legislative Assembly for Ontario and Quebec has been changed to five years by the *Legislative Assembly Act*, R.S.O. 1950, c. 202, and the *Legislature Act*, R.S.Q. 1941, c. 4, respectively.

4. NOVA SCOTIA AND NEW BRUNSWICK

88. The Constitution of the Legislature of each of the Provinces of Nova Scotia and New Brunswick shall, subject to the Provisions of this Act, continue as it exists at the Union until altered under Authority of this Act.[37]

Constitutions of Legislatures of Nova Scotia and New Brunswick

89. Repealed.[38]

6. THE FOUR PROVINCES

90. The following Provisions of this Act respecting the Parliament of Canada, namely,—the Provisions relating to Appropriation and Tax Bills, the Recommendation of Money Votes, the Assent to Bills, the Disallowance of Acts, and the Signification of Pleasure on Bills reserved,—shall extend and apply to the Legislatures of the several Provinces as if those Provisions were here re-enacted and made applicable in Terms to the respective Provinces and the Legislatures thereof, with the Substitution of the Lieutenant Governor of the Province for the Governor General, of the Governor General for the Queen and for a Secretary of State, of One Year for Two Years, and of the Province for Canada.

Application to Legislatures of Provisions respecting Money Votes, etc.

VI. *Distribution of Legislative Powers*

POWERS OF THE PARLIAMENT

91. It shall be lawful for the Queen, by and with the Advice and Consent of the Senate and House of Commons, to make Laws for the Peace, Order, and good Government of Canada, in relation to all Matters not coming within the Classes of Subjects by this Act assigned exclusively to the Legislatures of the Provinces; and for greater Certainty, but not so as to restrict the Generality of

Legislative Authority of Parliament of Canada

[37]Partially repealed by the *Statute Law Revision Act, 1893*, 56–57 Vict., c. 14 (U.K.) which deleted the following concluding words of the original enactment:
and the House of Assembly of New Brunswick existing at the passing of this Act shall, unless sooner dissolved, continue for the Period for which it was elected.
A similar provision was included in each of the instruments admitting British Columbia, Prince Edward Island, and Newfoundland. The Legislatures of Manitoba, Alberta and Saskatchewan were established by the statutes creating those provinces. See the footnotes to section 5, *supra*.

[38]Repealed by the *Statute Law Revision Act, 1893*, 56–57 Vict., c. 14 (U.K.). The section read as follows:
5. *Ontario, Quebec, and Nova Scotia.* 89. Each of the Lieutenant Governors of Ontario, Quebec and Nova Scotia shall cause Writs to be issued for the First Election of Members of the Legislative Assembly thereof in such Form and by such Person as he thinks fit, and at such Time and addressed to such Returning Officer as the Governor General directs, and so that the First Election of Member of Assembly for any Electoral District or any Subdivision thereof shall be held at the same Time and at the same Places as the Election for a Member to serve in the House of Commons of Canada for that Electoral District.

the foregoing Terms of this Section, it is hereby declared that (notwithstanding anything in this Act) the exclusive Legislative Authòrity of the Parliament of Canada extends to all Matters coming within the Classes of Subjects next herein-after enumerated; that is to say,—

1. The amendment from time to time of the Constitution of Canada, except as regards matters coming within the classes of subjects by this Act assigned exclusively to the Legislatures of the provinces, or as regards rights or privileges by this or any other Constitutional Act granted or secured to the Legislature or the Government of a province, or to any class of persons with respect to schools or as regards the use of the English or the French language or as regards the requirements that there shall be a session of the Parliament of Canada at least once each year, and that no House of Commons shall continue for more than five years from the day of the return of the Writs for choosing the House: provided, however, that a House of Commons may in time of real or apprehended war, invasion or insurrection be continued by the Parliament of Canada if such continuation is not opposed by the votes of more than one-third of the members of such House.[39]

1A. The Public Debt and Property.[40]

2. The Regulation of Trade and Commerce.

2A. Unemployment insurance.[41]

3. The raising of Money by any Mode or System of Taxation.

4. The borrowing of Money on the Public Credit.

5. Postal Service.

6. The Census and Statistics.

7. Militia, Military and Naval Service, and Defence.

8. The fixing of and providing for the Salaries and Allowances of Civil and other Officers of the Government of Canada.

9. Beacons, Buoys, Lighthouses, and Sable Island.

10. Navigation and Shipping.

11. Quarantine and the Establishment and Maintenance of Marine Hospitals.

12. Sea Coast and Inland Fisheries.

13. Ferries between a Province and any British or Foreign Country or between Two Provinces.

14. Currency and Coinage.

15. Banking, Incorporation of Banks, and the Issue of Paper Money.

16. Savings Banks.

17. Weights and Measures.

18. Bills of Exchange and Promissory Notes.

[39]Added by the *British North America (No. 2) Act, 1949*, 13 Geo. VI, c. 81 (U.K.).

[40]Re-numbered by the *British North America (No. 2) Act, 1949*.

[41]Added by the *British North America Act, 1940*, 3–4 Geo. VI, c. 36 (U.K.).

19. Interest.
20. Legal Tender.
21. Bankruptcy and Insolvency.
22. Patents of Invention and Discovery.
23. Copyrights.
24. Indians, and Lands reserved for the Indians.
25. Naturalization and Aliens.
26. Marriage and Divorce.
27. The Criminal Law, except the Constitution of Courts of Criminal Jurisdiction, but including the Procedure in Criminal Matters.
28. The Establishment, Maintenance, and Management of Penitentiaries.
29. Such Classes of Subjects as are expressly excepted in the Enumeration of the Classes of Subjects by this Act assigned exclusively to the Legislatures of the Provinces.

And any Matter coming within any of the Classes of Subjects enumerated in this Section shall not be deemed to come within the Class of Matters of a local or private Nature comprised in the Enumeration of the Classes of Subjects by this Act assigned exclusively to the Legislatures of the Provinces.[42]

[42]Legislative authority has been conferred on Parliament by other Acts as follows:

1. The *British North America Act, 1871*, 34–35 Vict., c. 28 (U.K.).
2. The Parliament of Canada may from time to time establish new Provinces in any territories forming for the time being part of the Dominion of Canada, but not included in any Province thereof, and may, at the time of such establishment, make provision for the constitution and administration of any such Province, and for the passing of laws for the peace, order, and good government of such Province, and for its representation in the said Parliament.
3. The Parliament of Canada may from time to time, with the consent of the Legislature of any Province of the said Dominion, increase, diminish, or otherwise alter the limits of such Province, upon such terms and conditions as may be agreed to by the said Legislature, and may, with the like consent, make provision respecting the effect and operation of any such increase or diminution or alteration of territory in relation to any Province affected thereby.
4. The Parliament of Canada may from time to time make provision for the administration, peace, order, and good government of any territory not for the time being included in any Province.
5. The following Acts passed by the said Parliament of Canada, and intituled respectively,—"An Act for the temporary government of Rupert's Land and the North Western Territory when united with Canada"; and "An Act to amend and continue the Act thirty-two and thirty-three Victoria, chapter three, and to establish and provide for the government of "the Province of Manitoba," shall be and be deemed to have been valid and effectual for all purposes whatsoever from the date at which they respectively received the assent, in the Queen's name, of the Governor General of the said Dominion of Canada."
6. Except as provided by the third section of this Act, it shall not be competent for the Parliament of Canada to alter the provisions of the last-mentioned Act of the said Parliament in so far as it relates to the Province of Manitoba, or of any other Act hereafter establishing new Provinces in the said Dominion, subject always to the right of the Legislature of the Province of Manitoba to alter from time to time the provisions of any law respecting the qualification of electors and members of the Legislative Assembly, and to make laws respecting elections in the said Province.
The *Rupert's Land Act, 1868*, 31–32 Vict., c. 105 (U.K.) (repealed by the *Statute Law Revision Act, 1893*, 56–57 Vict., c. 14 (U.K.)) had previously conferred similar authority in relation to Rupert's Land and the North-Western Territory upon admission of those areas.

2. The *British North America Act, 1886*, 49–50 Vict., c. 35, (U.K.).
1. The Parliament of Canada may from time to time make provision for the representation in the Senate and House of Commons of Canada, or in either of

EXCLUSIVE POWERS OF PROVINCIAL LEGISLATURES

92. In each Province the Legislature may exclusively make Laws in relation to Matters coming within the Classes of Subjects next herein-after enumerated; that is to say,— *Subjects of exclusive Provincial Legislation*

1. The Amendment from Time to Time, notwithstanding anything in this Act, of the Constitution of the Province, except as regards the Office of Lieutenant Governor.

2. Direct Taxation within the Province in order to the raising of a Revenue for Provincial Purposes.

3. The borrowing of Money on the sole Credit of the Province.

4. The Establishment and Tenure of Provincial Offices and the Appointment and Payment of Provincial Officers.

5. The Management and Sale of the Public Lands belonging to the Province and of the Timber and Wood thereon.

6. The Establishment, Maintenance, and Management of Public and Reformatory Prisons in and for the Province.

7. The Establishment, Maintenance, and Management of Hospitals, Asylums, Charities, and Eleemosynary Institutions in and for the Province, other than Marine Hospitals.

8. Municipal Institutions in the Province.

9. Shop, Saloon, Tavern, Auctioneer, and other Licences in order to the raising of a Revenue for Provincial, Local, or Municipal Purposes.

10. Local Works and Undertakings other than such as are of the following Classes: (*a*) Lines of Steam or other Ships, Railways, Canals, Telegraphs, and other Works and Undertakings connecting the Province with any other or others of the Provinces, or extending beyond the Limits of the Province; (*b*) Lines of Steam Ships between the Province and any British or Foreign Country; (*c*) Such Works as, although wholly situate within the Province, are before or after their Execution declared by the Parliament of Canada to be for the general Advantage of Canada or for the Advantage of Two or more of the Provinces.

11. The Incorporation of Companies with Provincial Objects.

12. The Solemnization of Marriage in the Province.

13. Property and Civil Rights in the Province.

14. The Administration of Justice in the Province, including the Constitution, Maintenance, and Organization of Provincial Courts, both of Civil and of Criminal Jurisdiction, and including Procedure in Civil Matters in those Courts.

15. The Imposition of Punishment by Fine, Penalty, or Imprisonment for enforcing any Law of the Province made in relation to any Matter coming within any of the Classes of Subjects enumerated in this Section.

---

them, of any territories which for the time being form part of the Dominion of Canada, but are not included in any province thereof.

3. The *Statute of Westminster, 1931*, 22 Geo. V, c. 4, (U.K.).

3. It is hereby declared and enacted that the Parliament of a Dominion has full power to make laws having extra-territorial operation.

16. Generally all Matters of a merely local or private Nature in the Province.

EDUCATION

93. In and for each Province the Legislature may exclusively make Laws in relation to Education, subject and according to the following Provisions:—

Legislation respecting Education

1. Nothing in any such Law shall prejudicially affect any Right or Privilege with respect to Denominational Schools which any Class of Persons have by Law in the Province at the Union:

2. All the Powers, Privileges, and Duties at the Union by Law conferred and imposed in Upper Canada on the Separate Schools and School Trustees of the Queen's Roman Catholic Subjects shall be and the same are hereby extended to the Dissentient Schools of the Queen's Protestant and Roman Catholic Subjects in Quebec:

3. Where in any Province a System of Separate or Dissentient Schools exists by Law at the Union or is thereafter established by the Legislature of the Province, an Appeal shall lie to the Governor General in Council from any Act or Decision of any Provincial Authority affecting any Right or Privilege of the Protestant or Roman Catholic Minority of the Queen's Subjects in relation to Education:

4. In case any such Provincial Law as from Time to Time seems to the Governor General in Council requisite for the due Execution of the Provisions of this Section is not made, or in case any Decision of the Governor General in Council on any Appeal under this Section is not duly executed by the proper Provincial Authority in that Behalf, then and in every such Case, and as far only as the Circumstances of each Case require, the Parliament of Canada may make remedial Laws for the due Execution of the Provisions of this Section and of any Decision of the Governor General in Council under this Section.[43]

[43]Altered for Manitoba by section 22 of the *Manitoba Act*, 33 Vict., c. 3 (Canada), (confirmed by the *British North America Act, 1871*), which reads as follows:

22. In and for the Province, the said Legislature may exclusively make Laws in relation to Education, subject and according to the following provisions:—
(1) Nothing in any such Law shall prejudicially affect any right or privilege with respect to Denominational Schools which any class of persons have by Law or practice in the Province at the Union:
(2) An appeal shall lie to the Governor General in Council from any Act or decision of the Legislature of the Province, or of any Provincial Authority, affecting any right or privilege of the Protestant or Roman Catholic minority of the Queen's subjects in relation to Education:
(3) In case any such Provincial Law, as from time to time seems to the Governor General in Council requisite for the due execution of the provisions of this section, is not made, or in case any decision of the Governor General in Council on any appeal under this section is not duly executed by the proper Provicial Authority in that behalf, then, and in every such case, and as far only as the circumstances of each case require, the Parliament of Canada may make remedial Laws for the due execution of the provisions of this section, and of any decision of the Governor General in Council under this section.

Altered for Alberta by section 17 of *The Alberta Act*, 4–5 Edw. VII, c. 3 which reads as follows:

APPENDIXES

UNIFORMITY OF LAWS IN ONTARIO, NOVA SCOTIA AND NEW
BRUNSWICK

94. Notwithstanding anything in this Act, the Parliament of Canada may make Provision for the Uniformity of all or any of the Laws relative to Property and Civil Rights in Ontario, Nova Scotia, and New Brunswick, and of the Procedure of all or any of the Courts in those Three Provinces, and from and after the passing of any Act in that Behalf the Power of the Parliament of Canada to make Laws in relation to any Matter comprised in any such Act shall, notwithstanding anything in this Act, be unrestricted; but any Act of the Parliament of Canada making Provision for such Uniformity shall not have effect in any Province unless and until it is adopted and enacted as Law by the Legislature thereof. **Legislation for Uniformity of Laws in Three Provinces**

17. Section 93 of The British North America Act, 1867, shall apply to the said province, with the substitution for paragraph (1) of the said section 93 of the following paragraph:—

(1) Nothing in any such law shall prejudicially affect any right or privilege with respect to separate schools which any class of persons have at the date of the passing of this Act, under the terms of chapters 29 and 30 of the Ordinances of the Northwest Territories, passed in the year 1901, or with respect to religious instruction in any public or separate school as provided for in the said ordinances.

2. In the appropriation by the Legislature or distribution by the Government of the province of any moneys for the support of schools organized and carried on in accordance with the said chapter 29 or any Act passed in amendment thereof, or in substitution therefor, there shall be no discrimination against schools of any class described in the said chapter 29.

3. Where the expression "by law" is employed in paragraph 3 of the said section 93, it shall be held to mean the law as set out in the said chapters 29 and 30, and where the expression "at the Union" is employed, in the said paragraph 3, it shall be held to mean the date at which this Act comes into force."

Altered for Saskatchewan by section 17 of *The Saskatchewan Act*, 4–5 Edw. VII, c. 42, which reads as follows:

17. Section 93 of the British North America Act, 1867, shall apply to the said province, with the substitution for paragraph (1) of the said section 93, of the following paragraph:—

(1) Nothing in any such law shall prejudicially affect any right or privilege with respect to separate schools which any class of persons have at the date of the passing of this Act, under the terms of chapters 29 and 30 of the Ordinances of the Northwest Territories, passed in the year 1901, or with respect to religious instruction in any public or separate school as provided for in the said ordinances.

2. In the appropriation by the Legislature or distribution by the Government of the province of any moneys for the support of schools organized and carried on in accordance with the said chapter 29, or any Act passed in amendment thereof or in substitution therefor, there shall be no discrimination against schools of any class described in the said chapter 29.

3. Where the expression "by law" is employed in paragraph (3) of the said section 93, it shall be held to mean the law as set out in the said chapters 29 and 30; and where the expression "at the Union" is employed in the said paragraph (3), it shall be held to mean the date at which this Act comes into force."

Altered by Term 17 of the Terms of Union of Newfoundland with Canada (confirmed by the *British North America Act, 1949*, 12–13 Geo. VI, c. 22 (U.K.)), which reads as follows:

17. In lieu of section ninety-three of the British North America Act, 1867, the following term shall apply in respect of the Province of Newfoundland:

In and for the Province of Newfoundland the Legislature shall have exclusive authority to make laws in relation to education, but the Legislature will not have authority to make laws prejudicially affecting any right or privilege with respect to denominational schools, common (amalgamated) schools, or denominational colleges, that any class or classes of persons have by law in Newfoundland at the date of Union, and out of public funds of the Province of Newfoundland, provided for education,

(a) all such schools shall receive their share of such funds in accordance with scales determined on a non-discriminatory basis from time to time by the Legislature for all schools then being conducted under authority of the Legislature; and

(b) all such colleges shall receive their share of any grant from time to time voted for all colleges then being conducted under authority of the Legislature, such grant being distributed on a non-discriminatory basis.

OLD AGE PENSIONS

94A. It is hereby declared that the Parliament of Canada may from time to time make laws in relation to old age pensions in Canada, but no law made by the Parliament of Canada in relation to old age pensions shall affect the operation of any law present or future of a Provincial Legislature in relation to old age pensions.[44]

AGRICULTURE AND.IMMIGRATION

95. In each Province the Legislature may make Laws in relation to Agriculture in the Province, and to Immigration into the Province; and it is hereby declared that the Parliament of Canada may from Time to Time make Laws in relation to Agriculture in all or any of the Provinces, and to Immigration into all or any of the Provinces; and any Law of the Legislature of a Province relative to Agriculture or to Immigration shall have effect in and for the Province as long and as far only as it is not repugnant to any Act of the Parliament of Canada.

(margin) Concurrent Powers of Legislation respecting Agriculture, etc.

VII. *Judicature*

96. The Governor General shall appoint the Judges of the Superior, District, and County Courts in each Province, except those of the Courts of Probate in Nova Scotia and New Brunswick.

(margin) Appointment of Judges

97. Until the Laws relative to Property and Civil Rights in Ontario, Nova Scotia, and New Brunswick, and the Procedure of the Courts in those Provinces, are made uniform, the Judges of the Courts of those Provinces appointed by the Governor General shall be selected from the respective Bars of those Provinces.

(margin) Selection of Judges in Ontario, etc.

98. The Judges of the Courts of Quebec shall be selected from the Bar of that Province.

(margin) Selection of Judges in Quebec

99.* The Judges of the Superior Courts shall hold Office during good Behaviour, but shall be removable by the Governor General on Address of the Senate and House of Commons.

(margin) Tenure of office of Judges of Superior Courts

100. The Salaries, Allowances, and Pensions of the Judges of the Superior, District, and County Courts (except the Courts of Probate in Nova Scotia and New Brunswick), and of the Admiralty Courts in Cases where the Judges thereof are for the Time being paid by Salary, shall be fixed and provided by the Parliament of Canada.[45]

(margin) Salaries etc., of Judges

101. The Parliament of Canada may, notwithstanding anything in this Act, from Time to Time provide for the Constitution, Main-

(margin) General Court of Appeal, etc.

[44]Added by the *British North America Act, 1951*, 14–15 Geo. VI, c. 32 (U.K.).

[45]Now provided for in the *Judges Act*, R.S.C. 1952, c. 159.

*See *infra*, p. 579.

tenance, and Organization of a General Court of Appeal for Canada, and for the Establishment of any additional Courts for the better Administration of the Laws of Canada.[46]

VIII. *Revenues; Debts; Assets; Taxation*

102. All Duties and Revenues over which the respective Legislatures of Canada, Nova Scotia, and New Brunswick before and at the Union had and have Power of Appropriation, except such Portions thereof as are by this Act reserved to the respective Legislatures of the Provinces, or are raised by them in accordance with the special Powers conferred on them by this Act, shall form One Consolidated Revenue Fund, to be appropriated for the Public Service of Canada in the Manner and subject to the Charges in this Act provided.

Creation of Consolidated Revenue Fund

103. The Consolidated Revenue Fund of Canada shall be permanently charged with the Costs, Charges, and Expenses incident to the Collection, Management, and Receipt thereof, and the same shall form the First Charge thereon, subject to be reviewed and audited in such Manner as shall be ordered by the Governor General in Council until the Parliament otherwise provides.

Expenses of Collection, etc.

104. The annual Interest of the Public Debts of the several Provinces of Canada, Nova Scotia, and New Brunswick at the Union shall form the Second Charge on the Consolidated Revenue Fund of Canada.

Interest of Provincial Public Debts

105. Unless altered by the Parliament of Canada, the Salary of the Governor General shall be Ten thousand Pounds Sterling Money of the United Kingdom of Great Britain and Ireland, payable out of the Consolidated Revenue Fund of Canada. and the same shall form the Third Charge thereon.[47]

Salary of Governor General

106. Subject to the several Payments by this Act charged on the Consolidated Revenue Fund of Canada, the same shall be appropriated by the Parliament of Canada for the Public Service.

Appropriation from Time to Time

107. All Stocks, Cash, Banker's Balances, and Securities for Money belonging to each Province at the Time of the Union, except as in this Act mentioned, shall be the Property of Canada, and shall be taken in Reduction of the Amount of the respective Debts of the Provinces at the Union.

Transfer of Stocks, etc.

108. The Public Works and Property of each Province, enumerated in the Third Schedule to this Act, shall be the Property of Canada.

Transfer of Property in Schedule

[46]See the *Supreme Court Act*, R.S.C. 1952, c. 259, and the *Exchequer Court Act*, R.S.C. 1952, c. 98.
[47]Now covered by the *Governor General's Act*, R.S.C. 1952, c. 139.

109. All Lands, Mines, Minerals, and Royalties belonging to the several Provinces of Canada, Nova Scotia, and New Brunswick at the Union, and all Sums then due or payable for such Lands, Mines, Minerals, or Royalties, shall belong to the several Provinces of Ontario, Quebec, Nova Scotia, and New Brunswick in which the same are situate or arise, subject to any Trusts existing in respect thereof, and to any Interest other than that of the Province in the same.[48]
Property in Lands, Mines, etc.

110. All Assets connected with such Portions of the Public Debt of each Province as are assumed by that Province shall belong to that Province.
Assets connected with Provincial Debts

111. Canada shall be liable for the Debts and Liabilities of each Province existing at the Union.
Canada to be liable for Provincial Debts

112. Ontario and Quebec conjointly shall be liable to Canada for the Amount (if any) by which the Debt of the Province of Canada exceeds at the Union Sixty-two million five hundred thousand Dollars, and shall be charged with Interest at the Rate of Five per Centum per Annum thereon.
Debts of Ontario and Quebec

113. The Assets enumerated in the Fourth Schedule to this Act belonging at the Union to the Province of Canada shall be the Property of Ontario and Quebec conjointly.
Assets of Ontario and Quebec

114. Nova Scotia shall be liable to Canada for the Amount (if any) by which its Public Debt exceeds at the Union Eight million Dollars, and shall be charged with Interest at the Rate of Five per Centum per Annum thereon.[49]
Debt of Nova Scotia

115. New Brunswick shall be liable to Canada for the Amount (if any) by which its Public Debt exceeds at the Union Seven million Dollars, and shall be charged with Interest at the Rate of Five per Centum per Annum thereon.
Debt of New Brunswick

116. In case the Public Debts of Nova Scotia and New Brunswick do not at the Union amount to Eight million and Seven million Dollars respectively, they shall respectively receive by half-yearly Payments in advance from the Government of Canada Interest at Five per Centum per Annum on the Difference between the actual Amounts of their respective Debts and such stipulated Amounts.
Payment of interest to Nova Scotia and New Brunswick

[48]The four western provinces were placed in the same position as the original provinces by the *British North America Act, 1930*, 21 Geo. V, c. 26 (U.K.).

[49]The obligations imposed by this section, sections 115 and 116, and similar obligations under the instruments creating or admitting other provinces, have been carried into legislation of the Parliament of Canada and are now to be found in the *Provincial Subsidies Act*, R.S.C. 1952, c. 221.

117. The several Provinces shall retain all their respective Public Property not otherwise disposed of in this Act, subject to the Right of Canada to assume any Lands or Public Property required for Fortifications or for the Defence of the Country. Provincial Public Property

118. Repealed.[50]

[50]Repealed by the *Statute Law Revision Act, 1950*, 14 Geo. VI, c. 6 (U.K.). As originally enacted, the section read as follows:

118. The following Sums shall be paid yearly by Canada to the several Provinces for the Support of their Governments and Legislatures:

	Dollars
Ontario	Eighty thousand.
Quebec	Seventy thousand.
Nova Scotia	Sixty thousand.
New Brunswick	Fifty thousand.

Two hundred and sixty thousand; and an annual Grant in aid of each Province shall be made, equal to Eighty Cents per Head of the Population as ascertained by the Census of One thousand eight hundred and sixty-one, and in the Case of Nova Scotia and New Brunswick, by each subsequent Decennial Census until the Population of each of those two Provinces amounts to Four hundred thousand Souls, at which Rate such Grant shall thereafter remain. Such Grants shall be in full Settlement of all future Demands on Canada, and shall be paid half-yearly in advance to each Province; but the Government of Canada shall deduct from such Grants, as against any Province, all Sums chargeable as Interest on the Public Debt of that Province in excess of the several Amounts stipulated in this Act.

The section was made obsolete by the *British North America Act, 1907*, 7 Edw. VII, c. 11 (U.K.) which provided:

1. (1) The following grants shall be made yearly by Canada to every province, which at the commencement of this Act is a province of the Dominion, for its local purposes and the support of its Government and Legislature:—
(a) A fixed grant—
where the population of the province is under one hundred and fifty thousand, of one hundred thousand dollars;
where the population of the province is one hundred and fifty thousand, but does not exceed two hundred thousand, of one hundred and fifty thousand dollars;
where the population of the province is two hundred thousand, but does not exceed four hundred thousand, of one hundred and eighty thousand dollars;
where the population of the province is four hundred thousand, but does not exceed eight hundred thousand, of one hundred and ninety thousand dollars;
where the population of the province is eight hundred thousand, but does not exceed one million five hundred thousand, of two hundred and twenty thousand dollars;
where the population of the province exceeds one million five hundred thousand, of two hundred and forty thousand dollars; and
(b) Subject to the special provisions of this Act as to the provinces of British Columbia and Prince Edward Island, a grant at the rate of eighty cents per head of the population of the province up to the number of two million five hundred thousand, and at the rate of sixty cents per head of so much of the population as exceeds that number.
(2) An additional grant of one hundred thousand dollars shall be made yearly to the province of British Columbia for a period of ten years from the commencement of this Act.
(3) The population of a province shall be ascertained from time to time in the case of the provinces of Manitoba, Saskatchewan, and Alberta respectively by the last quinquennial census or statutory estimate of population made under the Acts establishing those provinces or any other Act of the Parliament of Canada making provision for the purpose, and in the case of any other province by the last decennial census for the time being.
(4) The grants payable under this Act shall be paid half-yearly in advance to each province.
(5) The grants payable under this Act shall be substituted for the grants or subsidies (in this Act referred to as existing grants) payable for the like purposes at the commencement of this Act to the several provinces of the Dominion under the provisions of section one hundred and eighteen of the British North America Act 1867, or of any Order in Council establishing a province, or of any Act of the Parliament of Canada containing directions for the payment of any such grant or subsidy, and those provisions shall cease to have effect.
(6) The Government of Canada shall have the same power of deducting sums charged against a province on account of the interest on public debt in the case of the grant payable under this Act to the province as they have in the case of the existing grant.
(7) Nothing in this Act shall affect the obligation of the Government of Canada

119. New Brunswick shall receive by half-yearly Payments in advance from Canada for the Period of Ten Years from the Union an additional Allowance of Sixty-three thousand Dollars per Annum; but as long as the Public Debt. of that Province remains under Seven million Dollars, a Deduction equal to the Interest at Five per Centum per Annum on such Deficiency shall be made from that Allowance of Sixty-three thousand Dollars.[51]

Further Grant to New Brunswick

120. All Payments to be made under this Act, or in discharge of Liabilities created under any Act of the Provinces of Canada, Nova Scotia, and New Brunswick respectively, and assumed by Canada, shall, until the Parliament of Canada otherwise directs, be made in such Form and Manner as may from Time to Time be ordered by the Governor General in Council.

Form of Payments

121. All Articles of the Growth, Produce, or Manufacture of any one of the Provinces shall, from and after the Union, be admitted free into each of the other Provinces.

Canadian Manufactures, etc.

122. The Customs and Excise Laws of each Province shall, subject to the Provisions of this Act, continue in force until altered by the Parliament of Canada.[52]

Continuance of Customs and Excise Laws

123. Where Customs Duties are, at the Union, leviable on any Goods, Wares, or Merchandises in any Two Provinces, those Goods, Wares, and Merchandises may, from and after the Union, be imported from one of those Provinces into the other of them on Proof of Payment of the Customs Duty leviable thereon in the Province of Exportation, and on Payment of such further Amount (if any) of Customs Duty as is leviable thereon in the Province of Importation.[53]

Exportation and Importation as between Two Provinces

124. Nothing in this Act shall affect the Right of New Brunswick to levy the Lumber Dues provided in Chapter Fifteen of Title Three of the Revised Statutes of New Brunswick, or in any Act amending that Act before or after the Union, and not increasing

Lumber Dues in New Brunswick

---

to pay to any province any grant which is payable to that province, other than the existing grant for which the grant under this Act is substituted.

(8) In the case of the provinces of British Columbia and Prince Edward Island, the amount paid on account of the grant payable per head of the population to the provinces under this Act shall not at any time be less than the amount of the corresponding grant payable at the commencement of this Act, and if it is found on any decennial census that the population of the province has decreased since the last decennial census, the amount paid on account of the grant shall not be decreased below the amount then payable, notwithstanding the decrease of the population.

See the *Provincial Subsidies Act*, R.S.C. 1952, c. 221, *The Maritime Provinces Additional Subsidies Act*, 1942–43, c. 14, and the Terms of Union of Newfoundland with Canada, appended to the *British North America Act, 1949*, and also to *An Act to approve the Terms of Union of Newfoundland with Canada*, chapter 1 of the statutes of Canada, 1949.

[51]Spent.

[52]Spent. Now covered by the *Customs Act*, R.S.C. 1952, c. 58, the *Customs Tariff*, R.S.C. 1952, c. 60, the *Excise Act*, R.S.C. 1952, c. 99 and the *Excise Tax Act*, R.S.C. 1952, c. 100.

[53]Spent.

the Amount of such Dues; but the Lumber of any of the Provinces other than New Brunswick shall not be subject to such Dues.[54]

125. No Lands or Property belonging to Canada or any Province shall be liable to Taxation.

Exemption of Public Lands, etc.

126. Such Portions of the Duties and Revenues over which the respective Legislatures of Canada, Nova Scotia, and New Brunswick had before the Union Power of Appropriation as are by this Act reserved to the respective Governments or Legislatures of the Provinces, and all Duties and Revenues raised by them in accordance with the special Powers conferred upon them by this Act, shall in each Province form One Consolidated Revenue Fund to be appropriated for the Public Service of the Province.

Provincial Consolidated Revenue Fund

IX. *Miscellaneous Provisions*

GENERAL

127. Repealed.[55]

128. Every Member of the Senate or House of Commons of Canada shall before taking his Seat therein take and subscribe before the Governor General or some Person authorized by him, and every Member of a Legislative Council or Legislative Assembly of any Province shall before taking his Seat therein take and subscribe before the Lieutenant Governor of the Province or some Person authorized by him, the Oath of Allegiance contained in the Fifth Schedule to this Act; and every Member of the Senate of Canada and every Member of the Legislative Council of Quebec shall also, before taking his Seat therein, take and subscribe before the Governor General, or some Person authorized by him, the Declaration of Qualification contained in the same Schedule.

Oath of Allegiance, etc.

129. Except as otherwise provided by this Act, all Laws in force in Canada, Nova Scotia, or New Brunswick at the Union, and all Courts of Civil and Criminal Jurisdiction, and all legal Commissions, Powers, and Authorities, and all Officers, Judicial, Administrative, and Ministerial, existing therein at the Union, shall

Continuance of existing Laws, Courts, Officers, etc.

[54]These dues were repealed in 1873 by 36 Vict., c. 16 (N.B.). And see *An Act respecting the Export Duties imposed on Lumber*, etc., (1873) 36 Vict., c. 41 (Canada), and section 2 of the *Provincial Subsidies Act*, R.S.C. 1952, c. 221.

[55]Repealed by the *Statute Law Revision Act, 1893*, 56–57 Vict., c. 14 (U.K.). The section read as follows:

127. If any Person being at the passing of this Act a Member of the Legislative Council of Canada, Nova Scotia, or New Brunswick to whom a Place in the Senate is offered, does not within Thirty Days thereafter, by Writing under his Hand addressed to the Governor General of the Province of Canada or to the Lieutenant Governor of Nova Scotia or New Brunswick (as the Case may be), accept the same, he shall be deemed to have declined the same; and any Person who, being at the passing of this Act a Member of the Legislative Council of Nova Scotia or New Brunswick, accepts a Place in the Senate, shall thereby vacate his Seat in such Legislative Council.

continue in Ontario, Quebec, Nova Scotia, and New Brunswick respectively, as if the Union had not been made; subject nevertheless (except with respect to such as are enacted by or exist under Acts of the Parliament of Great Britain or of the Parliament of the United Kingdom of Great Britain and Ireland,) to be repealed, abolished, or altered by the Parliament of Canada, or by the Legislature of the respective Province, according to the Authority of the Parliament or of that Legislature under this Act.[56]

130. Until the Parliament of Canada otherwise provides, all Officers of the several Provinces having Duties to discharge in relation to Matters other than those coming within the Classes of Subjects by this Act assigned exclusively to the Legislatures of the Province shall be Officers of Canada, and shall continue to discharge the Duties of their respective Offices under the same Liabilities, Responsibilities, and Penalties as if the Union had not been made.[57] *Transfer of Officers to Canada*

131. Until the Parliament of Canada otherwise provides, the Governor General in Council may from Time to Time appoint such Officers as the Governor General in Council deems necessary or proper for the effectual Execution of this Act. *Appointment of new Officers*

132. The Parliament and Government of Canada shall have all Powers necessary or proper for performing the Obligations of Canada or of any Province thereof, as Part of the British Empire, towards Foreign Countries, arising under Treaties between the Empire and such Foreign Countries. *Treaty Obligations*

133. Either the English or the French Language may be used by any Person in the Debates of the Houses of the Parliament of Canada and of the Houses of the Legislature of Quebec; and both those Languages shall be used in the respective Records and Journals of those Houses; and either of those Languages may be used by any Person or in any Pleading or Process in or issuing from any Court of Canada established under this Act, and in or from all or any of the Courts of Quebec. *Use of English and French Languages*
The Acts of the Parliament of Canada and of the Legislature of Quebec shall be printed and published in both those Languages.

ONTARIO AND QUEBEC

134. Until the Legislature of Ontario or of Quebec otherwise provides, the Lieutenant Governors of Ontario and Quebec may each appoint under the Great Seal of the Province the following Officers, to hold Office during Pleasure, that is to say,—the *Appointment of Executive Officers for Ontario and Quebec*

[56]The restriction against altering or repealing laws enacted by or existing under statutes of the United Kingdom was removed by the *Statute of Westminster, 1931*, 22 Geo. V, c. 4 (U.K.).
[57]Spent.

Attorney General, the Secretary and Registrar of the Province, the Treasurer of the Province, the Commissioner of Crown Lands, and the Commissioner of Agriculture and Public Works, and in the Case of Quebec the Solicitor General, and may, by Order of the Lieutenant Governor in Council, from Time to Time prescribe the Duties of those Officers, and of the several Departments over which they shall preside or to which they shall belong, and of the Officers and Clerks thereof, and may also appoint other and additional Officers to hold Office during Pleasure, and may from Time to Time prescribe the Duties of those Officers, and of the several Departments over which they shall preside or to which they shall belong, and of the Officers and Clerks thereof.[58]

135. Until the Legislature of Ontario or Quebec otherwise provides, all Rights, Powers, Duties, Functions, Responsibilities, or Authorities at the passing of this Act vested in or imposed on the Attorney General, Solicitor General, Secretary and Registrar of the Province of Canada, Minister of Finance, Commissioner of Crown Lands, Commissioner of Public Works, and Minister of Agriculture and Receiver General, by any Law, Statute, or Ordinance of Upper Canada, Lower Canada, or Canada, and not repugnant to this Act, shall be vested in or imposed on any Officer to be appointed by the Lieutenant Governor for the Discharge of the same or any of them; and the Commissioner of Agriculture and Public Works shall perform the Duties and Functions of the Office of Minister of Agriculture at the passing of this Act imposed by the Law of the Province of Canada, as well as those of the Commissioner of Public Works.[59] *Powers, Duties, etc. of Executive Officers*

136. Until altered by the Lieutenant Governor in Council, the Great Seals of Ontario and Quebec respectively shall be the same, or of the same Design, as those used in the Provinces of Upper Canada and Lower Canada respectively before their Union as the Province of Canada. *Great Seals*

137. The Words "and from thence to the End of the then next ensuing Session of the Legislature," or Words to the same Effect, used in any temporary Act of the Province of Canada not expired before the Union, shall be construed to extend and apply to the next Session of the Parliament of Canada if the Subject Matter of the Act is within the Powers of the same as defined by this Act, or to the next Sessions of the Legislatures of Ontario and Quebec respectively if the Subject Matter of the Act is within the Powers of the same as defined by this Act. *Construction of temporary Acts*

[58]Spent. Now covered in Ontario by the *Executive Council Act*, R.S.O. 1950, c. 121 and in Quebec by the *Executive Power Act*, R.S.Q. 1941, c. 7.
[59]Probably spent.

138. From and after the Union the Use of the Words "Upper Canada" instead of "Ontario," or "Lower Canada" instead of "Quebec," in any Deed, Writ, Process, Pleading, Document, Matter, or Thing, shall not invalidate the same. As to Errors in Names

139. Any Proclamation under the Great Seal of the Province of Canada issued before the Union to take effect at a Time which is subsequent to the Union, whether relating to that Province, or to Upper Canada, or to Lower Canada, and the several Matters and Things therein proclaimed, shall be and continue of like Force and Effect as if the Union had not been made.[60] As to issue of Proclamations before Union, to commence after Union

140. Any Proclamation which is authorized by any Act of the Legislature of the Province of Canada to be issued under the Great Seal of the Province of Canada, whether relating to that Province, or to Upper Canada, or to Lower Canada, and which is not issued before the Union, may be issued by the Lieutenant Governor of Ontario or of Quebec, as its Subject Matter requires, under the Great Seal thereof; and from and after the Issue of such Proclamation the same and the several Matters and Things therein proclaimed shall be and continue of the like Force and Effect in Ontario or Quebec as if the Union had not been made.[61] As to Issue of Proclamations after Union

141. The Penitentiary of the Province of Canada shall, until the Parliament of Canada otherwise provides, be and continue the Penitentiary of Ontario and of Quebec.[62] Penitentiary

142. The Division and Adjustment of the Debts, Credits, Liabilities, Properties, and Assets of Upper Canada and Lower Canada shall be referred to the Arbitrament of Three Arbitrators, One chosen by the Government of Ontario, One by the Government of Quebec, and One by the Government of Canada; and the Selection of the Arbitrators shall not be made until the Parliament of Canada and the Legislatures of Ontario and Quebec have met; and the Arbitrator chosen by the Government of Canada shall not be a Resident either in Ontario or in Quebec.[63] Arbitration respecting Debts, etc.

143. The Governor General in Council may from Time to Time order that such and so many of the Records, Books, and Documents of the Province of Canada as he thinks fit shall be appropriated and delivered either to Ontario or to Quebec, and the same shall thenceforth be the Property of that Province; and any Copy thereof or Extract therefrom, duly certified by the Officer having charge of the Original thereof, shall be admitted as Evidence.[64] Division of Records

[60]Probably spent.
[61]Probably spent.
[62]Spent. Penitentiaries are now provided for by the *Penitentiary Act*, R.S.C. 1952, c. 206.
[63]Spent. See pages (xi) and (xii) of the Public Accounts, 1902–03.
[64]Probably spent. Two orders were made under this section on the 24th of January, 1868.

144. The Lieutenant Governor of Quebec may from Time to Time, by Proclamation under the Great Seal of the Province, to take effect from a Day to be appointed therein, constitute Townships in those Parts of the Province of Quebec in which Townships are not then already constituted, and fix the Metes and Bounds thereof.

Constitution of Townships in Quebec

145. Repealed.[65]

XI. *Admission of Other Colonies*

146. It shall be lawful for the Queen, by and with the Advice of Her Majesty's Most Honourable Privy Council, on Addresses from the Houses of the Parliament of Canada, and from the Houses of the respective Legislatures of the Colonies or Provinces of Newfoundland, Prince Edward Island, and British Columbia, to admit those Colonies or Provinces, or any of them, into the Union, and on Address from the Houses of the Parliament of Canada to admit Rupert's Land and the North-western Territory, or either of them, into the Union, on such Terms and Conditions in each Case as are in the Addresses expressed and as the Queen thinks fit to approve, subject to the Provisions of this Act; and the Provisions of any Order in Council in that Behalf shall have effect as if they had been enacted by the Parliament of the United Kingdom of Great Britain and Ireland[66]

Power to admit Newfoundland, etc., into the Union

147. In case of the Admission of Newfoundland and Prince Edward Island, or either of them, each shall be entitled to a Representation in the Senate of Canada of Four Members, and (notwithstanding anything in this Act) in case of the Admission of Newfoundland the normal Number of Senators shall be Seventy-six and their maximum Number shall be Eighty-two; but Prince Edward Island when admitted shall be deemed to be comprised in the Third of the Three Divisions into which Canada is, in relation to the Constitution of the Senate, divided by this Act, and accordingly, after the Admission of Prince Edward Island, whether Newfoundland is admitted or not, the Representation of

As to Representation of Newfoundland and Prince Edward Island in Senate

[65]Repealed by the *Statute Law Revision Act, 1893*, 56–57 Vict., c. 14, (U.K.). The section read as follows:

X. *Intercolonial Railway*
145. Inasmuch as the Provinces of Canada, Nova Scotia, and New Brunswick have joined in a Declaration that the Construction of the Intercolonial Railway is essential to the Consolidation of the Union of British North America, and to the Assent thereto of Nova Scotia and New Brunswick, and have consequently agreed that Provision should be made for its immediate Construction by the Government of Canada: Therefore, in order to give effect to that Agreement, it shall be the Duty of the Government and Parliament of Canada to provide for the Commencement, within Six Months after the Union, of a Railway connecting the River St. Lawrence with the City of Halifax in Nova Scotia, and for the Construction thereof without Intermission, and the Completion thereof with all practicable Speed.

[66]All territories mentioned in this section are now part of Canada. See the notes to section 5, *supra*.

Nova Scotia and New Brunswick in the Senate shall, as Vacancies occur, be reduced from Twelve to Ten Members respectively, and the Representation of each of those Provinces shall not be increased at any Time beyond Ten, except under the Provisions of this Act for the Appointment of Three or Six additional Senators under the Direction of the Queen.[67]

[67]Spent. See the notes to sections 21, 22, 26, 27 and 28, *supra*.

Appendix B

THE BRITISH NORTH AMERICA ACT, 1960*

AN ACT to amend the British North America Act, 1867

20 December, 1960

WHEREAS the Senate and House of Commons of Canada in Parliament assembled have submitted addresses to Her Majesty praying that Her Majesty may graciously be pleased to cause a measure to be laid before the Parliament of the United Kingdom for the enactment of the provisions hereinafter set forth:

BE IT THEREFORE enacted by the Queen's most Excellent Majesty, by and with the advice and consent of the Lord Spiritual and Temporal, and Commons, in this present Parliament assembled, and by the authority of the same, as follows:—

1. Section ninety-nine of the British North America Act, 1867, is hereby repealed and the following substituted therefor:—

    99. (1) Subject to subsection (2) of this section, the judges of the superior courts shall hold office during good behaviour, but shall be removeable by the Governor General on address of the Senate and House of Commons.

    (2) A judge of a superior court, whether appointed before or after the coming into force of this section, shall cease to hold office upon attaining the age of seventy-five years, or upon the coming into force of this section if at that time he has already attained that age.

2. This Act may be cited as the British North America Act, 1960, and the British North America Acts, 1867 to 1952, and this Act may be cited together as the British North America Acts, 1867 to 1960.

3. This Act shall come into force on the first day of March, nineteen hundred and sixty-one.

*9 Eliz. II, c. 2, enacted by the Parliament of the United Kingdom and reprinted here by permission of the Queen's Printer.

Appendix C

THE STATUTE OF WESTMINSTER, 1931*

AN ACT to give effect to certain resolutions passed by Imperial Conferences held in the years 1926 and 1930.

11th December, 1931

WHEREAS the delegates to His Majesty's Governments in the United Kingdom, the Dominion of Canada, the Commonwealth of Australia, the Dominion of New Zealand, the Union of South Africa, the Irish Free State and Newfoundland, at Imperial Conferences holden at Westminster in the years of our Lord nineteen hundred and twenty-six and nineteen hundred and thirty did concur in making the declarations and resolutions set forth in the Reports of the said Conferences:

And whereas it is meet and proper to set out by way of preamble to this Act that, inasmuch as the Crown is the symbol of the free association of the members of the British Commonwealth of Nations, and as they are united by a common allegiance to the Crown, it would be in accord with the established constitutional position of all the members of the Commonwealth in relation to one another that any alteration in the law touching the Succession to the Throne or the Royal Style and Titles shall hereafter require the assent as well of the Parliaments of all the Dominions as of the Parliament of the United Kingdom:

And whereas it is in accord with the established constitutional position that no law hereafter made by the Parliament of the United Kingdom shall extend to any of the said Dominions as part of the law of that Dominion otherwise than at the request and with the consent of that Dominion:

And whereas it is necessary for the ratifying, confirming and establishing of certain of the said declarations and resolutions of the said Conferences that a law be made and enacted in due form by authority of the Parliament of the United Kingdom:

And whereas the Dominion of Canada, the Commonwealth of Australia, the Dominion of New Zealand, the Union of South Africa, the Irish Free State and Newfoundland have severally requested and consented to the submission of a measure to the Parliament of the United Kingdom for making such provision with regard to the matters aforesaid as is hereafter in this Act contained:

Now, THEREFORE, BE IT ENACTED by the King's Most Excellent Majesty, by and with the advice and consent of the Lords Spiritual and Temporal, and Commons, in this present Parliament assembled, and by the authority of the same, as follows:—

*British Statutes, 22 George V, Chapter 4.

210

1. In this Act the expression "Dominion" means any of the following Dominions, that is to say, the Dominion of Canada, the Commonwealth of Australia, the Dominion of New Zealand, the Union of South Africa, the Irish Free State and Newfoundland.

2. 1. The Colonial Laws Validity Act, 1865, shall not apply to any law made after the commencement of this Act by the Parliament of a Dominion.

2. No law and no provision of any law made after the commencement of this Act by the Parliament of a Dominion shall be void or inoperative on the ground that it is repugnant to the law of England, or to the provisions of any existing or future Act of Parliament of the United Kingdom, or to any order, rule, or regulation made under any such Act, and the powers of the Parliament of a Dominion shall include the power to repeal or amend any such Act, order, rule or regulation in so far as the same is part of the law of the Dominion.

3. It is hereby declared and enacted that the Parliament of a Dominion has full power to make laws having extra-territorial operation.

4. No Act of Parliament of the United Kingdom passed after the commencement of this Act shall extend or be deemed to extend, to a Dominion as part of the law of that Dominion, unless it is expressly declared in that Act that that Dominion has requested, and consented to, the enactment thereof.

5. Without prejudice to the generality of the foregoing provisions of this Act, sections seven hundred and thirty-five and seven hundred and thirty-six of the Merchant Shipping Act, 1894, shall be construed as though reference therein to the Legislature of a British possession did not include reference to the Parliament of a Dominion.

6. Without prejudice to the generality of the foregoing provisions of this Act, section four of the Colonial Courts of Admiralty Act, 1890 (which requires certain laws to be reserved for the signification of His Majesty's pleasure or to contain a suspending clause), and so much of section seven of that Act as requires the approval of His Majesty in Council to any rules of Court for regulating the practice and procedure of a Colonial Court of Admiralty, shall cease to have effect in any Dominion as from the commencement of this Act.

7. 1. Nothing in this Act shall be deemed to apply to the repeal, amendment or alteration of the British North America Acts, 1867 to 1930, or any order, rule or regulation made thereunder.

2. The provisions of section two of this Act shall extend to laws made by any of the Provinces of Canada and to the powers of the legislatures of such Provinces.

3. The powers conferred by this Act upon the Parliament of Canada or upon the legislatures of the Provinces shall be restricted to the enactment

JUDICIAL COMMITTEE AND B.N.A. ACT

of laws in relation to matters within the competence of the Parliament of Canada or of any of the legislatures of the Provinces respectively.

8. Nothing in this Act shall be deemed to confer any power to repeal or alter the Constitution or the Constitution Act of the Commonwealth of Australia or the Constitution Act of the Dominion of New Zealand otherwise than in accordance with the law existing before the commencement of this Act.

9. 1. Nothing in this Act shall be deemed to authorize the Parliament of the Commonwealth of Australia to make laws on any matter within the authority of the States of Australia, not being a matter within the authority of the Parliament or Government of the Commonwealth of Australia.

2. Nothing in this Act shall be deemed to require the concurrence of the Parliament or Government of the Commonwealth of Australia, in any law made by the Parliament of the United Kingdom with respect to any matter within the authority of the States of Australia, not being a matter within the authority of the Parliament or Government of the Commonwealth of Australia, in any case where it would have been in accordance with the constitutional practice existing before the commencement of this Act that the Parliament of the United Kingdom should make that law without such concurrence.

3. In the application of this Act to the Commonwealth of Australia the request and consent referred to in section four shall mean the request and consent of the Parliament and Government of the Commonwealth.

10. 1. None of the following sections of this Act, that is to say, sections two, three, four, five and six, shall extend to a Dominion to which this section applies as part of the law of that Dominion unless that section is adopted by the Parliament of the Dominion, and any Act of that Parliament adopting any section of this Act may provide that the adoption shall have effect either from the commencement of this Act or from such later date as is specified in the adopting Act.

2. The Parliament of any such Dominion as aforesaid may at any time revoke the adoption of any section referred to in sub-section (1) of this section.

3. The Dominions to which this section applies are the Commonwealth of Australia, the Dominion of New Zealand, and Newfoundland.

11. Notwithstanding anything in the Interpretation Act, 1889, the expression "Colony" shall not, in any Act of the Parliament of the United Kingdom passed after the commencement of this Act, include a Dominion or any Province or State forming part of a Dominion.

12. This Act may be cited as the Statute of Westminster, 1931.

Appendix D

ANALYTICAL TABLE OF THE MAJOR JUDICIAL COMMITTEE JUDGMENTS

Key to numbers in Column D

1. Exhaustion Theory
2. Introductory words of s. 91
3. Deeming paragraph
4. Three-compartment view
5. Two-compartment view
6. Ambit of s. 92(16)
7. Ambit of s. 91(2)

8. Ambit of s. 92(13)
9. Ambit of s. 91(27)
10. Ambit of s. 92(15)
11. Ambit of s. 91(3)
12. Ambit of s. 92(2)
13. Ambit of s. 132
14. Severability Doctrine

15. Aspect Principle
16. Ancillary Doctrine
17. Occupied Field Doctrine
18. Co-operation Doctrine
19. Dimensions Doctrine
20. Emergency Doctrine

[The question marks after certain numbers imply that their inclusion is debatable. The "Exhaustion Theory" references are either to that theory as such, or else to the closely related problem of extra-territorial powers.]

A Case	B Date and Case No.	C Heads and Sections Referred to	D Issues
The Queen v. Coote (courts)	(1873), 4 A.C. 599	92(14), 96	
L'Union St. Jacques de Montréal v. Bélisle (federal railways)	(1874), 6 A.C. 31	91(7), 91(9), 91(21), 92(16)	3, 4(?), 6, 15(?), 16
Dow v. Black (local or private matter)	(1875), 6 A.C. 272	91(3), 92(2), 92(10), 92(16)	3, 4(?), 6, 11, 12
A.-G. Que. v. Queen Insurance Co. (indirect taxation)	(1878), 3 A.C. 1090	92(2), 92(9)	12

213

A Case	B Date and Case No.	C Heads and Sections Referred to	D Issues
Valin v. *Langlois* (controverted Election Act)	(1879), 5 A.C. 115	41, 92(14)	2, 4(?), 5(?)
Bourgoin v. *La Compagnie de Chemin de Fer de Montréal* (federal railways)	(1880), 5 A.C. 381	92(10)	
Cushing v. *Dupuis* (bankruptcy and insolvency)	(1880), 5 A.C. 409	91(21), 92(13), 92(14)	4(?), 5(?), 8, 16
Citizens Insurance Co. v. *Parsons* (insurance contracts)	(1881), 7 A.C. 96	91(2), 91(3), 91(26), 92(2), 92(11), 92(12), 92(13), 94	1, 2, 3, 4(?), 7, 8, 11, 12, 15(?)
Dobie v. *Temporalities Board* (pre-Confederation statutes)	(1881), 7 A.C. 136	92(2), 92(7), 92(11), 92(13), 129	2, 4(?), 8, 12, 15(?), 17
The Queen v. *Belleau* (B.N.A. Act – s. 111)	(1882), 7 A.C. 473	111	
Russell v. *The Queen* (Canada Temperance Act)	(1882), 7 A.C. 829	91(2), 91(27), 92(9), 92(13), 92(15), 92(16)	2, 4(?), 6, 7, 8, 9, 10, 15(?), 17, 19(?), 20(?)
A.-G. Ont. v. *Mercer* (escheats)	(1883), 8 A.C. 767	92(5), 92(13), 102, 109, 117, 125, 126	8
Hodge v. *The Queen* (Liquor Licence Act)	(1883), 9 A.C. 117	91(2), 92(8), 92(13), 92(15), 92(16)	6, 7, 8, 10, 15
Colonial Building and Investment Association v. *A.-G. Que.* (federal companies)	(1883), 9 A.C. 157	92(13)	2, 8, 17
A.-G. Que. v. *Reed* (indirect taxation)	(1884), 10 A.C. 141	65, 92(2), 92(14)	12
Bank of Toronto v. *Lambe* (indirect taxation)	(1887), 12 A.C. 575	91(2), 91(3), 91(15), 92(2), 92(9)	1, 7, 11, 12

214

Case	Citation	References	
St. Catherine's Milling and Lumber Co. v. The Queen (Indian lands)	(1889), 14 A.C. 46	91(24), 102, 108, 109, 117, 125, 142	
A.-G. B.C. v. A.-G. Can. (precious metals)	(1889), 14 A.C. 295	109, 146	
Liquidators of the Maritime Bank of Canada v. Receiver-Gen. of N.B. (status of provincial government)	[1892] A.C. 437	9, 58, 109, 126	1
Winnipeg v. Barrett (schools)	[1892] A.C. 445	93	
Tennant v. Union Bank (banking)	[1894] A.C. 31	91(15), 91(21), 91(22), 91(23), 92(13)	3, 4, 8, 16, 17
A.-G. Ont. v. A.-G. Can. (voluntary assignments)	[1894] A.C. 189	91(21), 92(13), 92(14)	8, 16, 17
Brophy v. A.-G. Man. (education)	[1895] A.C. 202	93	
A.-G. Ont. v. A.-G. Can. (Liquor Licence Act —local prohibition)	[1896] A.C. 348	91(2), 92(8), 92(9), 92(13), 92(16), 94, 129	2, 3, 4, 6, 7, 8, 15(?), 16, 17, 19
Esquimalt and Nanaimo Railway v. Bainbridge (precious metals)	[1896] A.C. 561	146	
Fielding v. Thomas (immunity of members of N.S. Assembly)	[1896] A.C. 600	18, 88, 91(27), 92(1)	1, 9
A.-G. Can. v. A.-G. Ont. (Indian annuities)	[1897] A.C. 199	109, 111, 112, 142	
Brewers' and Maltsters' Association v. A.-G. Ont. (indirect taxation)	[1897] A.C. 231	92(2), 92(9)	12
A.-G. Can. v. A.-G. Ont. (Queen's Counsel)	[1898] A.C. 247	65, 92(1), 92(4), 92(14), 96, 100, 101	
A.-G. Can. v. A.'s-G. Ont., Que., N.S. (fisheries)	[1898] A.C. 700	91(3), 91(10), 91(12), 91(21), 91(23), 92(5), 92(9), 92(13), 108	2, 4, 8, 11, 16, 17

Appendix D (continued)

A Case	B Date and Case No.	C Heads and Sections Referred to	D Issues
Canadian Pacific Railway v. *Notre Dame de Bonsecours* (federal railway)	[1899] A.C. 367	91(29), 92(2), 92(10), 92(16)	6, 12, 17
Union Colliery Co. v. *Bryden* (naturalization and aliens)	[1899] A.C. 580	91(25), 92(10), 92(13)	1, 3, 8, 15(?), 17
Madden v. *Nelson and Fort Sheppard Railway* (federal railway)	[1899] A.C. 626	91(29), 92(10), 92(16)	6, 17
A.-G. Man. v. *Manitoba Licence Holders' Association* (Manitoba Liquor Act)	[1902] A.C. 73	91(3), 92(8), 92(9), 92(13), 92(16)	2, 4, 6, 8, 11, 17
Lambe v. *Manuel* (succession duty)	[1903] A.C. 68	92(2)	12
Ontario Mining Co. v. *Seybold* (Indian lands)	[1903] A.C. 73	91(24), 109	1
Cunningham v. *Tomey Homma* (naturalization and aliens)	[1903] A.C. 151	91(25), 92(1)	
A.-G. Ont. v. *Hamilton Street Railway* (Lord's Day observance)	[1903] A.C. 524	91(27)	9
A.-G. P.E.I. v. *A.-G. Can.* (Parliamentary representation)	[1905] A.C. 37	1, 3, 8, 51, 146	
Toronto v. *Bell Telephone* (interprovincial works)	[1905] A.C. 52	91(29), 92(10)	17
A.-G. B.C. v. *C.P.R.* (railway—harbours—provincial property)	[1906] A.C. 204	91(29), 92(10), 108	
A.-G. Can. v. *Cain* (aliens)	[1906] A.C. 542	91(25)	1
Grand Trunk Railway v. *A.-G. Can.* (federal railway)	[1907] A.C. 65	91(29), 92(10), 92(13)	8, 16, 17

216

McGregor v. *Esquimalt and Nanaimo Railway* (local works—property rights)	[1907] A.C. 462	91(1), 92(10), 92(13)	8
Toronto v. *C.P.R.* (federal railway)	[1908] A.C. 54	91(29), 92(8), 92(10), 92(13)	8, 16, 17
Crown Grain Co. v. *Day* (courts)	[1908] A.C. 504	92(13)	8, 17
Woodruff v. *A.-G. Ont.* (extra-provincial taxes)	[1908] A.C. 508	92(2)	12
Watts v. *Watts* (divorce)	[1908] A.C. 573	91 (26)	
La Compagnie Hydraulique de St. François v. *Continental Heat and Light Co.* (federal companies)	[1909] A.C. 194	91(29), 92(11)	5(?), 17
Dominion of Canada v. *Province of Ontario* (Indian annuities)	[1910] A.C. 637	91(24)	
Burrard Power Co. v. *The King* (public property)	[1911] A.C. 87	91(1), 91(10), 146	
Wyatt v. *A.-G. Que.* (fishing rights)	[1911] A.C. 489	108	
The King v. *Lovitt* (succession duty)	[1912] A.C. 212	92(2)	12
Montreal v. *Montreal Street Railway* (local railway)	[1912] A.C. 333	91(2), 91(29), 92(10), 92(16)	2, 3, 6, 7, 16, 17, 18
A.-G. Ont. v. *A.-G. Canada* (companies)	[1912] A.C. 571	101	1, 2, 4
Toronto and Niagara Power Co. v. *North Toronto* (federal works)	[1912] A.C. 834	91(29), 92(10)	
In re Marriage Reference to Supreme Court (marriage and divorce)	[1912] A.C. 880	91(26), 92(12)	
Royal Bank of Canada v. *The King* (extra-provincial civil rights)	[1913] A.C. 283	91(12), 91(15), 92(2), 92(10), 92(13), 92(16)	6, 8, 12

Appendix D (*continued*)

A Case	B Date and Case No.	C Heads and Sections Referred to	D Issues
A.-G. B.C. v. *A.-G. Can.* (fishing rights)	[1914] A.C. 153	91(1), 91(10), 92(2), 92(5), 108, 146	12
Cotton v. *The King* (succession duty)	[1914] A.C. 176	92(2)	12
John Deere Plow Co. v. *Wharton* (federal companies)	[1915] A.C. 330	91(2), 92(11), 92(13)	2, 4, 7, 8, 15, 17
A.-G. Alta. v. *A.-G. Can.* (railway crossing)	[1915] A.C. 363	91(29), 92(10)	
Bonanza Creek Gold Mining Co. v. *The King* (dominion companies)	[1916] 1 A.C. 566	9, 12, 14, 15, 16, 58, 64, 65, 92(11), 129	
A.-G. Can. v. *A.-G. Alta.* (Insurance Act)	[1916] 1 A.C. 588	91(2), 91(12), 91(15), 91(25), 92(11), 92(13), 92(16)	2, 4, 6, 7, 8, 15, 16, 20
A.-G. Ont. v. *A.-G. Can.* (companies)	[1916] 1 A.C. 598	92(11)	
Smith v. *Vermillion Hills Rural Council* (B.N.A. Act—s. 125)	[1916] 2 A.C. 569	92(2), 125	12
Hamilton, Grimsby, and Beamsville Railway v. *A.-G. Ont.* (works for general advant-age of Canada)	[1916] 2 A.C. 583	91(29), 92(10)	
Ottawa Roman Catholic Separate Schools Trustees v. *Mackell* (schools)	[1917] A.C. 62	92(16), 93	1, 6
Ottawa Roman Catholic Separate Schools Trustees v. *Ottawa* (schools)	[1917] A.C. 76	93	
Toronto General Trusts Corporation v. *The King* (succession duty)	[1919] A.C. 679	92(2)	12

Case	Citation	Sections	Notes
In re the Initiative and Referendum Act (legislative power of province—office of Lt. Gov.)	[1919] A.C. 935	9, 12, 58, 65, 69, 90, 91(2)	14
Walker v. Walker (divorce)	[1919] A.C. 947	91(26), 92(14)	
Board v. Board (divorce—imperial laws in force in Canada)	[1919] A.C. 956	91(26), 92(14)	
A.-G. Can. v. Ritchie Contracting and Supply Co. (public harbours)	[1919] A.C. 999	91(10), 108, 109	
Workmen's Compensation Board v. C.P.R. (legislative power of province)	[1920] A.C. 184	91(10), 91(29), 92(2), 92(10), 92(13)	8, 12, 17
Ottawa Roman Catholic Separate Schools Trustees v. Quebec Bank (schools)	[1920] A.C. 230	92(13), 93	8
Toronto Railway v. Toronto (federal railway)	[1920] A.C. 426	91(29), 92(8), 92(10)	9, 16
Toronto Railway v. Toronto (Ontario Railway Act)	[1920] A.C. 446	91(27), 92(15), 96	10
Paquet v. Quebec Pilots' Corporation (pilotage dues)	[1920] A.C. 1029	91(2), 91(10), 92(13)	7, 8, 15
A.-G. Que. v. A.-G. Can. (Indian lands—Star Chrome)	[1921] 1 A.C. 401	91(24), 109	
A.-G. Can. v. A.-G. Que. (fisheries)	[1921] 1 A.C. 413	91(10), 92(2), 92(5), 92(13), 92(16), 109	6, 8, 12, 15(?)
Great West Saddlery Co. v. The King (dominion companies)	[1921] 2 A.C. 91	91(2), 91(26), 91(29), 92(2), 92(9), 92(10), 92(11), 92(12), 92(13), 92(14), 92(15), 92(16)	1, 2, 3, 4, 6, 7, 8, 10, 12, 14, 15(?), 16, 17
Canadian Pacific Wine Co. v. Tuley (liquor)	[1921] 2 A.C. 417	91(27), 92(8), 92(9), 92(13), 92(14), 92(15), 92(16)	4(?), 6, 8, 9, 10
In re the Board of Commerce Act, 1919, and the Combines and Fair Prices Act, 1919 (legislative power of the dominion)	[1922] 1 A.C. 191	91(2), 91(6), 91(27), 92(13), 101	1, 2, 4, 7, 8, 9, 15(?), 20

A Case	B Date and Case No.	C Heads and Sections Referred to	D Issues
Wilson v. *Esquimalt and Nanaimo Railway* (federal railway)	[1922] 1 A.C. 202	56, 90, 91(29), 92(10), 92(13)	8
Burland v. *The King* (succession duty)	[1922] 1 A.C. 215	92(2)	12
The King v. *Nat Bell Liquors* (liquor referendum legislation)	[1922] 2 A.C. 128	91(2), 91(27), 92(1), 92(15), 92(16), 121	6, 7, 9, 10, 17
McColl v. *C.P.R.* (federal railway)	[1923] A.C. 126	92(10), 92(13)	8, 17
Montreal v. *A.-G. Can.* (taxation)	[1923] A.C. 136	92(2), 125	12
Brooks–Bidlake and Whittall v. *A.-G. B.C.* (Chinese labour)	[1923] A.C. 450	91(25), 92(5), 109	
Fort Frances Pulp and Power Co. v. *Manitoba Free Press Co.* (power of Parliament during war)	[1923] A.C. 695	92(13)	2, 4, 8, 15(?), 20
A.-G. B.C. v. *A.-G. Can.* (Japanese Treaty Act—employment of Japanese)	[1924] A.C. 203	91(25), 92(5), 132	13
The King v. *A.-G. B.C.* (bona vacantia)	[1924] A.C. 213	102, 109	
A.-G. B.C. v. *A.-G. Can.* (liquor import—customs duty—provincial Crown)	[1924] A.C. 222	91(2), 91(3), 125	7, 11
A.-G. Ont. v. *Reciprocal Insurers* (provincial legislative authority—reciprocal insurance contracts)	[1924] A.C. 328	91(2), 91(25), 91(27), 92(8), 92(9), 92(10), 92(11), 92(12), 92(13), 95	1, 7, 8, 9, 15, 17
Caron v. *The King* (income tax)	[1924] A.C. 999	91(3), 91(8), 92(2)	11, 12

220

Case	Citation	Sections	No.
Brassard v. Smith (succession duty)	[1925] A.C. 371	92(2)	12
Lord's Day Alliance v. A.-G. Man. (Lord's Day Act)	[1925] A.C. 384	91(27), 92(13), 92(15), 92(16)	6, 8, 9, 10, 14
∨ Toronto Electric Commissioners v. Snider (Industrial Disputes Investigation Act)	[1925] A.C. 396	91(2), 91(27), 92(8), 92(13), 92(15), 101	2, 4, 7, 8, 9, 10, 14, 15(?), 20
A.-G. Man. v. A.-G. Can. (grain futures—indirect taxation)	[1925] A.C. 561	92(2), 121	12, 14
A.-G. Ont. v. A.-G. Can. (court appointment—judges)	[1925] A.C. 750	92(14), 96, 99, 100	
A.-G. N.B. v. C.P.R. (Ashburton Treaty—existing provincial right)	[1925] 2 D.L.R. 732	91(10), 92(10), 132	13
Toronto v. Toronto Roman Catholic Separate Schools Trustees (schools)	[1926] A.C. 81	92(8), 92(16), 93	6
Montreal v. Montreal Harbour Commissioners (navigation and shipping—harbours)	[1926] A.C. 299	91(10), 91(29), 92(10), 108, 109	
Nadan v. The King (criminal appeals to Privy Council)	[1926] A.C. 482	91(27), 92(15)	1, 9, 10
A.-G. Que. v. Nipissing Central Railway (expropriation)	[1926] A.C. 715	65, 91(29), 92(10), 109, 117	
Minister of Finance v. Smith (income tax)	[1927] A.C. 193	91(3)	11
Luscar Collieries v. McDonald (railway branch lines)	[1927] A.C. 925	91(29), 92(10)	
A.-G. B.C. v. C.P.R. (gasoline tax—indirect tax—fuel oil)	[1927] A.C. 934	92(2)	12
A.-G. N.S. v. Legislative Council of Nova Scotia (legislative council—tenure of office)	[1928] A.C. 107	88, 92(1)	
Halifax v. Fairbanks' Estate (indirect taxation—business tax)	[1928] A.C. 117	92(2), 125	12

A Case	B Date and Case No.	C Heads and Sections Referred to	D Issues
Royal Bank of Canada v. *Larue* (bankruptcy)	[1928] A.C. 187	91(21), 92(13)	8, 16, 17
Hirsch v. *Protestant School Commissioners of Montreal* (schools)	[1928] A.C. 200	93	
The King v. *Caledonian Collieries* (indirect taxation)	[1928] A.C. 358	92(2)	12
Tiny Roman Catholic Separate School Trustees v. *The King* (schools)	[1928] A.C. 363	93, 129	
A.-G. Alta. v. *A.-G. Can.* (bona vacantia— escheats—royalties)	[1928] A.C. 475	91(1), 92(13), 109	8, 15(?), 17
A.-G. Man. v. *A.-G. Can.* (sale of company shares)	[1929] A.C. 260	91(27), 92(2), 92(13), 92(16)	6, 8, 9, 12, 15(?), 17
A.-G. Can. v. *A.-G. B.C.* (fish canneries)	[1930] A.C. 111	91(2), 91(3), 91(10), 91(12), 92(13)	2, 4, 7, 8, 11, 16, 17, 18, 20
Edwards v. *A.-G. Can.* (Senate—women— persons)	[1930] A.C. 124	11, 21, 23, 24, 33, 133	
Erie Beach Co. v. *A.-G. Ont.* (succession duty)	[1930] A.C. 161	92(2)	12
A.-G. B.C. v. *McDonald Murphy Lumber Co.* (export tax—customs and excise—in-direct taxation)	[1930] A.C. 357	121, 122, 123, 124	12, 15(?)
Proprietary Articles Trade Association v. *A.-G. Can.* (Combines Investigation Act)	[1931] A.C. 310	91(2), 91(3), 91(22), 91(27), 92(13), 92(14), 122	2, 3, 4(?), 7, 8, 9, 11, 15(?), 16
In re Transfer of Natural Resources to Saskatchewan (dominion alienations—provincial claim)	[1932] A.C. 28	109, 146	

Case	Citation	Sections	Principles
In re the Insurance Act of Canada (Quebec insurance)	[1932] A.C. 41	91(2), 91(3), 91(25), 91(27), 92(13), 95	4, 7, 8, 9, 11, 15(?)
In re the Regulation and Control of Aeronautics in Canada (aerial navigation—international convention)	[1932] A.C. 54	91(2), 91(5), 91(7), 91(9), 91(10), 92(13), 92(16), 132	2, 3, 4, 6, 7, 8, 13, 16, 17, 19
Toronto v. The King (fines)	[1932] A.C. 98	91(27), 92(13), 109	2, 8, 9
Martineau and Sons v. Montreal (courts)	[1932] A.C. 113	92(13), 92(14), 96, 99, 100, 129	8
In re the Regulation and Control of Radio Communication in Canada (radio)	[1932] A.C. 304	92(10), 92(13), 92(16), 132	2, 4, 6, 8, 13, 19
Lymburn v. Mayland (securities fraud prevention)	[1932] A.C. 318	91(27), 92(13)	8, 9, 14, 17
In re Silver Brothers (priority of claims for taxes)	[1932] A.C. 514	91(3), 91(21)	11, 17
Croft v. Dunphy (extra-territorial legislation)	[1933] A.C. 156	91(3), 122	1, 2, 11
Lower Mainland Dairy Products Sales Adjustment Committee v. Crystal Dairy (indirect taxation)	[1933] A.C. 168	91(2), 91(3), 92(2), 92(13), 92(16), 95	3, 6, 7, 8, 11, 12
Consolidated Distilleries v. The King (federal courts)	[1933] A.C. 508	92(13), 92(14), 101	8
Provincial Treasurer of Alberta v. Kerr (succession duty)	[1933] A.C. 710	92(2)	12
A.-G. B.C. v. Kingcome Navigation Co. (direct taxation)	[1934] A.C. 45	91(2), 91(3), 92(2), 92(9), 122	7, 11, 12, 15(?)
Canadian Electrical Association v. C.N.R. (interprovincial railway)	[1934] A.C. 551	91(29), 92(10), 92(13)	2, 8, 17
British Coal Corporation v. The King (appeals to Privy Council—Statute of Westminster)	[1935] A.C. 500	91(27), 92(14), 101	1, 2, 9

Appendix D (*continued*)

A Case	B Date and Case No.	C Heads and Sections Referred to	D Issues
Forbes v. *A.-G. Man.* (provincial income tax)	[1937] A.C. 260	91(3), 91(8), 92(2)	1, 11, 12, 17, 18(?)
A.-G. Can. v. *A.-G. Ont.* (labour conventions)	[1937] A.C. 326	92(13), 132	1, 2, 8, 13, 18, 20
A.-G. Can. v. *A.-G. Ont.* (unemployment insurance)	[1937] A.C. 355	91(1), 91(3), 92(13)	2, 8, 11, 14, 15(?), 18, 20(?)
A.-G. B.C. v. *A.-G. Can.* (Criminal Code, s. 498A)	[1937] A.C. 368	91(27), 92(13), 92(15)	8, 9, 10, 15(?
A.-G. B.C. v. *A.-G. Can.* (Natural Products Marketing Act)	[1937] A.C. 377	91(2), 92(27), 92(13)	1, 4, 7, 8, 9, 15(?), 16, 18, 20
A.-G. B.C. v. *A.-G. Can.* (Farmers' Creditors Arrangement Act)	[1937] A.C. 391	91(19), 91(21), 92(13), 92(16)	6, 8, 15(?)
A.-G. Ont. v. *A.-G. Can.* (Dominion Trade and Industry Commission Act)	[1937] A.C. 405	91(2), 91(27), 92(13), 92(14)	7, 8, 9
Judges v. *A.-G. Sask.* (provincial income tax)	(1937), 53 T.L.R. 464	91(8), 92(2), 96, 99, 100	12, 17, 18(?)
Toronto v. *York* (judges)	[1938] A.C. 415	92(14), 96, 99, 100	14, 15(?)
Shannon v. *Lower Mainland Dairy Products Board* (natural products marketing legislation)	[1938] A.C. 708	91(2), 91(3), 91(23), 92(2), 92(9), 92(13), 92(16)	6, 7, 8, 11, 12, 14, 15(?), 16
A.-G. Alta. v. *A.-G. Can.* (Alberta bank taxation)	[1939] A.C. 117	91(14), 91(15), 91(18), 91(22), 92(2), 92(10), 92(13)	3, 8, 12, 15(?), 17
Ladore v. *Bennett* (municipal institutions—insolvency)	[1939] A.C. 468	91(19), 91(21), 92(8), 92(13), 92(16)	6, 8, 15(?), 16

Case	Citation	Sections	
Lethbridge Northern Irrigation District Board of Trustees v. I.O.F. (interest on provincial securities)	[1940] A.C. 513	91(19), 92(13), 92(16)	6, 8, 15(?), 16, 17
The King v. Williams (succession duty)	[1942] A.C. 541	92(2)	12
A.-G. Alta. v. A.-G. Can. (Debt Adjustment Act)	[1943] A.C. 356	91(2), 91(15), 91(16), 91(18), 91(19), 91(21), 92(8), 92(13), 92(14), 92(16), 122	1, 3, 4, 6, 7, 8, 15(?), 16
Abitibi Power and Paper Co. v. Montreal Trust Co. (moritorium legislation)	[1943] A.C. 536	91(21), 92(13)	8
Atlantic Smoke Shops v. Conlon (taxation)	[1943] A.C. 550	92(2), 121	12
A.-G. Ont. v. Canada Temperance Federation (Canada Temperance Act)	[1946] A.C. 193		2, 5(?), 15, 19
British Columbia Electric Railway v. The King (taxation of non-residents)	[1946] A.C. 527	91(3)	11
Treasurer of Ontario v. Blonde (succession duty)	[1947] A.C. 24	92(2)	12
A.-G. Can. v. A.-G. Que. (vacant property— bank deposits)	[1947] A.C. 33	91(15), 92(13)	3, 8, 16, 17
Montreal v. Montreal Locomotive Works (municipal taxation of Crown agent)	[1947] 1 D.L.R. 161	125	
Co-operative Committee on Japanese Canadians v. A.-G. Can. (emergency powers)	[1947] A.C. 87	92(13)	2, 8, 20
A.-G. Ont. v. A.-G. Can. (appeals to Privy Council)	[1947] A.C. 127	3, 91(27), 92(14), 94, 101, 129	1, 2, 3, 9
A.-G. Alta. v. A.-G. Can. (Alberta Bill of Rights Act)	[1947] A.C. 503	91(15), 92(13)	3, 8, 14
A.-G. Sask. v. A.-G. Can. (Farm Security Act)	[1949] A.C. 110	91(18), 91(19), 91(21), 92(13), 95	8, 15(?)

225

A Case	B Date and Case No.	C Heads and Sections Referred to	D Issues
Labour Relations Board of Saskatchewan v. John East Iron Works (courts)	[1949] A.C. 134	92(14), 96, 99, 100, 129	
A.-G. B.C. v. Esquimalt and Nanaimo Railway (direct taxation)	[1950] A.C. 87	92(2)	12, 15
C.P.R. v. A.-G. B.C. (Hours of Work Act—railway hotels)	[1950] A.C. 122	91(29), 92(13)	2, 4, 9, 15(?), 17, 20
Canadian Federation of Agriculture v. A.-G. Que. (Dairy Industry Act—margarine)	[1951] A.C. 179	91(2), 91(27), 92(13), 95	2, 8, 9, 10, 15(?), 20
Bennett and White v. Sugar City (taxation—Crown property)	[1951] A.C. 786	125	
A.-G. Can. v. Hallett and Carey (emergency powers)	[1952] A.C. 427	92(13)	2, 8
Huggard Assets v. A.-G. Alta. (legislative power in new province)	[1953] A.C. 420	109	
West Canadian Collieries v. A.-G. Alta. (Alberta Natural Resources Acts)	[1953] A.C. 453	109	14
†*A.-G. Sask. v. C.P.R.* (business tax—construction contract—exemption of property)	[1953] A.C. 594	92(2)	12
A.-G. Ont. v. Israel Winner (international and interprovincial bus lines)	[1954] A.C. 541	92(10)	17

*Both these judgments were concerned with the B.N.A. Act of 1930 [21 Geo. V, c. 26] by which the "Natural Resources Agreement Acts'' of 1930 [c. 3 (Can.) and c. 21 (Alta.)] were confirmed.

†This judgment was concerned with the use of the phrase "Peace, Order, and good Government'' in the B.N.A. Act of 1871 [34 and 35 Vict., c. 28].

SELECT BIBLIOGRAPHY

Source Materials

CANADA, *Constitutional Conference of Federal and Provincial Governments, Ottawa and Quebec, 1950, Proceedings, January 10–12, 1950* and *Proceedings, September 25–28, 1950.* Ottawa, 1950.

CANADA, *Dominion Liquor License Acts, 1883–4, Report of the Proceedings before the Judicial Committee of the Privy Council on the Hearing of the Petition of the Governor-General of Canada in relation to the Dominion License Acts of 1883 and 1884* (copy in the Privy Council Office, London).

CANADA, *Dominion-Provincial and Interprovincial Conferences from 1887 to 1926.* Ottawa, 1951.

CANADA, *Dominion-Provincial Conferences, 1927, 1935, 1941.* Ottawa, 1951.

CANADA, *Dominion-Provincial Conference (1945), Dominion and Provincial Submissions and Plenary Conference Discussions.* Ottawa, 1946.

CANADA, *Dominion-Provincial Conference, 1957.* Ottawa, 1958.

CANADA, *Federal and Provincial Governments, Proceedings of the Conference of, 1950.* Ottawa, 1951.

CANADA, *Federal-Provincial Conference, 1955, Preliminary Meeting and Proceedings.* Ottawa, 1955.

CANADA, DEPARTMENT OF JUSTICE, *Memorandum on Dominion Power of Disallowance of Provincial Legislation, 1937.* Ottawa, 1946.

CANADA, DEPARTMENT OF JUSTICE, *Memorandum on Office of Lieutenant-Governor of a Province: Its Constitutional Character and Functions, 1937.* Ottawa, 1946.

CANADA, PARLIAMENT, HOUSE OF COMMONS, SPECIAL COMMITTEE ON THE BRITISH NORTH AMERICA ACT, *Proceedings and Evidence and Report.* Ottawa, 1935.

CANADA, PARLIAMENT, SENATE, *Report Pursuant to Resolution of the Senate to the Honourable the Speaker by the Parliamentary Counsel Relating to the Enactment of the British North America Act, 1867, any lack of consonance between its terms and judicial construction of them and cognate matters* [the *O'Connor Report*]. Ottawa, 1939.

CANADA, ROYAL COMMISSION ON GOVERNMENT ORGANIZATION, *Report* [the *Glassco Report*]. Ottawa, 1962.

CANADA, ROYAL COMMISSION ON DOMINION-PROVINCIAL RELATIONS, *Report* [the *Rowell-Sirois Report*]. Ottawa, 1954.

227

CANADA (UNITED PROVINCE OF), PARLIAMENT, *Parliamentary Debates on the Subject of the Confederation of the British North American Provinces*. Quebec, 1865.

CARDWELL PAPERS, P.R.O., 30/48.

CARNARVON PAPERS, P.R.O., 30/6/132, 136, 137, 138, 139, 140, 149, 151, 157, 163, 166, 167, 169.

DRIEDGER, E. A., ed. *A Consolidation of the British North America Acts, 1867–1952*. Ottawa, 1962.

LEAR, W. E., ed. *Canadian Reports, Appeal Cases*. Toronto, 1910–16.

LEFROY, A. H. F., ed. *Leading Cases in Canadian Constitutional Law*. Toronto, 1920.

OLMSTED, R. A., ed. *Decisions of the Judicial Committee of the Privy Council Relating to the British North America Act, 1867 and the Canadian Constitution 1867–1954*. 3 Vols. Ottawa, 1954.

QUEBEC (PROVINCE OF), ROYAL COMMISSION OF INQUIRY ON CONSTITUTIONAL PROBLEMS, *Report* [the *Tremblay Report*]. Quebec, 1956.

UNITED KINGDOM, PARLIAMENT, HOUSE OF COMMONS, *Debates*, vol. 185 (1867).

UNITED KINGDOM, PARLIAMENT, HOUSE OF LORDS, *Debates*, vol. 185 (1867).

Books

ALLEN, SIR C. K. *Law in the Making* (6th ed.). Oxford, 1958.

ANDERSON, V., ed. *Problems in Canadian Unity*. Toronto, 1938.

AUSTIN, J. *The Province of Jurisprudence Determined*. London, 1954.

BAKER, P. J. N. *The Present Juridical Status of the British Dominions in International Law*. London, 1929.

BEAUCHAMP, J. J. *The Jurisprudence of the Privy Council*. Montreal, 1891.

BENTWICH, N. D. *The Practice of the Privy Council in Judicial Matters*. London, 1926.

BIRCH, A. H. *Federalism, Finance and Social Legislation in Canada, Australia, and the United States*. Oxford, 1955.

BLAKE, E. *The Ontario Insolvency Case in the Privy Council*. Toronto, 1894.

BORDEN, SIR R. L. *Canadian Constitutional Studies*. Toronto, 1922.

BOURINOT, A. S. *How Canada is Governed*. Toronto, 1928.

BOURINOT, SIR J. G. *Federal Government in Canada*. Baltimore, 1889.

—— *A Manual of the Constitutional History of Canada from the Earliest Period to 1901*. Toronto, 1901.

BRYCE, J. *Studies in History and Jurisprudence*. London, 1901.

BUCK, A. E. *Financing Canadian Government*. Chicago, 1949.

CAMERON, E. R. *The Canadian Constitution as Interpreted by the Judicial Committee of the Privy Council in Its Judgments*. Winnipeg, 1915.

—— *The Supreme Court of Canada*. Toronto, 1924.

CANADIAN BROADCASTING CORPORATION. *The Canadian Constitution*. Toronto, 1938.

Canadian Problems. Toronto, 1933.

CARDOZO, B. N. *The Nature of the Judicial Process.* New Haven, 1921.

CARTWRIGHT, J. R., ed. *Cases Decided on the British North America Act, 1867.* Toronto, 1882–1897.

CASSIDY, H. M. (Canadian Welfare Council). *The Rowell-Sirois Report and the Social Services in Survey.* Ottawa, n.d.

CITIZENS' FORUM. *Confederation—A Century Later: Does It Still Work?* (Canadian Association for Adult Education Pamphlet No. 2). Toronto, 1963.

COLBY, C. C. *Parliamentary Government in Canada.* Montreal, 1886.

CONGRESS ON CANADIAN AFFAIRS. *The Canadian Experiment, Success or Failure?* Quebec, 1962.

CLEMENT, W. H. P. *The Law of the Canadian Constitution* (2nd ed.). Toronto, 1916.

CLOKIE, H. M. *Canadian Government and Politics.* Toronto, 1944.

CORRY, J. A. *Democratic Government and Politics* (3rd ed.). Toronto, 1946.

——— *Law and Policy.* Toronto, 1959.

CREIGHTON, D. G. *The Road to Confederation.* Toronto, 1964.

CRÉPEAU, P. A. and C. B. MACPHERSON. *The Future of Canadian Federalism.* Toronto, 1965.

CROSS, R. *Precedent in English Law.* Oxford, 1961.

DAWSON, R. M. *Constitutional Issues in Canada, 1900–1931.* Oxford, 1933.

——— *Democratic Government in Canada* (3rd ed.). Toronto, 1963.

DENNING (LORD). *From Precedent to Precedent.* London, 1959.

EGERTON, H. E. *The Federation of Canada, 1867–1917.* Toronto, 1917.

——— *Federations and Unions within the British Empire.* London, 1924.

EGERTON, H. E., and W. L. GRANT. *Canadian Constitutional Development.* London, 1907.

EGGLESTON, W. *The Road to Nationhood, a Chronicle of Dominion-Provincial Relations.* Toronto, 1946.

EGGLESTON, W., and C. T. KRAFT. *Dominion-Provincial Subsidies and Grants.* Ottawa, 1939.

ELAZER, D. J. *The American Partnership.* Chicago, 1962.

FARIBAULT, M., and R. M. FOWLER. *Ten to One: The Confederation Wager.* Toronto, Montreal, 1965.

FRANKFURTER, F. *Mr. Justice Holmes and the Supreme Court.* Cambridge, Mass., 1938.

FRIEDMANN, W. G. *Law and Social Change in Contemporary Britain.* London, 1951.

——— *Legal Theory.* (4th ed.). London, 1960.

——— *Law in a Changing Society.* London, 1959.

GÉRIN-LAJOIE, P. *Constitutional Amendment in Canada.* Toronto, 1950.

GETTYS, C. L. *The Administration of Canadian Conditional Grants.* Chicago, 1937.

GRAY, J. C. *The Nature and Sources of the Law.* New York, 1931.

HART, H. L. A. *The Concept of Law.* Oxford, 1961.

HENDRY, J. M. *Treaties and Federal Constitutions.* Washington, 1955.

JACKETT, W. R. *Chart of Privy Council Decisions with Reference to the*

British North America Act (printed, but with no facts of publication; copy in Carleton University Library, Ottawa).

JENNINGS, SIR W. I. *The Law and the Constitution* (5th ed.). London, 1959.

KEITH, SIR A. B. *The Constitutional Law of the British Dominions.* London, 1933.

―――― *Federation, Its Nature and Conditions.* London, 1942.

KENNEDY, W. P. M. *The Nature of Canadian Federalism.* Toronto, 1921.

―――― *Some Aspects of Canadian and Australian Federal Constitutional Law.* Ithaca, 1930.

―――― *Some Aspects of the Theories and Workings of Constitutional Law.* New York, 1932.

―――― *Essays in Constitutional Law* (2nd ed.). London, 1934.

―――― *The Constitution of Canada, 1534–1937, an Introduction to Its Development, Law and Custom* (2nd ed.). Oxford, 1938.

KENNEDY, W. P. M., and D. C. WELLS. *The Law of the Taxing Power in Canada.* Toronto, 1931.

KONEFSKY, S. J. *The Legacy of Holmes and Brandeis.* New York, 1956.

LA FOREST, G. V. *Disallowance and Reservation of Provincial Legislation.* Ottawa, 1955.

LAMONTAGNE, M. *La fédéralisme canadien, évolution et problèmes.* Quebec, 1954.

LASKIN, B. *Canadian Constitutional Law.* Toronto, 1951.

LEAGUE OF NATIONS SOCIETY IN CANADA. *The Treaty-making Power in Canada.* Ottawa, 1938.

LEDERMAN, W. R. ed. *The Courts and the Canadian Constitution.* Toronto, 1964.

LEFROY, A. H. F. *The Law of Legislative Power in Canada.* Toronto, 1897–8.

―――― *Canada's Federal System.* Toronto, 1913.

―――― *A Short Treatise on Canadian Constitutional Law.* Toronto, 1918.

―――― *Leading Cases in Canadian Constitutional Law.* Toronto, 1920.

LEVI, E. H. *An Introduction to Legal Reasoning.* Chicago, 1961.

LIVINGSTON, W. S. *Federalism and Constitutional Change.* Oxford, 1956.

LORANGER, T. J. J. *Letters Upon the Interpretation of the Federal Constitution Known as the British North America Act, (1867).* Quebec, 1884.

LOWER, A. R. M., *et al. Evolving Canadian Federalism.* Durham, 1958.

MALLORY, J. R. *Social Credit and the Federal Power in Canada.* Toronto, 1954.

McCLOSKEY, R. G., ed. *Essays in Constitutional Law.* New York, 1957.

―――― *The American Supreme Court.* Chicago, 1960.

MACDONALD, V. C. *Legislative Power and the Supreme Court in the Fifties.* Toronto, 1961.

McWHINNEY, E. *Canadian Jurisprudence.* London, 1959.

―――― *Judicial Review in the English-Speaking World* (2nd ed.). Toronto, 1960.

MAXWELL, J. A. *Federal Subsidies to the Provincial Governments in Canada.* Cambridge, Mass., 1937.

―――― *Recent Developments in Dominion-Provincial Relations in Canada.* New York, 1948.

MOORE, A. M., and J. H. Perry. *Financing Canadian Federation.* Toronto, 1953.
MORTON, W. L. *The Critical Years: The Union of British North America, 1857–1873.* Toronto, 1964.
MUNRO, W. B. *American Influences on Canadian Government.* Toronto, 1929.
ODGERS, SIR C. E. *Craies on Statute Law.* London, 1952.
O HEARN, P. J. T. *Peace, Order and Good Government.* Toronto, 1964.
OLLIVIER, M. *Problems of Canadian Sovereignty from the British North America Act, 1867 to the Statute of Westminster, 1931.* Toronto, 1945.
PATON, G. W. *A Textbook of Jurisprudence* (2nd ed.). Oxford, 1951.
PERRY, J. H. *Taxes, Tariffs, and Subsidies: A History of Canadian Fiscal Development.* Toronto, 1955.
PIERSON, C. G. *Canada and the Privy Council.* London, 1960.
PLAXTON, C. P. *Canadian Constitutional Decisions of the Judicial Committee of the Privy Council, 1930 to 1939.* Ottawa, 1939.
POLLOCK, SIR F. *First Book of Jurisprudence* (6th ed.). London, 1929.
PORRITT, E. *Evolution of the Dominion of Canada, Its Government and Politics.* Yonkers-on-Hudson, 1918.
POUND, R. *Interpretations of Legal History.* Cambridge, 1923.
PRESTON, T. *A Manual Showing the Practice and Procedure in the Colonial and Indian Appeals before the Lords of the Judicial Committee of Her Majesty's Most Honourable Privy Council.* London, 1900.
RIDDELL, W. R. *The Canadian Constitution in Form and Fact.* New York, 1923.
—— *The Constitution of Canada in Its History and Practical Working.* New Haven, 1917.
ROSS, SIR G. *The Senate of Canada.* Toronto, 1914.
RUMILLY, R. *L'Autonomie provinciale.* Montreal, 1948.
SAUNDERS, S. A., and E. BLACK. *The Rowell-Sirois Commission.* Toronto, 1940.
SAYWELL, J. T. *The Office of Lieutenant-Governor.* Toronto, 1957.
SCOTT, F. R. *Canada Today.* London, 1939.
—— *Civil Liberties and Canadian Federalism.* Toronto, 1959.
SCOTT, W. S. *The Canadian Constitution Historically Explained.* Toronto, 1918.
SILCOX, C. E. *Must Canada Split?* Toronto, 1944.
SMITH, H. A. *Federalism in North America, a Comparative Study of Institutions in the United States and Canada.* Boston, 1928.
SWISHER, C. B. *The Growth of Constitutional Power in the United States.* (2nd ed.). Chicago, 1963.
—— *The Supreme Court in Modern Role.* New York, 1958.
TAYLOR, F. *Are Legislatures Parliaments?* Montreal, 1879.
TROTTER, R. G. *Canadian Federation, Its Origins and Achievements.* Toronto, 1924.
VARCOE, F. P. *The Distribution of Legislative Power in Canada.* Toronto, 1954.
VILE, M. J. C. *The Structure of American Federalism.* London, 1961.

WAITE, P. W. *The Life and Times of Confederation, 1864–1867.* (2nd ed.). Toronto, 1962.
WAMBAUGH, E. *Study of Cases.* (2nd ed.). Boston, 1894.
WHEARE, K. C. *Federal Government.* (3rd ed.). London, 1953.
—— *The Statute of Westminster and Dominion Status.* (5th ed.). Oxford, 1953.
WHEELER, G. P. *Privy Council Law.* London, 1893.
WHELAN, E. *The Union of the British Provinces.* Quebec, 1927.
WILLIAMS, G., ed. *Salmond on Jurisprudence.* London, 1957.
WRONG, G. M., et al. *The Federation of Canada, 1867–1917.* Toronto, 1917.

Articles

"A." "Some Problems of Federal Government," *CLT*, III (1941).
A.B.C. "Provincial Labour Legislation and Dominion Railway Companies," *CBR*, XXII (1944).
ANGUS, H. F. "An Analysis of the Report of the Royal Commission on Dominion-Provincial Relations," *Industrial Canada*, XLI (1940).
"Back to the Constitution," *Round Table*, No. 116 (1939).
BALLEM, J. B. "Constitutional Law: Delegation, Approach of Supreme Court of Canada to the B.N.A. Act," *CBR*, XXIX (1951).
—— "Constitutional Law: Marketing Legislation," *CBR*, XXX (1952).
—— "Constitutional Law: Interprovincial Trade over Provincial Highways," *CBR*, XXXII (1954).
—— "Constitutional Law: The Trade and Commerce Power," *CBR*, XXXIV (1956).
BASTEDO, F. L. "Amending the British North America Act," *CBR*, XII (1934).
BEAUCHESNE, A. "The Provincial Legislatures are not Parliaments," *CBR*, XXII (1944).
BENTWICH, N. D. "The Judicial Committee of the Privy Council in the War," *CBR*, XXV (1947).
BIGGAR, O. M. "Legislative Jurisdiction over Flying," *CBR*, VIII (1930).
B.L. "Constitutional Law: Insurance," *CBR*, XXII (1944).
BLADEN, V. W. "The Economics of Federalism," *CJEPS*, I (1935).
BOURINOT, SIR J. G. "Federal Government in Canada," *CLT*, IX (1889).
BOURNE, C. B. "Delegation between Federal Parliament and Provincial Legislature," *CBR*, XXXIV (1956).
BRADY, A. "Report of the Royal Commission on Dominion-Provincial Relations," *CHR*, XXI (1920).
—— "The Critical Problems of Canadian Federalism," *American Political Science Review*, XXXII (1958).
—— "Quebec and Canadian Federalism," *CJEPS*, XXV (1959).
BREBNER, J.B., et al. "On Some Appendices to the Rowell-Sirois Report," *CJEPS*, VII (1941).
BREWIN, F. A. "Constitutional Law: Canada Temperance Act Reference," *CBR*, XXIV (1946).

232

—— "Legislative History: Constitutional Law," *CBR*, XXX (1952).
BROSSARD, R., and H. F. ANGUS. "The Working of Confederation," CJEPS, III (1937).
BURNS, R. N. "The Royal Commission on Dominion-Provincial Relations," in R. M. CLARK, ed. *Canadian Issues: Essays in Honour of Henry F. Angus.* Toronto, 1961.
CAMERON, E. R. "The House of Lords and the Judicial Committee," *CBR*, I (1923).
"Canada and the Privy Council," *Round Table*, XXVII (1937).
"Canada, Federalism and Finance," *Round Table*, No. 181 (1955).
CARROTHERS, W. A. "Problems of the Canadian Federation," *CJEPS*, I (1935).
CASSIDY, H. M. "The Dominion-Provincial Impasse," *Canada in a New World.* Toronto, 1948.
CLAXTON, B. "Social Reform and the Constitution," *CJEPS*, I (1935).
CLOKIE, H. M. "Basic Problems of the Canadian Constitution," CBR, XX (1942).
—— "Judicial Review, Federalism and the Canadian Constitution," *CJEPS*, VIII (1942).
COHEN, M. "The MacQuarrie Report: The Background, Main Features and Problems," *CBR*, XXX (1952).
COLMANS, C. K. "Constitutional Law: Co-operation between Legislatures in a Federation," *CBR*, XXXI (1953).
CORRY, J. A. "Administrative Law and the Interpretation of Statutes," *UTLJ*, I (1936).
—— "Dominion-Provincial Relations," *Public Affairs*, VI (1943).
—— "Statutory Powers," in J. A. CORRY, F. C. CRONKITE, and E. F. WHITMORE, eds. *Legal Essays in Honour of Arthur Moxon.* Toronto, 1953.
—— "The Use of Legislative History in the Interpretation of Statutes," *CBR*, XXXII (1954).
—— "The Prospects for the Rule of Law," *CJEPS*, XXI (1955).
—— "Constitutional Trends and Federalism," in R. M. CLARK, ed. *Essays in Honour of Henry F. Angus.* Toronto, 1961.
COULTEE, L. W. "Privy Council Decisions Respecting the Powers of the Dominion and Provincial Legislatures from 1867 to 1910," *CLT*, XXXI (1911).
"Courts: *Stare Decisis*, Authority of Decisions of Full Court of Appeal and of Division Thereof," *CBR*, XXIII (1945).
CREIGHTON, D. G. "Federal Relations in Canada since 1914," *Canada in Peace and War.* London, 1941.
CRONKITE, F. C. "The Social Legislation References," *CBR*, XV (1937).
CROWLE, H. E. "Constitutional Remedies," *CBR*, XXVI (1948).
CURTIS, G. F. "The Stresses and Strains of Confederation," in V. ANDERSON, ed. *Problems in Canadian Unity.* Toronto, 1938.
DAFOE, J. W. "Revising the Constitution," *QQ*, XXXVII (1930).
—— "The Canadian Federal System under Review," *Foreign Affairs*, XVIII (1940).
DAGGETT, A. P. "Treaty Legislation in Canada," *CBR*, XVI (1938).

233

DAVIES, D. J. L. "Interpretation of Statutes in the Light of Their Policy," *Columbia Law Review*, XXXV (1935).

DAVISON, J. F. "The Problem of Liquor Legislation in Canada," *CBR*, IV (1926).

DEACON, W. S. "Canadians and the Privy Council," *CLT*, XXXI (1911).

DEAN, E. P. "Towards a More Perfect Canadian Union," *Pacific Affairs*, XIII (1940).

"Decline of the Judicial Committee of the Privy Council: Current Status of Appeals from the British Dominions," *Harvard Law Review*, LX (1947).

DEHEM, R., and J. N. WOLFE. "The Principles of Federal Finance and the Canadian Case," *CJEPS*, XXI (1955).

DE SMITH, S. A. "Constitutional Law: Trade and Commerce," *CBR*, XXIX (1951).

DEXTER, G. "Commerce and the Canadian Constitution," *QQ*, XXXIX (1932).

"The Dominions and the Judicial Committee (as an Appellate Tribunal)," *CLT*, XL (1920).

DRIEDGER, E. A. "A New Approach to Statutory Interpretation," *CBR*, XXIX (1951).

DUFF, SIR L. P. "The Privy Council," *CBR*, III (1925).

EGGLESTON, W. "Amending the Canadian Constitution," *QQ*, LVI (1949).

———— "Recent Trends in Dominion-Provincial Relations," *Canadian Banker*, LXI (1952).

EWART, J. S. "The Judicial Committee," *CLT*, XXXIV (1914).

———— "The Aeronautics Case," *CBR*, IX (1931).

———— "Some Further Comments on Dominion-Provincial Relations," *PPCPSA*, III (1931).

EWART, J. S., and G. H. SEDGWICK. "Judicial Appeals to the Privy Council," *QQ*, XXXVII (1930).

FALCONER, A. "British North America: Agreement or Grant?" *CLT*, XXXIX (1919).

FERGUSON, G. H. "Memorandum to the Prime Minister of Canada, 10 September, 1930," *Toronto Globe*, 20 September, 1930.

FLEMING, D. "Social Credit and the Federal Power in Canada," *CBR*, XXXIV (1956).

FLINT, T. B. "The Theory and Practice of the Constitution," *CLT*, XXVIII (1908).

FORSEY, E. A. "Disallowance: A Contrast," *Canadian Forum*, XVIII (1938).

———— "Disallowance of Provincial Acts, Reservation of Provincial Bills, and Refusal of Assent by Lieutenant Governors since 1867," *CJEPS*, IV (1938).

———— "Lieutenant-Governors Are not Ambassadors," *Saturday Night*, LXIII (1948).

———— "Are Provinces to have Dominion Status?" *Saturday Night*, LXIII (1948).

———— "B.N.A. Act is No Case for Nine Nations" *Saturday Night*, LXIII (1948).

———— "Should a Legislature have Plenary Power?" *Saturday Night*, LXIII (1948).

———— "Disallowance and Reservation of Provincial Legislation," *CBR*, XXXIV (1956).

FRIEDMANN, W. G. "Statute Law and Its Interpretation in the Modern State," *CBR*, XXVI (1948).

———— "Judges, Politics and the Law," *CBR*, XXIX (1951).

———— "*Stare Decisis* and the Civil Code of Quebec," *CBR*, XXXI (1953).

GALT, A. C. "Privy Council Appeals," *CLT*, XLI (1921).

GARDINER, G., and F. E. JONES. "The Administration of Justice," in G. GARDINER and A. MARTIN, eds. *Law Reform Now*. London, 1963.

GÉRIN-LAJOIE, P. "Du pouvoir d'amendement constitutionnel au Canada," *CBR*, XXIX (1951).

GOLDENBERG, H. "Social and Economic Problems in Canadian Federalism," *CBR*, XII (1934).

———— "Constitutional Amendment in Canada," *PPCPSA*, VI (1934).

GOODERSON, R. N. "*Ratio Decidendi* and Rules of Law," *CBR*, XXX (1952).

GOODHART, A. L. "Determining the *Ratio Decidendi* of a Case," *Yale Law Journal*, XL (1930).

———— "Precedent in English and Continental Law," *LQR*, L (1934).

———— "Case Law: A Short Replication," *LQR*, L (1934).

GOODMAN, W. D. "Constitutional Law: British North America Act, s. 92(2)," *CBR*, XXVIII (1950).

GORDON, D. M., *et al.* "Abolition of Appeals to the Privy Council: a Symposium," *CBR*, XXV (1947).

GRAY, V. E. " 'The O'Connor Report' on the British North America Act 1867," *CBR*, XVII (1939).

———— "More on the Regulation of Insurance in Canada," *CBR*, XXIV (1946).

GREY, R. "Conditional Grants in Aid," in INSTITUTE OF PUBLIC ADMINISTRATION OF CANADA, *Proceedings of the Fifth Annual Conference*. Toronto, 1953.

HANSARD, H. "The MacQuarrie Report . . . Combines, 'Criminal' Law and the Constitution," *CBR*, XXX (1952).

HAYWORTH, A. "Bona Vacantia," *CBR*, II (1924).

HEIGHINGTON, A. C. "Constitutional Aspect of Insurance Legislation," *CBR*, II (1924).

HEIGHINGTON, W. "Parliamentary Status and Provincial Legislatures," *CBR*, II (1924).

HENDERSON, G. F. "Eligibility of Women for the Senate," *CBR*, VII (1929).

HODGINS, F. E. "Judicial Committee Differences," *CBR*, II (1924).

HOLDSWORTH, SIR W. "Case Law," *LQR*, L (1934).

HOPKINS, E. R. "The Literal Canon and the Goldon Rule," *CBR*, XV (1937).

HUMPHREY, J. P. "Privy Council as a Legislative Body," *Canadian Forum*, XIX (1940).

HUNTER, A. T. "Proposal for Statutory Relief from Privy Council Controversy," *CBR*, IV (1926).

HYDE, C. C. "Canada's Water-tight Compartments," *American Journal of International Law*, XXXI (1957).

INNIS, H. A. "The Rowell-Sirois Report," *CJEPS*, VI (1940).

JACKETT, W. R. "Sections 91 and 92 of the British North America Act and the Privy Council," in J. A. CORRY, F. C. CRONKITE, and E. F. WHITMORE, eds. *Legal Essays in Honour of Arthur Moxon*. Toronto, 1953.

JENKS, C. W. "The Dominion Jurisdiction in Respect of Criminal Law as a Basis for Social Legislation in Canada," *CBR*, XIII (1935).

—— "The Present Status of the Bennett Ratifications of International Labour Conventions," *CBR*, XV (1937).

JENNINGS, J. W. "Dominion Legislation and Treaties," *CBR*, XV (1937).

JENNINGS, SIR W. I. "The Statute of Westminster and Appeals to the Privy Council," *LQR*, LII (1936).

—— "Constitutional Interpretation: The Experience of Canada," *Harvard Law Review*, LI (1937).

JOANES, A. "*Stare Decisis* in the Supreme Court of Canada," *CBR*, XXXVI (1958).

KEIRSTEAD, B. S. "The Sirois Report, an Evaluation," *Public Affairs*, IV (1940).

KEITH, SIR A. B. "Recent Cases on the Canadian Constitution," *CLT*, XXXIV (1914).

—— "Privy Council Decisions: A Comment from Great Britain," *CBR*, XV (1937).

KELLY, J. G. "The Dominions and the Judicial Committee," *Nineteenth Century*, CV (1929).

KEMP, H. R. "Is a Revision of Taxing Powers Necessary?" *PPCPSA*, III (1931).

KENNEDY, G. D. "*Stare Decisis*: Are Decisions of English Court of Appeal Binding on Canadian Trial Judges?" *CBR*, XXVI (1948).

—— "*Stare Decisis*: Authority of Court of Appeal Decisions from England or another Canadian Province," *CBR*, XXVII (1949).

—— "*Stare Decisis*: Five Recent Judicial Comments," *CBR*, XXIX (1951).

—— "*Stare Decisis*: Provincial Court of Appeal Overruling Itself," *CBR*, XXXI (1953).

—— "*Stare Decisis*: . . . ," *CBR*, XXXI (1953).

—— "Supreme Court of Canada: *Stare Decisis* . . . ," *CBR*, XXXIII (1955).

—— "Supreme Court of Canada: Canada's Final Court," *CBR*, XXXIII (1955).

KENNEDY, W. P. M. "The Nature of Canadian Federalism," *CHR*, II (1921).

—— "Canadian Legislation on Trade Marks, Is It *Ultra Vires*?" *CBR*, VIII (1930).

—— "Lord Haldane (a Personal Note)," *CBR*, VI (1928).

—— "Three Views of Constitutional Law," *CBR*, IX (1931).

—— "The British North America Act: Past and Future," *CBR*, XV (1937).

———— "Interpretation of the British North America Act," *Cambridge Law Journal*, VIII (1943).

KILGOUR, D. G. "The Rule against the Use of Legislative History: 'Canon of Construction or Counsel of Caution?' " *CBR*, XXX (1952).

KRAFT, T. "The Dominion-Provincial Tax Agreements in Canada," *American Political Science Review*, XXXVII (1943).

LA BRIE, F. E. "Constitutional Law: Alberta Bill of Rights Act," *CBR*, XXV (1947).

———— "Canadian Constitutional Interpretation and Legislative Review," *UTLJ*, VIII (1950).

LA FOREST, G. V. "Disallowance of Provincial Legislation," *CBR*, XXXIV (1956).

LAIRD, D. H. "The Doctrine of *Stare Decisis*," *CBR*, XIII (1935).

LASH, Z. A. "The Working of Federal Institutions in Canada," *CLT*, XXXVII (1917).

LASKIN, B. "Tests for the Validity of Legislation: What's the 'Matter'?" *UTLJ*, II (1944).

———— " 'Peace, Order and Good Government' Re-Examined," *CBR*, XXV (1947).

———— "The Supreme Court of Canada: A Final Court of and for Canadians," *CBR*, XXIX (1951).

———— "Constitutional Law: Provincial Legislation Implementing Reciprocal Enforcement Arrangements with Foreign State . . . ," *CBR*, XXXIV (1956).

———— "Constitutional Law: Peace, Order and Good Government," *CBR*, XXXV (1957).

———— "Provincial Marketing Levies: Indirect Taxation and Federal Power," *UTLJ*, XIII (1959).

LEACH, R. H. "Interprovincial Co-operation," *Canadian Public Administration*, II (1959).

LEDERMAN, W. R. "Classification of Laws and the British North America Act," in J. A. CORRY, F. C. CRONKITE, and E. F. WHITMORE, eds. *Legal Essays in Honour of Arthur Moxon*. Toronto, 1953.

———— "The Independence of the Judiciary," *CBR*, XXXIV (1956).

LEFROY, A. H. F. "Canada's Federal Constitution," *CLT*, XXXIII (1913).

———— "Points of Special Interest in Canada's Federal Constitution," *PPCPSA*, I (1913).

———— "Prohibition: the Late Privy Council Decisions," *CLT*, XVI (1896).

LLOYD, D. "Reason and Logic in the Common Law," *LQR*, LXIV (1948).

LOWER, A. R. M. "Theories of Canadian Federalism, Yesterday and Today," in A. R. M. LOWER, *et al. Evolving Canadian Federalism*. Durham, 1958.

MACDONALD, R. ST. J. "Treaties and Federal Constitutions," *CBR*, XXXIV (1956).

MACDONALD, V. C. "Canada's Power to Perform Treaty Obligations," *CBR*, XI (1933).

———— "Judicial Interpretation of the Canadian Constitution," *UTLJ*, I (1936).

——— "The Canadian Constitution Seventy Years After," *CBR*, XV (1937).

——— "Constitutional Interpretation and Extrinsic Evidence," *CBR*, XVII (1939).

——— "The Constitution and the Courts in 1939," *CBR*, XVIII (1940).

——— "Taxation Powers in Canada," *CBR*, XIX (1941).

——— "The Regulation of Insurance in Canada," *CBR*, XXIV (1946).

——— "The Constitution in a Changing World," *CBR*, XXVI (1948).

——— "The Privy Council and the Canadian Constitution," *CBR*, XXIX (1951).

——— "The Privy Council and Statutory Interpretation," *CBR*, XXIX (1951).

——— "Bora Laskin's *Canadian Constitutional Law*," *CBR*, XXX (1952).

MacFarlane, R. O. "Provinces versus Dominion," *QQ*, XLII (1935).

McGeachy, J. B. "One Country or Nine? The Demands Made by the Provinces before the Rowell Commission," in V. Anderson, ed. *Problems in Canadian Unity*. Toronto, 1938.

McKagnen, W. A. "The Financial Problem in Dominion-Provincial Relations," in V. Anderson, ed. *Problems in Canadian Unity*. Toronto, 1938.

MacKenzie, N. A. M. "Constitutional Law: British North America Act, Section 132, Legislative Jurisdiction," *CBR*, IX (1931).

——— "Canada and the Treaty-Making Power," *CBR*, XV (1937).

Mackintosh, W. A. "Federal Finance in Canada," in G. Sawer, ed. *Federalism: An Australian Study*. Melbourne, 1952.

McLeod, T. H., *et al.* "Federal-Provincial Relations, 1958," *Canadian Public Administration*, I (1958).

McMullen, J. E. "Constitutional Law: Provincial Taxation," *CBR*, VI (1928).

MacQuarrie, J. T. "The Use of Legislative History," *CBR*, XXX (1952).

McQueen, R. "Economic Aspects of Federalism," *CJEPS*, I (1935).

McWhinney, E. "Constitutional Law: Provincial Regulation of Commerce," *CBR*, XXX (1952).

——— "Judicial Positivism in Australia: The Communist Party Case," *Australian Journal of Comparative Legislation*, II (1953).

——— "Labour Conventions Case: Lord Wright's Undisclosed Dissent?" *CBR*, XXXIV (1956).

——— "Federal Constitutional Law and the Treaty-making Power," *CBR*, XXXV (1957).

McWilliams, R. F. "The Amendment of the Constitution," *CBR*, XVI (1938).

——— "The Privy Council and the Constitution," *CBR*, XVII (1939).

Mallory, J. R. "Disallowance and the National Interest: The Alberta Social Credit Legislation of 1937," *CJEPS*, XIV (1948).

——— "Disallowance of Provincial Legislation," *CBR*, XXXIV (1956).

Martin, C. "Sidelights on Practice before the Judicial Committee of the Privy Council," *CBR*, V (1927).

Maxwell, J. A. "Flexible Portion of the British North America Act," *CBR*, XI (1933).

———— "Federal Subsidies to Provincial Governments," *Canadian Forum*, XIII (1933).

———— "Better Terms," *QQ*, XL (1933).

———— "Provincial Conferences and Better Terms," *PPCPSA*, VI (1934).

———— "Petitions to London by Provincial Governments," *CBR*, XIV (1936).

———— "The Adjustment of Federal-Provincial Relations," *CJEPS*, II (1936).

MERCIER, J. "Immigration and Provincial Rights," *CBR*, XXII (1944).

MIGNAULT, P. B. "The Authority of Decided Cases," *CBR*, III (1925).

———— "Nos problèmes constitutionnels," *La Revue du Droit*, XVI (1938).

MILNER, J. B. "The Use of Legislative History," *CBR*, XXXI (1953).

MUNDELL, D. W. "Tests for Validity of Legislation under the British North America Act," *CBR*, XXXII (1954).

MURPHY, E. E. "The Wartime Power of the Dominion," *CBR*, XXX (1952).

NESBITT, W. "The Judicial Committee of the Privy Council," *CLT*, XXIX (1909).

NETTL, J. P. "The Treaty Enforcement Power in Federal Constitutions," *CBR*, XXVIII (1950).

NEWLANDS, H. W. "Appeals to the Privy Council," *CBR*, I (1923).

NICHOLLS, G. V. "British North America Acts and Selected Statutes: 1867–1948," *CBR*, XXVII (1949).

O'CONNOR, W. F. "Property and Civil Rights in the Province," *CBR*, XVIII (1940).

OSBORN, R. G. "Federalism in Canada," *Economic Record*, XVI (1940).

OYLER, P. A., *et al.* "British Coal Corporation v. The King: Three Comments," *CBR*, XIII (1935).

PATON, G. W. and G. SAWYER. "*Ratio Decidendi* and *Obiter Dictum*," *LQR*, LXVIII (1947).

PEARCE, H. J. "Problems Occasioned by Ministerial Government within the Federal State of Canada," *CHR*, VI (1925).

PERRY, J. H. "What Price Provincial Autonomy?" *CJEPS*, XXI (1955).

PIGEON, L.-P. "Are the Provincial Legislatures Governments?" *CBR*, XXI (1943).

———— "Delegation of Legislative Power to the Lieutenant-Governor in Council," *CBR*, XXVI (1948).

———— "The Meaning of Provincial Autonomy," *CBR*, XXIX (1951).

———— " 'Nonsense' and Provincial Autonomy," *CBR*, XXX (1952).

POLLOCK, SIR F. "Judicial Caution and Valour," *LQR*, XLV (1929).

RANEY, W. E. "Another Question of Dominion Jurisdiction Emerges," *CBR*, III (1925).

———— "Finality of Privy Council Decisions," *CBR*, IV (1926).

———— "The Appeal to Privy Council," *CBR*, V (1927).

READ, H. E. "Canada as a Treaty Maker," *CBR*, V (1927).

———— "Constitutional Law: Extra-territorial Operation of Dominion Legislation," *CBR*, X (1932).

READ, J. E. "The Constitutional Aspects of *Rex* v. *Nadan*," *CBR*, IV (1926).

———— "The Early Provincial Constitutions," *CBR*, XXVI (1948).

RICHARD, R. "Peace, Order and Good Government," *CBR*, XVIII (1940).
RIDDELL, W. R. "The Judicial Committee of the Privy Council," *CLT*, XXX (1910).
——— "The Constitutional History of Canada," *CLT*, XXXII (1912).
——— "Delegation of Powers of Parliament," *CBR*, VII (1929).
ROGERS, A. W. "Some Aspects of Treaty Legislation," *CBR*, IV (1926).
ROGERS, N. M. "The Compact Theory of Confederation," *CBR*, IX (1931).
——— "The Genesis of Provincial Rights," *CHR*, XIV (1933).
——— "The Political Principles of Federation," *CJEPS*, I (1935).
——— "The Constitutional Impasse," *QQ*, XLI (1943).
ROSS, G. R. "Interpreting the British North America Act," *CBR*, VII (1929).
ROWAT, D. C. "Recent Developments in Canadian Federalism," *PPCPSA*, III (1931).
ROWELL, N. W. "The Place and Functions of the Judiciary in our Canadian Constitution," *CBR*, XV (1937).
"The Rowell-Sirois Report, a Canadian Affirmation of the Democratic Faith in Social Progress," *International Labour Review* (1941).
RUSSELL, P. "The Supreme Court's Interpretation of the Constitution since 1949," in P. Fox, ed. *Politics: Canada.* Toronto, 1962.
RUTHERFORD, G. S. "Delegation of Legislative Powers to the Lieutenant-Governors in Council," *CBR*, XXVI (1948).
R. W. S. "Interpreting the Constitution," *CBR*, III (1925).
SANDWELL, B. K. "The Provinces and the Supremacy of the Treaty Power," *QQ*, XXXVII (1930).
——— "Constitutional Change in Canada," *QQ*, L (1943).
SCHMITTHOFF, C. M. "The Growing Ambit of the Common Law," *CBR*, XXX (1952).
SCHUMIATCHER, M. C. "Disallowance, the Constitution's Atomic Bomb," *Canadian Forum*, XXV (1945).
——— "Section 96 of the British North America Act Re-examined," *CBR*, XXVII (1949).
SCOTT, F. R. "The Privy Council and Minority Rights," *QQ*, XXXVII (1930).
——— "The Development of Canadian Federalism," *PPCPSA*, III (1931).
——— "Constitutional Law: Priority . . . ," *CBR*, X (1932).
——— "The Consequences of the Privy Council Decisions," *CBR*, XV (1937).
——— "The Privy Council and Mr. Bennett's 'New Deal' Legislation," *CJEPS*, III (1937).
——— "Section 94 of the British North America Act," *CBR*, XX (1942).
——— "The Special Nature of Canadian Federalism," *CJEPS*, XIII (1947).
——— "Constitutional Law: Delegation by Parliament to Provincial Legislatures and Vice-Versa," *CBR*, XXVI (1948).
——— "Dominion Jurisdiction over Human Rights and Fundamental Freedoms," *CBR*, XXVII (1949).
——— "Some Privy Counsel," *CBR*, XXVIII (1950).
——— "Centralization and Decentralization in Canadian Federalism," *CBR*, XXIX (1951).

—— "French Canada and Canadian Federalism," in A. R. M. Lower, et al. *Evolving Canadian Federalism*. Durham, 1958.

—— "Social Planning and Canadian Federalism," in M. Oliver, ed. *Social Purpose for Canada*. Toronto, 1961.

Scott, W. S. "Powers of Provincial Legislatures as to Marriage," *CBR*, II (1924).

S. E. S. "Constitutional Law: Criminal Law . . . ," *CBR*, X (1932).

Shannon, R. W. "Constitutional Law: The regulation of Trade and Commerce," *CBR*, IX (1931).

Smiley, D. V. "The Rowell-Sirois Report, Provincial Autonomy, and Post-War Canadian Federalism," *CJEPS*, XXVIII (1962).

Smith, H. A. "The Residue of Power in Canada," *CBR*, IV (1926).

—— "Interpretation in English and Continental Law," *Journal of Comparative Legislation*, IX (1927).

Stanley, G. F. G. "Act or Pact? Another Look at Confederation," in Canadian Historical Association, *Annual Report*, 1956.

Stewart, R. B. "Canada and International Labour Conventions," *American Journal of International Law*, XXXII (1938).

Stout, R. "Is the Privy Council a Legislative Body?" *LQR*, XXI (1905).

Stuart, C. A. "Our Constitution Outside of the British North America Act," *CBR*, III (1925).

"Symposium, The Criminal Law Power in Canada," *University of Toronto Faculty of Law Review*, XV (1959).

Tennant, N. B. "Dominion Companies and the Trade and Commerce Clause," *CBR*, V (1927).

Thompson, B. "The Constitution of Canada," *CLT*, XXXIX (1919).

—— "Canada's Distorted Constitution," *CLT*, XL (1920).

Tuck, R. "Canada and the Judicial Committee of the Privy Council," *UTLJ*, IV (1941).

—— "Delegation: A Way over the Constitutional Hurdle," *CBR*, XXIII (1945).

—— "Social Security . . . ," *CJEPS*, XIII (1947).

Tupper, C. H. "The Position of the Privy Council (Question of Abolition of Appeals from Canada)," *Journal of the Society of Comparative Legislation*, III (1921).

Underhill, F. H. "The Conception of National Interest," *CJEPS*, I (1935).

—— "Some Observations upon Nationalism and Provincialism in Canada," in V. Anderson, ed. *Problems in Canadian Unity*. Toronto, 1938.

"Various Aspects of Canadian Federalism," *CJEPS*, I (1935).

Viator. "Privy Council Appeals," *CLT*, XLI (1921).

Wahn, I. G. "Constitutional Law: Delegation of Authority by a Provincial Parliament," *CBR*, XIV (1936).

Waines, W. J. "Dominion-Provincial Financial Arrangements," *CJEPS*, XIX (1953).

Wegenast, F. W. "The Federal System," *CLT*, XXX (1910).

—— "The Judgment of the Judicial Committee delivered by Viscount Haldane in the case of *Fort Frances Pulp and Paper Company, Limited* v. *Manitoba Free Press Co. Limited* . . . ," *CBR*, I (1923).

241

WILLIAMS, E. K. *"Stare Decisis," CBR,* IV (1926).

WILLIS, J. "Statutory Interpretation in a Nutshell," *CBR,* XVI (1938).

―――― "Section 96 of the British North America Act," *CBR,* XVIII (1940).

WOODS, H. D. "The Sirois Report before the Ottawa Conference," *Public Affairs,* IV (1941).

WRIGHT, P. *"Canadian Constitutional Law,* by Bora Laskin," *CBR,* XXX (1952).

―――― " 'Nonsense' and Provincial Autonomy," *CBR,* XXX (1952).

WRIGHT, (LORD). "Precedents," *UTLJ,* IV (1942).

―――― "Precedents," *Cambridge Law Journal,* VIII (1944).

―――― Obituary notice on L. P. Duff, *CBR,* XXXIII (1955).

YOUNG, M. "Disallowance of Provincial Statutes," *CLT,* XXX (1910).

INDEX